The Constitution of
The State of Oklahoma:
A Quick Reference Guide

Bootblack Budget Books
Copyright 2018 ©
ISBN-13: 978-1720780427
ISBN-10: 1720780420

Article IV: Distribution of Powers – Page 78

Section 1. Departments of Government - Separation and Distinction

Article V: Legislative Department – Page 79

Initiative and Referendum:

Section 1. Legislature - Authority and Composition - Powers Reserved to People

Section 2. Designation and Definition of Reserved Powers - Determination of Percentages

Section 3. Petitions - Veto Power - Elections - Time of Taking Effect - Style of Bills - Duty of Legislature

Section 4. Referendum Against Part of Act

Section 5. Reservation of Powers to Voters of Counties and Districts - Manner of Exercising

Section 6. Subsequent Proposal of Rejected Measure

Section 7. Powers of Legislature not Affected

Section 8. Prevention of Corruption

The Senate:

Section 9. Repealed

Section 9a. Senatorial Districts – Tenure

The House Of Representatives:

Section 10a. House of Representatives - Number of Members - Formula – Tenure

Legislative Appointment:

Section 11a. Legislature to Apportion Legislature - Failure to Make Apportionment - Apportionment Commission

Section 11b. Order of Apportionment Rendered by Commission

Section 11c. Review of Apportionment Orders - Failure to Seek Review

Section 11d. Determination by Supreme Court

Section 11e. Compelling Commission to Act - Consolidation Of Proceedings

Qualifications and Rights Of Members:

Section 17. Age - Qualified Electors - Residents

Section 17a. Limitation of Time Served in the Legislature

Section 18. Ineligibility - Federal and State Officers - Conviction of Felony

Section 19. Expelled Member Ineligible - Punishment not to Bar Indictment

Section 20. Vacancies

Section 21. Conflict of Interests Prohibited - Board on Legislative Compensation

Section 22. Privileges - Arrest - Speeches or Debates

Section 23. Ineligibility to Appointment to Office - Interest in Contracts

Section 63. Continuity of Governmental Operations in Periods of Emergency

Article VI: Executive Department – Page 103

General Provisions:

Section 1. Executive Officers Enumerated - Offices and Records - Duties

Section 2. Supreme Power Vested in Governor

Section 3. Eligibility to Certain State Offices

Section 4. Terms of Office - Succession

Section 5. Returns of Election - Tie Votes

The Governor:

Section 6. Commander-In-Chief Of Militia - Calling Out Militia

Section 7. Extraordinary Sessions of Legislature

Section 8. Execution of Laws - Intercourse With Other States and United States - Conservator of Peace

Section 10. Reprieves, Commutations, Paroles and Pardons

Section 11. Approval or Veto Of Bills - Passage Over Veto - Failure to Return Bill

Section 12. Appropriation Bills - Approval or Disapproval - Emergency Bills

Section 13. Officers Commissions - Vacancies

Section 14. Adjournment of Legislature - Changing Place of Meeting

Department of Mines:

Commissioner of Charities and Corrections:

Board of Agriculture:

Commissioners Of The Land Office:

The State Seal:

Section 35. Description of Seal

18

Article VII: Judicial Department – Page 117

Article VIII: Impeachment and Removal From Office – Page 139

Public Indebtedness:

Article XI: State and School Lands – Page 252

Article XII-A: Homestead Exemption from Taxation – Page 258

Section 1. Exemption from Ad Valorem Taxation Authorized

Section 2. Duration of Exemption - Increase of Homestead

Article XIII: Education – Page 259

Section 1. Establishment and Maintenance of Public Schools

Section 1a. Appropriation and Allocation of Funds for Support of Common Schools

Section 2. Institutions for Deaf, Dumb and Blind

Section 4. Compulsory School Attendance

Section 5. Board of Education

Section 6. Textbook System for Common Schools - Official Multiple Textbook Lists

Section 7. Instruction in Agriculture, Horticulture, Stock Feeding and Domestic Science

Section 8. Board of Regents Of University Of Oklahoma

Article XIIIA: Oklahoma State System of Higher Education – Page 262

Section 1. Oklahoma State System of Higher Education

Section 2. Oklahoma State Regents for Higher Education - Establishment - Membership - Appointment - Terms - Vacancy - Powers as Coordinating Board Of Control

Section 3. Appropriations - Allocation

Section 4. Co-Ordination of Private, Denominational and Other Institutions of Higher Learning

Article XIIIB: Board of Regents of Oklahoma Colleges – Page 264

Section 1. Board of Regents of Oklahoma Colleges - Creation, Members, Terms, Etc

Section 2. Powers and Duties of Board - Officers, Supervisors, Etc

Section 3. Successor to Existing Governing Boards - Records, Papers, Etc

Section 4. Salaries and Expenses - Allocation of Funds for Payment

Article XIV: Banks and Banking – Page 267

Section 1. Banking Department

Section 2. Classification of Loans and Lenders - Licenses - Maximum Rates of Interest

Section 3. Excessive Rate - Forfeiture of Interest - Recovery of Double Interest

Article XVII: Counties – Page 271

Article XVIII: Municipal Corporations – Page 307

Section 1. Creation - General or Special Laws - Classification

Section 2. Existing Municipal Corporations Continued - Rights and Powers

Section 3.

(a) Framing and Adoption of Charter - Approval by Governor - Effect - Record - Amendment

(b). Election of Board Of Freeholders

Section 4.

(a) Reservation of Powers

(b). Petition - Signatures - Filing

(c). Presentation of Petition to Legislative Body - Submission to Voters

(d). Submission to Referendum Vote

(e). Submission of Amendment to Charter

Section 5.

(a). Grant, Extension or Renewal - Approval by Voters - Term

(b). Petition - Calling Election - Result of Election

Section 6. Business or Enterprise - Right to Engage In

Section 7. Control and Regulation not Divested - Surrender of Powers - Exclusive Franchises

Article XIX: Insurance – Page 312

Section 1. Foreign Insurance Companies - Conditions of Doing Business

Section 2. Entrance Fees - Annual Tax

Section 3. Non-Profit Insurance Organizations

Section 4. Fees Paid to State Treasurer

43

Article XX: Manufacture and Commerce – Page 314

Section 1. Denaturized Alcohol - Manufacture and Sale

Section 2. Kerosene Oil - Flash Test - Specific Gravity Test

Article XXI: Public Institutions – Page 315

Section 1. Establishment and Support

Article XXII: Alien and Corporate Ownership of Lands – Page 316

Section 1. Aliens - Ownership of Land Prohibited - Disposal of Lands Acquired

Section 2. Corporations - Buying, Acquiring or Dealing in Real Estate

Article XXIV: Constitutional Amendments – Page 321

Section 1. Amendments Proposed by Legislature - Submission to Vote

Section 2. Constitutional Convention to Propose Amendments or New Constitution

Section 3. Right of Amendment by Initiative Petition not Impaired

Article XXVI: Department of Wildlife Conservation – Page 324

Section 1. Creation of Department - Wildlife Conservation Commission - Membership - Appointment - Tenure - Vacancies - Oath and Bonds

Section 2. Game and Fish Laws not Repealed - Acquisition of Property

Section 3. Director of Wildlife Conservation

Section 4. Disposition of Funds

Article XXVIII: Alcoholic Beverage
Laws and Enforcement – Page 327

Section 1. Creation of Commission - Appointment - Membership - Powers – Tenure / Repealed

Section 1.A. Transition from The Alcoholic Beverage Control Board To The Alcoholic Beverage Laws Enforcement Commission / Repealed

Section 2. Exclusion of Beer or Cereal Malt Beverages Containing not More than 3.2% Of Alcohol by Weight / Repealed

Section 3. Enactment of Laws by Legislature - Indiscriminate Sales to Licensed Wholesale Distribution / Repealed

Section 4. Retail Sales by Package Stores and by the Individual Drink / Repealed

Section 5. Prohibition of Sales to Certain Persons - Limitation on Advertising - Penalties / Repealed

Section 6. Prohibition of Sales on Certain Days - Penalties / Repealed

Section 7. Taxation and Licensing - Distribution of Funds / Repealed

Section 8. State and Political Subdivisions Prohibited from Engaging in Business / Repealed

Section 9. Occupation Tax / Repealed

Section 10. Restrictions on Issuance of Licenses / Repealed

Section 11. Repealed

Article XXIX: Ethics Commission – Page 328

Section 1. Ethics Commission - Appointments - Qualifications - Terms – Vacancies - Quorum

Section 2. Appropriation - Compensation - Staff

Section 3. Ethics Rules

Section 4. Investigation - Decision - Subpoena Power

Section 5. Ethics Interpretations

Section 6. Criminal Penalties

Section 7. Removal

Schedule – Page 332

Preamble:

Section 1. Existing Rights, Actions, Proceedings, Contracts, Claims, and Processes

Section 2. Laws of the Territory of Oklahoma – Extended and to Remain in Force

Section 3. Debts, Fines, Penalties and Forfeitures Accruing to the Territory of Oklahoma

Section 4. Constitution Takes Effect and Force – When

Section 5. Notaries Public - Continuation of Duties of Office

Section 6. Female Persons as Notaries - Females Eligible to Office of County Superintendent of Public Instruction

Section 7. Property, Credits, Claims, and Choses in Action Belonging to Territory of Oklahoma

Section 8. Judgments and Property Records in Indian Territory and Osage Reservation Effectual to Impart Notice

Section 9. Judgments and Property Records of Oklahoma Territory Effectual to Impart Notice

Section 10. Continued Corporate Existence of Cities and Towns - Officers – Ordinances

Section 11. Taxes Assessed or Due in Incorporated Cities and Towns

Section 12. Local Improvements and Public Buildings Being Made or Constructed in Indian Territory

Section 42. Officers Elected at Time of Adoption of Constitution - Official Bonds

Section 43. Filing and Preservation of Constitution - Secretary of State

Preamble:

Invoking the guidance of Almighty God, in order to secure and perpetuate the blessing of liberty; to secure just and rightful government; to promote our mutual welfare and happiness, we, the people of the State of Oklahoma, do ordain and establish this Constitution.

ARTICLE I: FEDERAL REGULATIONS

Section 1. Supreme Law of Land

The State of Oklahoma is an inseparable part of the Federal Union, and the Constitution of the United States is the supreme law of the land.

Section 2. Religious Liberty - Polygamous or Plural Marriages

Perfect toleration of religious sentiment shall be secured, and no inhabitant of the State shall ever be molested in person or property on account of his or her mode of religious worship; and no religious test shall be required for the exercise of civil or political rights. Polygamous or plural marriages are forever prohibited.

Section 3. Unappropriated Public Lands - Indian Lands - Jurisdiction of United States

The people inhabiting the State do agree and declare that they forever disclaim all right and title in or to any unappropriated public lands lying within the boundaries thereof, and to all lands lying within said limits owned or held by any Indian, tribe, or nation; and that until the title to any such public land shall have been extinguished by the United States, the same shall be and remain subject to the jurisdiction, disposal, and control of the United States. Land belonging to citizens of the United States residing without the limits of the State shall never be taxed at a higher rate than the land belonging to residents thereof. No taxes shall be imposed by the State on lands or property belonging to or which may hereafter be purchased by the United States or reserved for its use.

Section 4. Territorial Debts and Liabilities

The debts and liabilities of the Territory of Oklahoma are hereby assumed, and shall be paid by the State.

Section 5. Public Schools - Separate Schools

Provisions shall be made for the establishment and maintenance of a system of public schools, which shall be open to all the children of the state and free from sectarian control; and said schools shall always be conducted in English: Provided, that nothing herein shall preclude the teaching of other languages in said public schools.

Section 6. Right of Suffrage

The State shall never enact any law restricting or abridging the right of suffrage on account of race, color, or previous condition of servitude.

Section 7. Repealed

ARTICLE II: BILL OF RIGHTS

Section 1. Political Power - Purpose of Government - Alteration or Reformation

All political power is inherent in the people; and government is instituted for their protection, security, and benefit, and to promote their general welfare; and they have the right to alter or reform the same whenever the public good may require it: Provided, such change be not repugnant to the Constitution of the United States.

Section 2. Inherent Rights

All persons have the inherent right to life, liberty, the pursuit of happiness, and the enjoyment of the gains of their own industry.

Section 3. Right of Assembly and Petition

The people have the right peaceably to assemble for their own good, and to apply to those invested with the powers of government for redress of grievances by petition, address, or remonstrance.

Section 4. Interference with Right of Suffrage

No power, civil or military, shall ever interfere to prevent the free exercise of the right of suffrage by those entitled to such right.

Section 5. Public Money or Property - Use for Sectarian Purposes

No public money or property shall ever be appropriated, applied, donated, or used, directly or indirectly, for the use, benefit, or support of any sect, church, denomination, or system of religion, or for the use, benefit, or support of any priest, preacher, minister, or other religious teacher or dignitary, or sectarian institution as such.

Section 6. Courts of Justice Open - Remedies for Wrongs - Sale, Denial or Delay

The courts of justice of the State shall be open to every person, and speedy and certain remedy afforded for every wrong and for every injury to person, property, or reputation; and right and justice shall be administered without sale, denial, delay, or prejudice.

Section 7. Due Process of Law

No person shall be deprived of life, liberty, or property, without due process of law.

Section 8. Right to Bail – Exceptions

A. All persons shall be bailable by sufficient sureties, except that bail may be denied for:

1. capital offenses when the proof of guilt is evident, or the presumption thereof is great;

2. violent offenses;

3. offenses where the maximum sentence may be life imprisonment or life imprisonment without parole;

4. felony offenses where the person charged with the offense has been convicted of two or more felony offenses arising out of different transactions; and

5. controlled dangerous substances offenses where the maximum sentence may be at least ten (10) years imprisonment. On all offenses specified in paragraphs 2 through 5 of this section, the proof of guilt must be evident, or the presumption must be great, and it must be on the grounds that no condition of release would assure the safety of the community or any person.

B. The provisions of this resolution shall become effective on July 1, 1989.

Section 9. Excessive Bail or Fines - Cruel or Unusual Punishment

Excessive bail shall not be required, nor excessive fines imposed, nor cruel or unusual punishments inflicted.

Section 9a. Death Penalty

All statutes of this state requiring, authorizing, imposing or relating to the death penalty are in full force and effect, subject to legislative amendment or repeal by statute, initiative or referendum. Any method of execution shall be allowed, unless prohibited by the United States Constitution. Methods of execution may be designated by the Legislature. A sentence of death shall not be reduced on the basis that a method of execution is invalid. In any case in which an execution method is declared invalid, the death sentence shall remain in force until the sentence can be lawfully executed by any valid method. The death penalty provided for under such statutes shall not be deemed to be, or to constitute, the infliction of cruel or unusual punishments, nor shall such punishment be deemed to contravene any other provision of this Constitution.

Section 10. Habeas Corpus – Suspension

The privilege of the writ of habeas corpus shall never be suspended by the authorities of this State.

Section 11. Officers - Personal Attention to Duties – Intoxication

Every person elected or appointed to any office or employment of trust or profit under the laws of the State, or under any ordinance of any municipality thereof, shall give personal attention to the duties of the office to which he is elected or appointed. Drunkenness and the excessive use of intoxicating liquors while in office shall constitute sufficient cause for impeachment or removal therefrom.

Section 12. Officers of United States or Other States - Ineligibility to Office

No member of Congress from this State, or person holding any office of trust or profit under the laws of any other State, or of the United States, shall hold any office of trust or profit under the laws of this State; provided, neither the provisions of this section nor any other provision of this Constitution or state law shall be construed to prohibit the following officeholders from holding at the same time any other office of trust or profit:

1. Officers and enlisted members of the National Guard;

2. Officers and enlisted members of the National Guard Reserve;

3. Officers of the Officers Reserve Corps of the United States;

4. Enlisted members of the Organized Reserves of the United States; and

5. Officers and enlisted members of the Oklahoma State Guard and any other active militia or military force organized under state law.

The Legislature shall have the power to enact laws to further implement the provisions of this section.
Amendments

Section 12A. Candidacy as United States Representative or Senator - Term Limits – Write-ins

Beginning January 1, 1995, persons wanting to become a candidate for election to the United States Congress from this State for a term beginning on or after January 1, 1995, shall be subject to the following provisions:

A. Any person seeking to have his or her name placed on the ballot for election to the United States House of Representatives shall be eligible if, by the end of the then current term of office, that person has served in that office for three (3) two-year terms.

B. Any person seeking to have his or her name placed on the ballot for election to the United States Senate shall be ineligible if, by the end of the then current term of office, that person has served in that office for two (2) six-year terms.

C. A person elected to serve as member of the United States Congress shall be eligible to serve as a Representative for a total of six (6) years and as a Senator for a total of twelve (12) years for a maximum total of eighteen (18) years as a member of Congress from this State.

D. The provisions of this section shall not be applicable to or include:

1. The years served by any person as a member of the United States House of Representatives or as a member of the United States Senate which began prior to the election at which this measure was enacted.

2. The years served by a person who served on complete the remainder of a vacated term.

E. The provisions of this Section shall not be construed so as to prevent casting a ballot for any person regardless of the number of years previously served in the United States Congress by writing the name of that person on the ballot, or from having such ballot counted or to prevent a person from campaigning by means of a "write-in" campaign if that procedure is otherwise authorized in this Constitution or by law.

Section 13. Imprisonment for Debt

Imprisonment for debt is prohibited, except for the non-payment of fines and penalties imposed for the violation of law.

Section 14. Military Subordinate to Civil Authorities - Quartering without Owner's Consent

The military shall be held in strict subordination to the civil authorities. No soldier shall be quartered in any house, in time of peace, without the consent of the owner, nor in time of war, except in a manner to be prescribed by law.

Section 15. Bills of Attainder - Ex post Facto Laws - Obligation of Contracts – Forfeitures

No bill of attainder, ex post facto law, nor any law impairing the obligation of contracts, shall ever be passed. No conviction shall work a corruption of blood or forfeiture of estate: Provided, that this provision shall not prohibit the imposition of pecuniary penalties.

Section 16. Treason

Treason against the State shall consist only in levying war against it or in adhering to its enemies, giving them aid and comfort. No person shall be convicted of treason, unless on the testimony of two witnesses to the same overt act, or on confession in open court.

Section 17. Indictment or Information - Preliminary Examination - Prosecutions in Courts Not of Record

No person shall be prosecuted criminally in courts of record for felony or misdemeanor otherwise than by presentment or indictment or by information. No person shall be prosecuted for a felony by information without having had a preliminary examination before an examining magistrate, or having waived such preliminary examination. Prosecutions may be instituted in courts not of record upon a duly verified complaint.

Section 18. Grand Jury

A grand jury shall be composed of twelve (12) persons, any nine (9) of whom concurring may find an indictment or true bill. A grand jury shall be convened upon the order of a district judge upon his own motion; or such grand jury shall be ordered by a district judge upon the filing of a petition therefore signed by qualified electors of the county equal to the number of signatures required to propose legislation by a county by initiative petition as provided in Section 5 of Article V of the Oklahoma Constitution, with the minimum number of required signatures being five hundred (500) and the maximum being five thousand (5000); and further providing that in any calendar year in which a grand jury has been convened pursuant to a petition therefore, then any subsequent petition filed during the same calendar year shall require double the minimum number of signatures as were required hereunder for the first petition; or such grand jury shall be ordered convened upon the filing of a verified application by the Attorney General of the State of Oklahoma who shall have authority to conduct the grand jury in investigating crimes which are alleged to have been committed in said county or involving multi-county criminal activities; when so assembled such grand jury shall have power to inquire into and return indictments for all character and grades of crime. All other provisions of the Constitution or the laws of this state in conflict with the provisions of this constitutional amendment are hereby expressly repealed.

The legislature shall enact laws to prevent corruption in making, filing, circulating, and submitting petitions calling for convening a grand jury.

Section 19. Trial by Jury

The right of trial by jury shall be and remain inviolate, except in civil cases wherein the amount in controversy does not exceed One Thousand Five Hundred Dollars ($1,500.00), or in criminal cases wherein punishment for the offense charged is by fine only, not exceeding One Thousand Five Hundred Dollars ($1,500.00). Provided, however, that the Legislature may provide for jury trial in cases involving lesser amounts. Juries for the trial of civil cases, involving more than Ten Thousand Dollars ($10,000.00), and felony criminal cases shall consist of twelve (12) persons. All other juries shall consist of six (6) persons. However, in all cases the parties may agree on a lesser number of jurors than provided herein.

In all criminal cases where imprisonment for more than six (6) months is authorized the entire number of jurors must concur to render a verdict. In all other cases three-fourths (3/4) of the whole number of jurors concurring shall have power to render a verdict. When a verdict is rendered by less than the whole number of jurors, the verdict shall be signed by each juror concurring therein.

Section 20. Rights of Accused in Criminal Cases

In all criminal prosecutions the accused shall have the right to a speedy and public trial by an impartial jury of the county in which the crime shall have been committed or, where uncertainty exists as to the county in which the crime was committed, the accused may be tried in any county in which the evidence indicates the crime might have been committed. Provided, that the venue may be changed to some other county of the state, on the application of the accused, in such manner as may be prescribed by law. He shall be informed of the nature and cause of the accusation against him and have a copy thereof, and be confronted with the witnesses against him, and have compulsory process for obtaining witnesses in his behalf. He shall have the right to be heard by himself and counsel; and in capital cases, at least two days before the case is called for trial, he shall be furnished with a list of the witnesses that will be called in chief, to prove the allegations of the indictment or information, together with their post office addresses.

Section 21. Self-Incrimination - Double Jeopardy

No person shall be compelled to give evidence which will tend to incriminate him, except as in this Constitution specifically provided; nor shall any person, after having been once acquitted by a jury, be again put in jeopardy of life or liberty for that of which he has been acquitted. Nor shall any person be twice put in jeopardy of life or liberty for the same offense.

Section 22. Liberty of Speech and Press - Truth as Evidence in Prosecution for Libel

Every person may freely speak, write, or publish his sentiments on all subjects, being responsible for the abuse of that right; and no law shall be passed to restrain or abridge the liberty of speech or of the press. In all criminal prosecutions for libel, the truth of the matter alleged to be libelous may be given in evidence to the jury, and if it shall appear to the jury that the matter charged as libelous be true, and was written or published with good motives and for justifiable ends, the party shall be acquitted.

Section 23. Private Property - Taking or Damaging for Private Use

No private property shall be taken or damaged for private use, with or without compensation, unless by consent of the owner, except for private ways of necessity, or for drains and ditches across lands of others for agricultural, mining, or sanitary purposes, in such manner as may be prescribed by law.

Section 24. Private Property - Public Use - Character of Use a Judicial Question

Private property shall not be taken or damaged for public use without just compensation. Just compensation shall mean the value of the property taken, and in addition, any injury to any part of the property not taken. Any special and direct benefits to the part of the property not taken may be offset only against any injury to the property not taken. Such compensation shall be ascertained by a board of commissioners of not less than three freeholders, in such manner as may be prescribed by law. Provided however, in no case shall the owner be required to make any payments should the benefits be judged to exceed damages. The commissioners shall not be appointed by any judge or court without reasonable notice having been served upon all parties in interest. The commissioners shall be selected from the regular jury list of names prepared and made as the Legislature shall provide. Any party aggrieved shall have the right of appeal, without bond, and trial by jury in a court of record. Until the compensation shall be paid to the owner, or into court for the owner, the property shall not be disturbed, or the proprietary rights of the owner divested. When possession is taken of property condemned for any public use, the owner shall be entitled to the immediate receipt of the compensation awarded, without prejudice to the right of either party to prosecute further proceedings for the judicial determination of the sufficiency or insufficiency of such compensation. The fee of land taken by common carriers for right of way, without the consent of the owner, shall remain in such owner subject only to the use for which it is taken. In all cases of condemnation of private property for public or private use, the determination of the character of the use shall be a judicial question.

Section 25. Contempt - Definition - Jury trial – Hearing

The legislature shall pass laws defining contempts and regulating the proceedings and punishment in matters of contempt: Provided, that any person accused of violating or disobeying, when not in the presence or hearing of the court, or judge sitting as such, any order of injunction, or restraint, made or entered by any court or judge of the State shall, before penalty or punishment is imposed, be entitled to a trial by jury as to the guilt or innocence of the accused. In no case shall a penalty or punishment be imposed for contempt, until an opportunity to be heard is given.

Section 26. Bearing Arms - Carrying Weapons

The right of a citizen to keep and bear arms in defense of his home, person, or property, or in aid of the civil power, when thereunto legally summoned, shall never be prohibited; but nothing herein contained shall prevent the Legislature from regulating the carrying of weapons.

Section 27. Witnesses Not Excused from Testifying - Immunity from Prosecution

Any person having knowledge or possession of facts that tend to establish the guilt of any other person or corporation under the laws of the state shall not be excused from giving testimony or producing evidence, when legally called upon so to do, on the ground that it may tend to incriminate him under the laws of the state; but no person shall be prosecuted or subjected to any penalty or forfeiture for or on account of any transaction, matter, or thing concerning which he may so testify or produce evidence. All other provisions of the Constitution or the laws of this state in conflict with the provisions of this constitutional amendment are hereby expressly repealed.

Section 28. Corporate Records, Books and Files

The records, books, and files of all corporations shall be, at all times, liable and subject to the full visitorial and inquisitorial powers of the State, notwithstanding the immunities and privileges in this Bill of Rights secured to the persons, inhabitants, and citizens thereof.

Section 29. Transportation Out of State

No person shall be transported out of the State for any offense committed within the State, nor shall any person be transported out of the State for any purpose, without his consent, except by due process of law; but nothing in this provision shall prevent the operation of extradition laws, or the transporting of persons sentenced for crime, to other states for the purpose of incarceration.

Section 30. Unreasonable Searches or Seizures - Warrants, Issuance of

The right of the people to be secure in their persons, houses, papers, and effects against unreasonable searches or seizures shall not be violated; and no warrant shall issue but upon probable cause supported by oath or affirmation, describing as particularly as may be the place to be searched and the person or thing to be seized.

Section 31. State - Engagement in Occupation or Business
The right of the State to engage in any occupation or business for public purposes shall not be denied nor prohibited, except that the State shall not engage in agriculture for any other than educational and scientific purposes and for the support of its penal, charitable, and educational institutions.

Section 32. Perpetuities - Monopolies - Primogeniture - Entailments
Perpetuities and monopolies are contrary to the genius of a free government, and shall never be allowed, nor shall the law of primogeniture or entailments ever be in force in this State.

Section 33. Effect of Enumeration of Rights
The enumeration in this Constitution of certain rights shall not be construed to deny, impair, or disparage others retained by the people.

Section 34. Rights of Victims

A. To preserve and protect the rights of victims to justice and due process, and ensure that victims are treated with fairness, respect and dignity, and are free from intimidation, harassment, or abuse, throughout the criminal justice process, any victim or family member of a victim of a crime has the right to know the status of the investigation and prosecution of the criminal case, including all proceedings wherein a disposition of a case is likely to occur, and where plea negotiations may occur. The victim or family member of a victim of a crime has the right to know the location of the defendant following an arrest, during a prosecution of the criminal case, during a sentence to probation or confinement, and when there is any release or escape of the defendant from confinement. The victim or family member of a victim of a crime has a right to be present at any proceeding where the defendant has a right to be present, to be heard at any sentencing or parole hearing, to be awarded restitution by the convicted person for damages or losses as determined and ordered by the court, and to be informed by the state of the constitutional rights of the victim.

B. An exercise of any right by a victim or family member of a victim or the failure to provide a victim or family member of a victim any right granted by this section shall not be grounds for dismissing any criminal proceeding or setting aside any conviction or sentence.

C. The Legislature, or the people by initiative or referendum, has the authority to enact substantive and procedural laws to define, implement, preserve and protect the rights guaranteed to victims by this section, including the authority to extend any of these rights to juvenile proceedings and if enacted by the Legislature, youthful offender proceedings.

D. The enumeration in the Constitution of certain rights for victims shall not be construed to deny or disparage other rights granted by the Legislature or retained by victims.

Section 35. "Marriage" Defined - Marriage Between Persons of Same Gender Not Valid or Recognized

A. Marriage in this state shall consist only of the union of one man and one woman. Neither this Constitution nor any other provision of law shall be construed to require that marital status or the legal incidents thereof be conferred upon unmarried couples or groups.

B. A marriage between persons of the same gender performed in another state shall not be recognized as valid and binding in this state as of the date of the marriage.

C. Any person knowingly issuing a marriage license in violation of this section shall be guilty of a misdemeanor.

Section 36. Preferential treatment or discrimination

A. The state shall not grant preferential treatment to, or discriminate against, any individual or group on the basis of race, color, sex, ethnicity or national origin in the operation of public employment, public education or public contracting.

B. This section shall apply only to action taken after the effective date of this section.

C. Nothing in this section shall be interpreted as prohibiting bona fide qualifications based on sex that are reasonably necessary to the normal operation of public employment, public education or public contracting.

D. Nothing in this section shall be interpreted as invalidating any court order or consent decree that is in force as of the effective date of this section.

E. Nothing in this section shall be interpreted as prohibiting action that must be taken to establish or maintain eligibility for any federal program, where ineligibility would result in a loss of federal funds to the state.

F. For the purposes of this section, "state" shall include, but not be limited to, the state itself or an agency, institution, instrumentality, or political subdivision of the state.

G. The remedies available for violations of this section shall be the same, regardless of the injured party's race, color, sex, ethnicity or national origin, as are otherwise available for violations of the antidiscrimination laws of this state.

Section 37. Health Care Freedom Amendment

A. For purposes of this section:

1. "Compel" shall include penalties or fines;

2. "Direct payment or pay directly" means payment for lawful health care services without a public or private third party, not including an employer, paying for any portion of the service;

3. "Health care system" means any public or private entity whose function or purpose is the management of, processing of, enrollment of individuals for or payment for, in full or in part, health care services or health care data or health care information for its participants;

4. "Lawful health care services" means any health-related service or treatment to the extent that the service or treatment is permitted or not prohibited by law or regulation that may be provided by persons or businesses otherwise permitted to offer such services; and

5. "Penalties or fines" means any civil or criminal penalty or fine, tax, salary or wage withholding or surcharge or any named fee with a similar effect established by law or rule by a government-established, -created or -controlled agency that is used to punish or discourage the exercise of rights protected under this section.

B. To preserve the freedom of Oklahomans to provide for their health care:

1. A law or rule shall not compel, directly or indirectly, any person, employer or health care provider to participate in any health care system; and

2. A person or employer may pay directly for lawful health care services and shall not be required to pay penalties or fines for paying directly for lawful health care services. A health care provider may accept direct payment for lawful health care services and shall not be required to pay penalties or fines for accepting direct payment from a person or employer for lawful health care services.

C. Subject to reasonable and necessary rules that do not substantially limit a person's options, the purchase or sale of health insurance in private health care systems shall not be prohibited by law or rule.

D. This section shall not:

1. Affect which health care services a health care provider or hospital is required to perform or provide;

2. Affect which health care services are permitted by law;

3. Prohibit care related to workers' compensation;

4. Affect laws or rules in effect as of January 1, 2010; or

5. Affect the terms or conditions of any health care system to the extent that those terms and conditions do not have the effect of punishing a person or employer for paying directly for lawful health care services or a health care provider or hospital for accepting direct payment from a person or employer for lawful health care services.

ARTICLE III: SUFFRAGE

Section 1. Qualifications of Electors

Subject to such exceptions as the Legislature may prescribe, all citizens of the United States, over the age of eighteen (18) years, who are bona fide residents of this state, are qualified electors of this state.

Section 2. State Election Board - Creation – Membership

The Legislature shall create a State Election Board to be charged with the supervision of such elections as the Legislature shall direct. Not more than a majority of the members of said Board shall be selected from the same political party.

Section 3. Mandatory Primary System - Nomination of Candidates

The Legislature may enact laws providing for a mandatory primary system which shall provide for the nomination of all candidates in all elections for federal, state, county and municipal offices, for all political parties, except for the office of Presidential Elector, the candidates for which shall be nominated by the recognized political parties at their conventions. The Legislature also shall enact laws providing that citizens may, by petition, place on the ballot the names of independent, nonpartisan candidates for office, including the office of Presidential Elector.

Section 4. Manner of Holding and Conducting Elections - Registration of Electors

The Legislature shall prescribe the time and manner of holding and conducting all elections, and enact such laws as may be necessary to detect and punish fraud in such elections. The Legislature may provide by law for the registration of electors throughout the state and, when it is so provided, no person shall vote at any election unless he shall have registered according to law.

Section 5. Free and Equal Elections - Interference by Civil or Military Power - Privilege from Arrest

All elections shall be free and equal. No power, civil or military, shall ever interfere to prevent the free exercise of the right of suffrage, and electors shall, in all cases, except for treason, felony, and breach of the peace, be privileged from arrest during their attendance on elections and while going to and from the same.

ARTICLE IV: DISTRIBUTION OF POWERS

Section 1. Departments of Government - Separation and Distinction

The powers of the government of the State of Oklahoma shall be divided into three separate departments: The Legislative, Executive, and Judicial; and except as provided in this Constitution, the Legislative, Executive, and Judicial departments of government shall be separate and distinct, and neither shall exercise the powers properly belonging to either of the others.

ARTICLE V: LEGISLATIVE DEPARTMENT

Section 1. Legislature - Authority and Composition - Powers Reserved to People

The Legislative authority of the State shall be vested in a Legislature, consisting of a Senate and a House of Representatives; but the people reserve to themselves the power to propose laws and amendments to the Constitution and to enact or reject the same at the polls independent of the Legislature, and also reserve power at their own option to approve or reject at the polls any act of the Legislature.

Section 2. Designation and Definition of Reserved Powers - Determination of Percentages

The first power reserved by the people is the initiative, and eight per centum of the legal voters shall have the right to propose any legislative measure, and fifteen per centum of the legal voters shall have the right to propose amendments to the Constitution by petition, and every such petition shall include the full text of the measure so proposed. The second power is the referendum, and it may be ordered (except as to laws necessary for the immediate preservation of the public peace, health, or safety), either by petition signed by five per centum of the legal voters or by the Legislature as other bills are enacted. The ratio and per centum of legal voters hereinbefore stated shall be based upon the total number votes cast at the last general election for the Office of Governor.

Section 3. Petitions - Veto Power - Elections - Time of Taking Effect - Style of Bills - Duty of Legislature

Referendum petitions shall be filed with the Secretary of State not more than ninety (90) days after the final adjournment of the session of the Legislature which passed the bill on which the referendum is demanded. The veto power of the Governor shall not extend to measures voted on by the people. All elections on measures referred to the people of the state shall be had at the next election held throughout the state, except when the Legislature or the Governor shall order a special election for the express purpose of making such reference. Any measure referred to the people by the initiative or referendum shall take effect and be in force when it shall have been approved by a majority of the votes cast thereon and not otherwise.

The style of all bills shall be:

"Be it Enacted By the People of the State of Oklahoma."

Petitions and orders for the initiative and for the referendum shall be filed with the Secretary of State and addressed to the Governor of the state, who shall submit the same to the people. The Legislature shall make suitable provisions for carrying into effect the provisions of this article.

Section 4. Referendum Against Part of Act

The referendum may be demanded by the people against one or more items, sections, or parts of any act of the Legislature in the same manner in which such power may be exercised against a complete act. The filing of a referendum petition against one or more items, sections, or parts of an act shall not delay the remainder of such act from becoming operative.

Section 5. Reservation of Powers to Voters of Counties and Districts - Manner of Exercising

The powers of the initiative and referendum reserved to the people by this Constitution for the State at large, are hereby further reserved to the legal voters of every county and district therein, as to all local legislation, or action, in the administration of county and district government in and for their respective counties and districts. The manner of exercising said powers shall be prescribed by general laws, except that Boards of County Commissioners may provide for the time of exercising the initiative and referendum powers as to local legislation in their respective counties and districts.

The requisite number of petitioners for the invocation of the initiative and referendum in counties and districts shall bear twice, or double, the ratio to the whole number of legal voters in such county or district, as herein provided therefore in the State at large.

Section 5a. Township Organization or Government - Abolition and Restoration

Each county in the State of Oklahoma may by a majority of the legal voters of such county voting upon the proposition, abolish township organization or government. The Board of County Commissioners of such county, upon a petition signed by sixteen per centum of the total number of votes cast at the last general election for the county office receiving the highest number of votes, praying that the question of abolishing township organization or government be submitted to a vote of the county, shall within thirty days after the regular meeting of such board next convening after the filing of such petition, call a special election for such purpose, or the board may in their discretion submit such question at the next general election held after the filing of such petition. If such question shall be carried, township organization or government shall cease in such county, and all the duties theretofore performed by the township officers shall be cast upon and be performed by such county officers having like duties to perform in relation to the county at large as such township officers performed in relation to the township at large. At any general election after the abolition of township organization or government the question of returning to township government may be submitted as provided for the submission of the question of abolishing such government, and if a majority of the votes cast upon such question be in favor of township government the same shall thereupon be established, and the Board of County Commissioners shall appoint the full quota of township officers, who shall hold their offices and perform the duties thereof until their successors shall have been elected at the next general election and until they have been qualified. Except as otherwise specifically provided by this section, the law relating to carrying into effect the initiative and referendum provisions of the Constitution shall govern.

Section 6. Subsequent Proposal of Rejected Measure

Any measure rejected by the people, through the powers of the initiative and referendum, cannot be again proposed by the initiative within three years thereafter by less than twenty-five per centum of the legal voters.

Section 7. Powers of Legislature Not Affected

The reservation of the powers of the initiative and referendum in this article shall not deprive the Legislature of the right to repeal any law, propose or pass any measure, which may be consistent with the Constitution of the State and the Constitution of the United States.

Section 8. Prevention of Corruption

Laws shall be provided to prevent corruption in making, procuring, and submitting initiative and referendum petitions. The Senate

Section 9. Repealed

Section 9(a). Repealed

Section 9(b). Repealed

Section 9A. Senatorial Districts – Tenure

The state shall be apportioned into forty-eight senatorial districts in the following manner: the nineteen most populous counties, as determined by the most recent Federal Decennial Census, shall constitute nineteen senatorial districts with one senator to be nominated and elected from each district; the fifty-eight less populous counties shall be joined into twenty-nine two-county districts with one senator to be nominated and elected from each of the two-county districts. In apportioning the State Senate, consideration shall be given to population, compactness, area, political units, historical precedents, economic and political interests, contiguous territory, and other major factors, to the extent feasible.

Each senatorial district, whether single county or multi-county, shall be entitled to one senator, who shall hold office for four years; provided that any senator, serving at the time of the adoption of this amendment, shall serve the full time for which he was elected. Vitalization of senatorial districts shall provide for one-half of the senators to be elected at each general election.

The House of Representatives:

Section 10. Repealed

Section 10A. House of Representatives - Number of members - Formula – Tenure

The House of Representatives shall consist of the number of Representatives as determined by the formula and procedure set forth herein. The number of members of the House of Representatives to which each county shall be entitled shall be determined according to the following formula:

a. The total population of the state as ascertained by the most recent Federal Decennial Census shall be divided by the number one hundred and the quotient shall be the ratio of representation in the House of Representatives, except as otherwise provided in this Article.

b. Every county having a population less than one full ratio shall be assigned one Representative; every county containing an entire ratio but less than two ratios shall be assigned two Representatives; every county containing a population of two entire ratios but less than three ratios shall be assigned three Representatives; and every county containing a population of three entire ratios but less than four ratios shall be assigned four Representatives.

After the first four Representatives, a county shall qualify for additional representation on the basis of two whole ratios of population for each additional Representative.
Each Representative nominated and elected shall hold office for two years.

Legislative Apportionment:

Section 11. Repealed

Section 11A. Legislature to apportion Legislature - Failure to make apportionment - Apportionment Commission

The apportionment of the Legislature shall be accomplished by the Legislature according to the provisions of this article, within ninety (90) legislative days after the convening of the first regular session of the Legislature following each Federal Decennial Census. If the Legislature shall fail or refuse to make such apportionment within the time provided herein, then such apportionment shall be accomplished by the Bipartisan Commission on Legislative Apportionment, according to the provisions of this article. The Commission shall be composed of seven (7) members as follows: the Lieutenant Governor, who shall be nonvoting and the chair of the Commission; two members, one Republican and one democrat, appointed by the President Pro Tempore of the Senate; two members, one Republican and one democrat, appointed by the Speaker of the House of Representatives; and two members, one Republican and one democrat, appointed by the Governor.

Section 11B. Order of Apportionment Rendered by Commission

Each order of apportionment rendered by the Bipartisan Commission on Legislative Apportionment shall be in writing and shall be filed with the Secretary of State and shall be signed by at least four members of the Commission.

Section 11C. Review of Apportionment Orders - Failure to Seek Review

Any qualified elector may seek a review of any apportionment order of the Commission, or apportionment law of the legislature, within sixty days from the filing thereof, by filing in the Supreme Court of Oklahoma a petition which must set forth a proposed apportionment more nearly in accordance with this Article. Any apportionment of either the Senate or the House of Representatives, as ordered by the Commission, or apportionment law of the legislature, from which review is not sought within such time, shall become final. The court shall give all cases involving apportionment precedence over all other cases and proceedings; and if said court be not in session, it shall convene promptly for the disposal of the same.

Section 11D. Determination by Supreme Court

Upon review, the Supreme Court shall determine whether or not the apportionment order of the Commission or act of the legislature is in compliance with the formula as set forth in this Article and, if so, it shall require the same to be filed or refiled as the case may be with the Secretary of State forthwith, and such apportionment shall become final on the date of said writ. In the event the Supreme Court shall determine that the apportionment order of said Commission or legislative act is not in compliance with the formula for either the Senate or the House of Representatives as set forth in this Article, it will remand the matter to the Commission with directions to modify its order to achieve conformity with the provisions of this Article.

Section 11E. Compelling Commission to Act - Consolidation of Proceedings

The Supreme Court, upon petition of any qualified elector alleging failure of the Commission to timely act, is hereby vested with original jurisdiction to compel, and shall compel, the Commission to make the apportionment as herein provided. It shall also have exclusive jurisdiction of any review hereunder. If more than one petition be filed, the court shall consolidate such proceedings for hearing and disposition, and shall file its opinion and issue its writ within sixty days from the timely filing of such last petition. In the event any action filed hereunder shall be abandoned or dismissed, any other qualified elector shall be allowed to intervene within ten days thereof.

Section 12-16. Repealed

Qualifications and Rights of Members:

Section 17. Age - Qualified electors – Residents

Members of the Senate shall be at least twenty-five years of age, and members of the House of Representatives twenty-one years of age at the time of their election. They shall be qualified electors in their respective counties or districts and shall reside in their respective counties or districts during their term of office.

Section 17A. Limitation of Time Served in the Legislature

Any member of the Legislature who is elected to office after the effective date of this amendment shall be eligible to serve no more than 12 years in the Oklahoma State Legislature. Years in Legislative office need not be consecutive and years of service in both the Senate and the House of Representatives shall be added together and included in determining the total number of Legislative years in office. The years served by any member elected or appointed to serve less than a full Legislative term to fill a vacancy in office shall not be included in the 12-year limitation set forth herein; but no member who has completed 12 years in office shall thereafter be eligible to serve a partial term. Any member who is serving a Legislative term in office or who has been elected or appointed to serve a term in office on the effective date hereof shall be entitled to complete his or her term and shall be eligible to serve an additional 12 years thereafter. This amendment shall be effective on the 1st day of the year following its adoption.

Section 18. Ineligibility - Federal and State Officers - Conviction of Felony

No person shall serve as a member of the Legislature who is, at the time of such service, an officer of the United States or State government, or is receiving compensation as such; nor shall any person be eligible to election to the Legislature, who has been adjudged guilty of a felony.

Section 19. Expelled Member Ineligible - Punishment Not to Bar Indictment

A member of the Legislature expelled for corruption shall not thereafter be eligible to membership in either House. Punishment for contempt or disorderly conduct, or for any other cause, shall not bar an indictment for the same offense.

Section 20. Vacancies

The Governor shall issue writs of election to fill such vacancies as may occur in the Legislature.

Section 21. Conflict of Interests Prohibited - Board on Legislative Compensation

A. The Legislature shall enact laws to prohibit members of the Legislature from engaging in activities or having interests which conflict with the proper discharge of their duties and responsibilities.

B. The Board on Legislative Compensation is hereby created. Said Board shall be composed of five members appointed by the Governor, two members appointed by the President Pro Tempore of the Senate, and two members appointed by the Speaker of the House of Representatives. The members appointed by the Governor shall be from religious organizations, communications media, nonstate-supported educational institutions, labor organizations, and retail business; the members appointed by the President Pro Tempore of the Senate shall be from agricultural and civic organizations; and the members appointed by the Speaker of the House of Representatives shall be from manufacturing and from professional fields not otherwise specified. No member of the Legislature may be appointed to or serve on the Board. In addition to the members above provided for, the Chairman of the Oklahoma Tax Commission and the Director of State Finance shall serve as ex officio nonvoting members of said Board. The Chairman of said Board shall be designated by the Governor. Members of the Legislature shall receive such compensation as shall be fixed by the Board on Legislative Compensation. If a member of the Legislature is incarcerated due to being charged with a criminal offense and subsequently is found guilty of the offense or pleads guilty or nolo contendere to the offense, the legislator shall return to the state any compensation the legislator received from the state while the legislator was incarcerated prior to the guilty verdict or plea or nolo contendere plea and shall not receive any compensation from the state during any incarceration following such verdict or plea. Said Board shall each two years review the compensation paid to the members of the Legislature and shall be empowered to change such compensation; such change to become effective on the fifteenth day following the succeeding general election. The members of the Board shall serve without compensation, but shall be entitled to receive necessary travel and subsistence expense as provided by law for other state officers.

Section 22. Privileges - Arrest - Speeches or Debates

Senators and Representatives shall, except for treason, felony, or breach of the peace, be privileged from arrest during the session of the Legislature, and in going to and returning from the same, and, for any speech or debate in either House, shall not be questioned in any other place.

Section 23. Ineligibility to Appointment to Office - Interest in Contracts

No member of the Legislature shall, during the term for which he was elected, be appointed or elected to any office or commission in the State, which shall have been created, or the emoluments of which shall have been increased, during his term of office, nor shall any member receive any appointment from the Governor, the Governor and Senate, or from the Legislature, during the term for which he shall have been elected, nor shall any member, during the term for which he shall have been elected, or within two years thereafter, be interested, directly or indirectly, in any contract with the State, or any county or other subdivision thereof, authorized by law passed during the term for which he shall have been elected.

Section 24. Disclosure of Personal or Private Business
A member of the Legislature, who has a personal or private interest in any measure or bill, proposed or pending before the Legislature, shall disclose the fact to the House of which he is a member, and shall not vote thereon.

Legislative Sessions:

Section 25. Duration of First Session

The first session of the Legislature, held by virtue of this Constitution, shall not exceed one hundred and sixty days.

Section 26. Regular Sessions

The Legislature shall meet in regular session at the seat of government at twelve o'clock noon on the first Monday in February of each year and the regular session shall be finally adjourned sine die not later than five o'clock p.m. on the last Friday in May of each year.

The Legislature shall also meet in regular session at the seat of government on the First Tuesday after the First Monday in January of each odd numbered year, beginning at twelve o'clock noon for the purposes only of performing the duties as required by Section 5 of Article VI of the Constitution and organizing pursuant to the provisions of this Article and shall recess not later than five o'clock p.m. of that same day until the following first Monday in February of the same year, beginning at twelve o'clock noon.

Section 27. Special Sessions

The Legislature shall hold regular annual sessions as herein provided, but this shall not prevent the calling of special sessions of the Legislature by the Governor.

Section 27A. Method of Calling Special Sessions

(1) The Legislature may be called into special session by a written call for such purposes as may be specifically set out in the call, signed by two-thirds (2/3) of the members of the Senate and two-thirds (2/3) of the members of the House of Representatives when it is filed with the President Pro Tempore of the Senate and the Speaker of the House of Representatives who shall issue jointly an order for the convening of the special session.

(2) Nothing in this section shall prevent the calling of a special session of the Legislature by the Governor, as provided by the Constitution of the State of Oklahoma.

Leadership, Rules and Organization:

Section 28. Senate - President Pro Tempore - Standing Committees

The Senate shall, at the beginning of each regular session and at such other times as may be necessary, elect one of its members President pro tempore, who shall preside over its deliberations in the absence or place of the Lieutenant Governor; and the Senate shall provide for all its standing committees and, by a majority vote, elect the members thereof.

Section 29. Speaker of House of Representatives

The House of Representatives shall, at the beginning of each regular session and at such other times as may be necessary, elect one of its members Speaker.

Section 30. Judges of Election of Members - Quorum - Rules - Disorderly Behavior – Journal

Each House shall be the judge of the elections, returns, and qualifications of its own members, and a majority of each shall constitute a quorum to do business; but a smaller number may adjourn from day to day, and may be authorized to compel the attendance of absent members, in such manner and under such penalty as each House may provide.

Each House may determine the rules of its proceedings, punish its members for disorderly behavior, and, with the concurrence of two-thirds, expel a member.

Each House shall keep a journal of its proceedings, and from time to time publish the same. The yeas and nays of the members of either House on any question, at the desire of one-fifteenth of those present shall be entered upon its journal. Neither House, during the session of the Legislature, shall, without the consent of the other, adjourn for more than three days, nor to any other place than that in which the two Houses shall be sitting.

Section 31. Elections by Legislature - Voting and Entry in Journal

In all elections made by the Legislature, except for officers and employees thereof, the members thereof shall vote yea or nay, and each vote shall be entered upon the journal.

Section 32. Special and Local Laws - Notice of Intended Introduction

No special or local law shall be considered by the Legislature until notice of the intended introduction of such bill or bills shall first have been published for four consecutive weeks in some weekly newspaper published or of general circulation in the city or county affected by such law, stating in substance the contents thereof, and verified proof of such publication filed with the Secretary of State.

Section 33. Revenue Bills - Origination - Amendment - Limitations on Passage - Effective Date - Submission to Voters

A. All bills for raising revenue shall originate in the House of Representatives. The Senate may propose amendments to revenue bills.

B. No revenue bill shall be passed during the five last days of the session.

C. Any revenue bill originating in the House of Representatives shall not become effective until it has been referred to the people of the state at the next general election held throughout the state and shall become effective and be in force when it has been approved by a majority of the votes cast on the measure at such election and not otherwise, except as otherwise provided in subsection D of this section.

D. Any revenue bill originating in the House of Representatives may become law without being submitted to a vote of the people of the state if such bill receives the approval of three-fourths (3/4) of the membership of the House of Representatives and three-fourths (3/4) of the membership of the Senate and is submitted to the Governor for appropriate action. Any such revenue bill shall not be subject to the emergency measure provision authorized in Section 58 of this Article and shall not become effective and be in force until ninety days after it has been approved by the Legislature, and acted on by the Governor.

Section 34. Reading and Passage of Bills - Yeas and Nays Entered on Journal

Every bill shall be read on three different days in each House, and no bill shall become a law unless, on its final passage, it be read at length, and no law shall be passed unless upon a vote of a majority of all the members elected to each House in favor of such law; and the question, upon final passage, shall be taken upon its last reading, and the yeas and nays shall be entered upon the journal.

Section 35. Signing Bills and Resolutions - Entry on Journal

The presiding officer of each House shall, in the presence of the House over which he presides, sign all bills and joint resolutions passed by the Legislature, immediately after the same shall have been publicly read at length, and the fact of reading and signing shall be entered upon the journal, but the reading at length may be dispensed with by a two-thirds vote of a quorum present, which vote, by yeas and nays, shall also be entered upon the journal.

Legislative Authority and Duties:

Section 36. Extent of Legislative Authority - Specific Grants Not Limitations

The authority of the Legislature shall extend to all rightful subjects of legislation, and any specific grant of authority in this Constitution, upon any subject whatsoever, shall not work a restriction, limitation, or exclusion of such authority upon the same or any other subject or subjects whatsoever.

Section 37. Printing Plant and State Printer

The Legislature shall have the power to establish a state printing plant, and to provide for the election or appointment of a State Printer.

Section 38. Geological and Economic Survey
The Legislature shall provide for the establishment of a State Geological and Economic Survey.

Section 39. Boards of Health, Dentistry and Pharmacy - Pure Food Commission - Present Practitioners

The Legislature shall create a Board of Health, Board of Dentistry, Board of Pharmacy, and Pure Food Commission, and prescribe the duties of each. All physicians, dentists and pharmacists now legally registered and practicing in Oklahoma and Indian Territory shall be eligible to registration in the State of Oklahoma without examination or cost.

Section 40. Militia

The Legislature shall provide for organizing, disciplining, arming, maintaining, and equipping the Militia of the State.

Section 41. Firemen's Pensions

The Legislature may enact laws authorizing cities to pension meritorious and disabled firemen.

Section 42. Contempt, Disobedience of Process and Disorderly Conduct

In any legislative investigation, either House of the Legislature, or any committee thereof, duly authorized by the House creating the same, shall have power to punish as for contempt, disobedience of process, or contumacious or disorderly conduct, and this provision shall also apply to joint sessions of the Legislature, and also to joint committees thereof, when authorized by joint resolution of both Houses.

Section 43. Decennial Revision of Laws

The Legislature shall, in the year nineteen hundred and nine and each ten years thereafter, make provision by law for revising, digesting, and promulgating the statutes of the State.

Section 44. Unlawful Restraints of Trade

The Legislature shall define what is an unlawful combination, monopoly, trust, act, or agreement, in restraint of trade, and enact laws to punish persons engaged in any unlawful combination, monopoly, trust, act, or agreement, in restraint of trade, or composing any such monopoly, trust, or combination.

Section 45. Carrying Constitution into Effect
The Legislature shall pass such laws as are necessary for
carrying into effect the provisions of this Constitution.

Limitations on Legislative Powers:

Section 46. Local and Special Laws on Certain Subjects
Prohibited

The Legislature shall not, except as otherwise provided in this
Constitution, pass any local or special law authorizing:

The creation, extension, or impairing of liens;
Regulating the affairs of counties, cities, towns, wards, or school
districts;

Changing the names of persons or places;
Authorizing the laying out, opening, altering, or maintaining of
roads, highways, streets, or alleys;

Relating to ferries or bridges, or incorporating ferry or bridge
companies, except for the erection of bridges crossing streams
which form boundaries between this and any other state;
Vacating roads, town plats, streets, or alleys;

Relating to cemeteries, graveyards, or public grounds not owned
by the State;

Authorizing the adoption or legitimation of children;
Locating or changing county seats;

Incorporating cities, towns, or villages, or changing their
charters;

For the opening and conducting of elections, or fixing or
changing the places of voting;

Granting divorces;

Creating offices, or prescribing the powers and duties of officers, in counties, cities, towns, election or school districts;

Changing the law of descent or succession;

Regulating the practice or jurisdiction of, or changing the rules of evidence in judicial proceedings or inquiry before the courts, justices of the peace, sheriffs, commissioners, arbitrators, or other tribunals, or providing or changing the methods for the collection of debts, or the enforcement of judgments or prescribing the effect of judicial sales of real estate;

Regulating the fees, or extending the powers and duties of aldermen, justices of the peace, or constables;

Regulating the management of public schools, the building or repairing of school houses, and the raising of money for such purposes;

Fixing the rate of interest;

Affecting the estates of minors, or persons under disability; Remitting fines, penalties and forfeitures, and refunding moneys legally paid into the treasury;

Exempting property from taxation;

Declaring any named person of age;

Extending the time for the assessment or collection of taxes, or otherwise relieving any assessor or collector of taxes from due performance of his official duties, or his securities from liability;

Giving effect to informal or invalid wills or deeds;

Summoning or impaneling grand or petit juries;

For limitation of civil or criminal actions;

For incorporating railroads or other works of internal improvements;

Providing for change of venue in civil and criminal cases.

Section 47. Retirement of Officers

The Legislature shall not retire any officer on pay or part pay, or make any grant to such retiring officer.

Section 48. Bureau of Immigration

The Legislature shall have no power to appropriate any of the public money for the establishment and maintenance of a Bureau of Immigration in this State.

Section 49. Legislative employees - Number and Emoluments
The Legislature shall not increase the number or emolument of its employees, or the employees of either House, except by general law, which shall not take effect during the term at which such increase was made.

Section 50. Exemption of Property from Taxation

The Legislature shall pass no law exempting any property withis this State from taxation, except as otherwise provided in this Constitution.

Section 51. Exclusive Rights, Privileges or Immunities
The Legislature shall pass no law granting to any association, corporation, or individual any exclusive rights, privileges, or immunities within this State.

Section 52. Revival of Rights or Remedies - Taking Away Cause of Action or Defense

The Legislature shall have no power to revive any right or remedy which may have become barred by lapse of time, or by any statute of this State. After suit has been commenced on any cause of action, the Legislature shall have no power to take away such cause of action, or destroy any existing defense to such suit.

Section 53. Release or Extinguishment of Debts or Liabilities to State, County or Municipality

Except as to tax and assessment charges against real property remaining delinquent and unpaid for a period of time as long or longer than that provided by law to authorize the taking title to real property by prescription, the Legislature shall have no power to release or extinguish, or to authorize the releasing or extinguishing, in whole or in part, the indebtedness, liabilities, or obligations of any corporation or individual, to this State, or any county or other municipal corporation thereof.

Statutes, Bills, Acts, and Laws:

Section 54. Repeal of Statute – Effect

The repeal of a statute shall not revive a statute previously repealed by such statute, nor shall such repeal affect any accrued right, or penalty incurred, or proceedings begun by virtue of such repealed statute.

Section 55. Appropriations - Necessity and Requisites

No money shall ever be paid out of the treasury of this State, nor any of its funds, nor any of the funds under its management, except in pursuance of an appropriation by law, nor unless such payments be made within two and one-half years after the passage of such appropriation act, and every such law making a new appropriation, or continuing or reviving an appropriation, shall distinctly specify the sum appropriated and the object to which it is to be applied, and it shall not be sufficient for such law to refer to any other law to fix such sum.

Section 56. General Appropriation Bills - Salaries - Separate Appropriation Bills

The general appropriation bill shall embrace nothing but appropriations for the expenses of the executive, legislative, and judicial departments of the State, and for interest on the public debt. The salary of no officer or employee of the State, or any subdivision thereof, shall be increased in such bill, nor shall any appropriation be made therein for any such officer or employee, unless his employment and the amount of his salary, shall have been already provided for by law. All other appropriations shall be made by separate bills, each embracing but one subject.

Section 57. Subjects and Titles - Revival or Amendment by Reference - Extent of Invalidity

Every act of the Legislature shall embrace but one subject, which shall be clearly expressed in its title, except general appropriation bills, general revenue bills, and bills adopting a code, digest, or revision of statutes; and no law shall be revived, amended, or the provisions thereof extended or conferred, by reference to its title only; but so much thereof as is revived, amended, extended, or conferred shall be re-enacted and published at length: Provided, That if any subject be embraced in any act contrary to the provisions of this section, such act shall be void only as to so much of the law as may not be expressed in the title thereof.

Section 58. Time of Taking Effect of Statutes - Emergency Measures

No act shall take effect until ninety days after the adjournment of the session at which it was passed, except enactments for carrying into effect provisions relating to the initiative and referendum, or a general appropriation bill, unless, in case of emergency, to be expressed in the act, the Legislature, by a vote of two-thirds of all members elected to each House, so directs. An emergency measure shall include only such measures as are immediately necessary for the preservation of the public peace, health, or safety, and shall not include the granting of franchises or license to a corporation or individual, to extend longer than one year, nor provision for the purchase or sale of real estate, nor the renting or encumbrance of real property for a longer term than one year. Emergency measures may be vetoed by the Governor, but such measures so vetoed may be passed by a three-fourths vote of each House, to be duly entered on the journal.

Section 59. Uniform Operation of General Laws - Special Laws When General Law Applicable

Laws of a general nature shall have a uniform operation throughout the State, and where a general law can be made applicable, no special law shall be enacted.

Other Legislative Powers and Duties:

Section 60. System of Checks and Balances

The Legislature shall provide by law for the establishment and maintenace of an efficient system of checks and balances between the officers of the Executive Department, and all commissioners and superintendents, and boards of control of State institutions, and all other officers entrusted with the collection, receipt, custody, or disbursement of the revenue or moneys of the State whatsoever.

Section 61. Pensions to Police Officers

The legislature may enact laws authorizing cities to pension meritorious and disabled police officers.

Section 62. Retirement Benefits for Teachers and School Employees

The Legislature may enact laws to provide for the retirement for meritorious service of teachers and other employees in the public schools, colleges and universities in this State supported wholly or in part by public funds, and may provide for payments to be made and accumulated from public funds, either of the State or of the several school districts. Payments from public funds shall be made in conformity to equality and uniformity within the same classifications according to duration of service and remuneration received during such service.

Section 63. Continuity of Governmental Operations in Periods of Emergency

The Legislature, in order to insure continuity of State and local governmental operations in periods of emergency resulting from disasters caused by enemy attack or in periods of emergency resulting from the imminent threat of such disasters, shall have the power and the immediate duty

(1) to provide for prompt and temporary succession to the powers and duties of public offices, of whatever nature and whether filled by election or appointment, the incumbents of which may become unavailable for carrying on the powers and duties of such offices; and

(2) to adopt such other measures as may be necessary and proper for so insuring the continuity of governmental operations. In the exercise of the powers hereby conferred, the Legislature shall in all respects conform to the requirements of this Constitution.

ARTICLE VI: EXECUTIVE DEPARTMENT

General Provisions:

Section 1. Executive Officers Enumerated - Offices and Records – Duties

A. The Executive authority of the state shall be vested in a Governor, Lieutenant Governor, Secretary of State, State Auditor and Inspector, Attorney General, State Treasurer, Superintendent of Public Instruction, Commissioner of Labor, Commissioner of Insurance and other officers provided by law and this Constitution, each of whom shall keep his office and public records, books and papers at the seat of government, and shall perform such duties as may be designated in this Constitution or prescribed by law.

B. The Secretary of State shall be appointed by the Governor by and with the consent of the Senate for a term of four (4) years to run concurrently with the term of the Governor.

Section 2. Supreme Power Vested in Governor

The Supreme Executive power shall be vested in a Chief Magistrate, who shall be styled "The Governor of the State of Oklahoma."

Section 3. Eligibility to Certain State Offices

No person shall be eligible to the office of Governor, Lieutenant Governor, Secretary of State, State Auditor and Inspector, Attorney General, State Treasurer or Superintendent of Public Instruction except a citizen of the United States of the age of not less than thirty-one (31) years and who shall have been ten (10) years next preceding his or her election, or appointment, a qualified elector of this state.

Section 4. Terms of Office – Succession

A. The term of office of the Governor, Lieutenant Treasurer, Commissioner of Labor and Superintendent of Public Instruction shall be (4) years from the second Monday of January next after their election. The said officers shall be eligible to immediately succeed themselves except as otherwise provided in this section.

B. 1. No person shall be eligible to serve as Governor for a period of time in excess of eight (8) years. Such years need not be consecutive. Any years served by a person serving as Governor for less than full term to fill a vacancy in such office shall not be included in eight-year limitation set forth herein.

2. Notwithstanding the provisions of this amendment, any person serving as Governor at the time of passage of this amendment shall be eligible to complete the term of office to which he or she was elected but shall not be eligible to serve as Governor for a period of time in excess of eight (8) years, excluding years served for less than a full term to fill a vacancy in such office. The provisions of this paragraph shall apply regardless of whether such years were served prior to or after passage of this amendment.

C. No person shall be eligible to serve as Lieutenant Governor, State Auditor and Inspector, Attorney General, State Treasurer, Commissioner of Labor or Superintendent of Public Instruction for a period of time in excess of eight (8) years. Such years need not be consecutive. Any years served by a person elected or appointed to serve less than full term to fill a vacancy in any such office shall not be included in the limitations set forth herein. Any person serving in such position at the time of passage of this amendment shall be eligible to complete the term for which he or she has been elected and shall be eligible to serve an additional eight (8) years thereafter, notwithstanding the provisions of this amendment.

D. The Legislature is hereby authorized to enact laws to implement the provisions of subsections B and C of this section.

Section 5. Returns of Election - Tie Votes

The returns of every election for all elective state officers shall be sealed up and transmitted by the returning officers to the Secretary of State, directed to the Speaker of the House of Representatives, who shall, immediately after the organization of the House, and before proceeding to other business, open and publish the same in the presence of a majority of each branch of the Legislature, who shall for that purpose assemble in the hall of the House of Representatives. The persons respectively having the highest number of votes for either of the said offices shall be declared duly elected; but in case two or more shall have an equal and the highest number of votes for either of said offices, the Legislature shall, forthwith, by joint ballot, choose one of the said persons so having an equal and the highest number of votes for said office.

The Governor:

Section 6. Commander-in-Chief of Militia - Calling out Militia

The Governor shall be Commander-in-Chief of the militia of the State, except when in service of the United States, and may call out the same to execute the laws, protect the public health, suppress insurrection, and repel invasion.

Section 7. Extraordinary Sessions of Legislature

The Governor shall have power to convoke the Legislature, or the Senate only, on extraordinary occasions. At extraordinary sessions, no subject shall be acted upon, except such as the Governor may recommend for consideration.

Section 8. Execution of Laws - Intercourse with other States and United States - Conservator of Peace

The Governor shall cause the laws of the State to be faithfully executed, and shall conduct in person or in such manner as may be prescribed by law, all intercourse and business of the State with other states and with the United States, and he shall be a conservator of the peace throughout the State.

Section 9. Messages and Communications to Legislature

At every session of the Legislature, and immediately upon its organization, the Governor shall communicate by message, delivered to a joint session of the two Houses, upon the condition of the State; and shall recommend such matters to the Legislature as he shall judge expedient. He shall also transmit a copy, to each house, of the full report of each State officer and State commission. He shall communicate, from time to time, such matters as he may elect or the Legislature may require.

Section 10. Reprieves, Commutations, Paroles and Pardons
There is hereby created a Pardon and Parole Board to be composed of five members; three to be appointed by the Governor; one by the Chief Justice of the Supreme Court; one by the Presiding Judge of the Criminal Court of Appeals or its successor. An attorney member of the Board shall be prohibited from representing in the courts of this state persons charged with felony offenses. The appointed members shall hold their offices coterminous with that of the Governor and shall be removable for cause only in the manner provided by law for elective officers not liable to impeachment. It shall be the duty of the Board to make an impartial investigation and study of applicants for commutations, pardons or paroles, and by a majority vote make its recommendations to the Governor of all persons deemed worthy of clemency. Provided, the Pardon and Parole Board shall have no authority to make recommendations regarding parole for persons sentenced to death or sentenced to life imprisonment without parole. The Pardon and Parole Board

by majority vote shall have the power and authority to grant parole for nonviolent offenses after conviction, upon such conditions and with such restrictions and limitations as the majority of the Pardon and Parole Board may deem proper or as may be required by law.

The Pardon and Parole Board shall have no authority to grant but may recommend parole for persons sentenced pursuant to Section 13.1 of Title 21 of the Oklahoma Statutes or the exceptions to nonviolent offenses as defined by Section 571 of Title 57 of the Oklahoma Statutes.

The Governor shall have the power to grant, after conviction and after favorable recommendation by a majority vote of the Pardon and Parole Board, commutations, pardons and paroles for all offenses, except cases of impeachment, upon such conditions and with such restrictions and limitations as the Governor may deem proper, subject to such regulations as may be prescribed by law. Provided, the Governor shall not have the power to grant paroles if a person has been sentenced to death or sentenced to life imprisonment without parole. The Legislature shall have the authority to prescribe a minimum mandatory period of confinement which must be served by a person prior to being eligible to be considered for parole. The Governor shall have power to grant after conviction, reprieves, or leaves of absence not to exceed sixty (60) days, without the action of the Pardon and Parole Board.

The Governor shall communicate to the Legislature, at each regular session, each case of reprieve, commutation, parole or pardon, granted, stating the name of the person receiving clemency, the crime of which the person was convicted, the date and place of conviction, and the date of commutation, pardon, parole and reprieve.

The Pardon and Parole Board shall communicate to the Legislature, at each regular session, all paroles granted, stating the names of the persons paroled, the crimes of which the persons were convicted, the dates and places of conviction, and the dates of paroles.

Section 11. Approval or Veto of Bills - Passage over Veto - Failure to Return Bill

Every bill which shall have passed the Senate and House of Representatives, and every resolution requiring the assent of both branches of the Legislature, shall, before it becomes a law, be presented to the Governor; if he approve, he shall sign it; if not, he shall return it with his objections to the house in which it shall have originated, who shall enter the objections at large in the Journal and proceed to reconsider it. If, after such reconsideration, two-thirds of the members elected to that house shall agree to pass the bill or joint resolution, it shall be sent, together with the objections, to the other house, by which it shall likewise be reconsidered; and, if approved by two-thirds of the members elected to that house, it shall become a law, notwithstanding the objections of the Governor. In all such cases, the vote in both houses shall be determined by yeas and nays, and the names of the members voting shall be entered on the Journal of each house respectively. If any bill or resolution shall not be returned by the Governor within five days (Sundays excepted) after it shall have been presented to him, the same shall be a law in like manner as if he had signed it, unless the Legislature shall, by their adjournment, prevent its return, in which case it shall not become a law without the approval of the Governor. No bill shall become a law after the final adjournment of the Legislature, unless approved by the Governor within fifteen days after such adjournment.

Section 12. Appropriation Bills - Approval or Disapproval - Emergency Bills

Every bill passed by the Legislature, making appropriations of money embracing distinct items, shall, before it becomes a law, be presented to the Governor; if he disapproves the bill, or any item, or appropriation therein contained, he shall communicate such disapproval, with his reasons therefore, to the house in which the bill shall have originated, but all items not disapproved shall have the force and effect of law according to the original provisions of the bill. Any item or items so disapproved shall be void, unless repassed by a two-thirds vote, according to the rules and limitations prescribed in the preceding section in reference to other bills: Provided, That this section shall not relieve emergency bills of the requirement of the three-fourths vote.

Section 13. Officers' Commissions – Vacancies

The Governor shall commission all officers not otherwise commissioned by law. All commissions shall run in the name and by the authority of the "State of Oklahoma," be signed by the Governor, sealed with the Great Seal of the State of Oklahoma, and attested by the Secretary of State. When any office shall become vacant, he shall, unless otherwise provided by law, appoint a person to fill such vacancy, who shall continue in office until a successor shall have been duly elected or appointed, and qualified according to law.

Section 14. Adjournment of Legislature - Changing Place of Meeting

In case of a disagreement between the two houses of the Legislature, at a regular or special session, with respect to the time of adjournment, the Governor may, if the facts be certified to him, by the presiding officer of the house first moving the adjournment, adjourn them to such time as he shall deem proper, not beyond the day of the next stated meeting of the Legislature. He may convoke the Legislature at or adjourn it to another place, when, in his opinion, the public safety or welfare, or the safety or health of the members require it: Provided, however, That such change or adjournment shall be concurred in by a two-thirds vote of all the members elected to each branch of the Legislature.

The Lieutenant Governor:

Section 15. Qualifications - President of Senate - Impeachment, etc., during Vacancy in Governor's Office

The Lieutenant Governor shall possess the same qualifications of eligibility for office as the Governor. He shall be president of the Senate, but shall have only a casting vote therein, and also in joint vote of both houses. If, during a vacancy of the office of Governor, the Lieutenant Governor shall be impeached, displaced, resign, die or be absent from the State, or become incapable of performing the duties of the office, the president, pro tempore, of the Senate, shall act as Governor until the vacancy be filled or the disability shall cease; and if the president, pro tempore, of the Senate, for any of the above enumerated causes, shall become incapable of performing the duties pertaining to the office of Governor, the Speaker of the House of Representatives shall act as Governor until the vacancy be filled or the disability shall cease. Further provisions for succession to the office of Governor shall be prescribed by law.

Section 16. Devolution of Powers and Duties of Governor upon Lieutenant Governor

In case of impeachment of the Governor, or of his death, failure to qualify, resignation, removal from the State, or inability to discharge the powers and duties of the office, the said office, with its compensation, shall devolve upon the Lieutenant Governor for the residue of the term or until the disability shall be removed.

The Secretary of State:

Section 17. Duties Generally

The Secretary of State shall keep a register of the official acts of the Governor, and when necessary, shall attest them, and shall lay copies of the same, together with copies of all papers relative thereto, before either house of the Legislature when required to do so. He shall also perform such other duties as shall be prescribed by law.

Section 18. Custody and Use of Seal – Designation

The Secretary of State shall be the custodian of the Seal of the State, and authenticate therewith all official acts of the Governor except his approval of laws. The said seal shall be called "The Great Seal of the State of Oklahoma."

The State Auditor and Inspector:

Section 19. Qualifications, Powers and Duties

The State Auditor and Inspector must have had at least three years' experience as an expert accountant; his duties shall be, without notice to such treasurer, to examine the state and all county treasurers' books, accounts and cash on hand or in bank at least twice each year, and publish his report as to every such treasurer once each year. For the purpose of such examination he shall take complete possession of such treasurer's office. He shall also prescribe a uniform system of bookkeeping for the use of all treasurers. The State Auditor and Inspector shall perform such other duties and have such other powers as may be prescribed by law.

The Commissioner of Labor:

Section 20. Department Created – Duties

A Department of Labor is hereby created to be under the control of a Commissioner of Labor whose duties shall be prescribed by law.

Section 21. Board of Arbitration and Conciliation

The Legislature shall create a Board of Arbitration and Conciliation in the Department of Labor and the Commissioner of Labor shall be ex-officio chairman.

The Insurance Commissioner:

Section 22. Insurance Department Established – Function

There is hereby established an Insurance Department, which shall be charged with the execution of all laws now in force, or which shall hereafter be passed, in relation to insurance and insurance companies doing business in the State.

Section 23. Commissioner - Election - Term of office – Qualifications

There shall be elected by the qualified electors of the State, at the first general election, a chief officer of said department, who shall be styled "The Insurance Commissioner," whose term of office shall be four years: Provided, That the first term of the Insurance Commissioner so elected, shall expire at the time of the expiration of the term of office of the first Governor elected. Said Insurance Commissioner shall be at least twenty-five years of age and well versed in insurance matters.

Section 24. Bond of Commissioner - Additional Duties and Qualifications

The Insurance Commissioner shall give bond, perform such duties, and possess such further qualifications as may be prescribed by law.

Department of Mines:

Section 25. Creation of Office - Term and Qualifications - Duties, Oath and Bond

There is hereby created a Department of Mines, which shall be charged with the execution of all laws now in force or which shall hereafter be passed in relation to mining activities and corporations engaged in mining activities within the state.

Section 26. Repealed

Section 27. Repealed

Section 28. Repealed

Section 29. Repealed

Section 30. Repealed

Board of Agriculture:

Section 31. Creation and Membership - Status Authority and Duties

A Board of Agriculture is hereby created to be composed of five members all of whom shall be farmers and shall be selected in the manner prescribed by law.

Said Board shall be maintained as a part of the State government, and shall have jurisdiction over all matters affecting animal industry and animal quarantine regulation, and shall be the Board of Regents of all State Agricultural and Mechanical Colleges, and shall discharge such other duties and receive such compensation as now is, or may hereafter be, provided by law.

Section 31a. Board of Regents for Agricultural and Mechanical Schools and Colleges - Members - Vacancies - Removal – Terms

There is hereby created a Board of Regents for the Oklahoma Agricultural and Mechanical College and all Agricultural and Mechanical Schools and Colleges maintained in whole or in part by the State. The Board shall consist of nine (9) members, eight (8) members to be appointed by the Governor by and with the advice and consent of the Senate, a majority of whom shall be farmers, and the ninth member shall be the President of the State Board of Agriculture. Any vacancy occurring among the appointed members shall be filled by appointment of the Governor by and with the advice and consent of the Senate. The members of the Board shall be removable only for cause as provided by law for the removal of officers not subject to impeachment. The members shall be appointed for terms of eight (8) years each, with one term expiring each year, provided that the members of the first Board shall be appointed for terms of from one (1) to eight (8) years respectively. Provided that no State, National or County officer shall ever be appointed as a member of said Board of Regents until two years after his tenure as such officer has ceased.

Commissioners of the Land Office:

Section 32. Membership and Functions

A. The Governor, Lieutenant Governor, State Auditor, Superintendent of Public Instruction and the President of the Board of Agriculture shall constitute the Commissioners of the Land Office, who shall have charge of the sale, rental, disposal and managing of the school lands and other public lands of the state, and of the funds and proceeds derived therefrom, under rules and regulations prescribed by the Legislature.

B. Should the offices of State Examiner and Inspector and State Auditor be consolidated in the office of State Auditor and Inspector, the State Auditor shall be replaced as a member of the Commissioners of the Land Office by the State Auditor and Inspector. Should the offices not be so consolidated, the membership of the Board shall remain as prescribed in subsection A of this section.

Section 33. Accounts and Reports of Officers and Commissioners

An account shall be kept by the officers and commissioners of the State of all moneys and choses in action disbursed or otherwise disposed of severally by them, from all sources, and for every service performed; and a report thereof shall be made semi-annually and as often as may be required by law, to the Governor under oath. The Governor may, at any time, require information in writing, under oath, from all officers and commissioners of the State, and all officers of State institutions, penal, eleemosynary, educational, and industrial on any subject relating to their respective offices and institutions; which information, when so required, shall be furnished by such officers and managers; and any officer or manager who, at any time, shall make a false report, shall be punished as by law provided.

Section 34. Compensation of Officers

Each of the officers in this article named shall, at stated times, during his continuance in office, receive for his services a compensation, which shall not be increased or diminished during the term for which he shall have been elected; nor shall he receive to his use, any fees, cost, or perquisites of office or other compensation.

The State Seal:

Section 35. Description of Seal

In the center shall be a five pointed star, with one ray directed upward. The center of the star shall contain the central device of the seal of the Territory of Oklahoma, including the words, "Labor Omnia Vincit." The upper left hand ray shall contain the symbol of the ancient seal of the Cherokee Nation, namely: A seven pointed star partially surrounded by a wreath of oak leaves. The ray directed upward shall contain the symbol of the ancient seal of the Chickasaw Nation, namely: An Indian warrior standing upright with bow and shield. The lower left hand ray shall contain the symbol of the ancient seal of the Creek Nation, namely: A sheaf of wheat and a plow. The upper right hand ray shall contain the symbol of the ancient seal of the Choctaw Nation, namely: A tomahawk, bow, and three crossed arrows. The lower right hand ray shall contain the symbol of the ancient seal of the Seminole Nation, namely: A village with houses and a factory beside a lake upon which an Indian is paddling a canoe. Surrounding the central star and grouped between its rays shall be forty-five small stars, divided into five clusters of nine stars each, representing the forty-five states of the Union, to which the forty-sixth is now added. In a circular band surrounding the whole device shall be inscribed,

"GREAT SEAL OF THE STATE OF OKLAHOMA 1907."

ARTICLE VII: JUDICIAL DEPARTMENT

Section 1. Courts in which Judicial Power Vested

The judicial power of this State shall be vested in Senate, sitting as a Court of Impeachment, a Supreme Court, the Court of Criminal Appeals, the Court on the Judiciary, the State Industrial Court, the Court of Bank Review, the Court of Tax Review, and such intermediate appellate courts as may be provided by statute, District Courts, and such Boards, Agencies and Commissions created by the Constitution or established by statute as exercise adjudicative authority or render decisions in individual proceedings. Provided that the Court of Criminal Appeals, the State Industrial Court, the Court of Bank Review and the Court of Tax Review and such Boards, Agencies and Commissions as have been established by statute shall continue in effect, subject to the power of the Legislature to change or abolish said Courts, Boards, Agencies, or Commissions. Municipal Courts in cities or incorporated towns shall continue in effect and shall be subject to creation, abolition or alteration by the Legislature by general laws, but shall be limited in jurisdiction to criminal and traffic proceedings arising out of infractions of the provisions of ordinances of cities and towns or of duly adopted regulations authorized by such ordinances.

Section 2. Supreme Court Justices - Number - Terms - Vacancies - Qualifications - Chief Justice - Vice Chief Justice

The Supreme Court shall consist of nine Justices until the number shall be changed by statute and each Justice shall be from a separate district of the State. Each district shall remain as presently constituted until otherwise provided by Statute. The terms of office of the Justices of the Supreme Court shall be six years and shall commence on the second Monday of January following their election. Those appointed or elected to fill vacancies shall assume office immediately upon qualifying for the office. Each Justice, at the time of his election or appointment, shall have attained the age of thirty years, shall have been a qualified elector in the district for at least one year immediately prior to the date of filing or appointment, and shall have been a licensed practicing attorney or judge of a court of record, or both, in Oklahoma for five years preceding his election or appointment and shall continue to be a duly licensed attorney while in office to be eligible to hold the office. The Justices shall choose from among their members a Chief Justice and a Vice Chief Justice.

Section 3. Election of Justices and Judges – Vacancies

From each of the Supreme Court districts and Court of Criminal Appeals districts, the voters thereof shall elect a Justice of the Supreme Court and a Judge of the Court of Criminal Appeals at a nonpartisan election, in a manner provided by statute. In the event intermediate appellate courts are created, the judges thereof shall be elected at a nonpartisan election, in a manner provided by statute. In the event of a vacancy the Governor shall, by appointment from said district, fill such vacancy until the next election for State Officers, and at such election the vacancy for the unexpired term shall be filled by a nonpartisan election in a manner provided by statute.

Section 4. Jurisdiction of Supreme Court – Writs

The appellate jurisdiction of the Supreme Court shall be co-extensive with the State and shall extend to all cases at law and in equity; except that the Court of Criminal Appeals shall have exclusive appellate jurisdiction in criminal cases until otherwise provided by statute and in the event there is any conflict as to jurisdiction, the Supreme Court shall determine which court has jurisdiction and such determination shall be final. The original jurisdiction of the Supreme Court shall extend to a general superintendent control over all inferior courts and all Agencies, Commissions and Boards created by law. The Supreme Court, Court of Criminal Appeals, in criminal matters and all other appellate courts shall have power to issue, hear and determine writs of habeas corpus, mandamus, quo warranto, certiorari, prohibition and such other remedial writs as may be provided by law and may exercise such other and further jurisdiction as may be conferred by statute. Each of the Justices or Judges shall have power to issue writs of habeas corpus to any part of the State upon petition by or on behalf of any person held in actual custody and make such writs returnable before himself, or before the Supreme Court, other Appellate Courts, or before any District Court, or judge thereof in the State. The appellate and the original jurisdiction of the Supreme Court and all other appellate courts shall be invoked in the manner provided by law.

Section 5. Sessions - Quorum - Intermediate Appellate Courts - Form of Decisions - Clerk of Supreme Court

The sessions of the Supreme Court shall be held at the seat of government, and the sessions and duration thereof shall be fixed by rule of said Court. A majority of the members of the Supreme Court shall constitute a quorum and the concurrence of the majority of said Court shall be necessary to decide any question. The jurisdiction, powers, duties and procedures of intermediate appellate courts shall be as provided by rules of the Supreme Court until otherwise provided by statute. In the event of the creation of intermediate appellate courts, all appeals shall be made to the Supreme Court, which may, by rule, determine the method of assignment to, and recall from, the intermediate appellate courts until otherwise provided by statute. When the intermediate appellate courts acquire jurisdiction in any cause and make final disposition of same, such disposition shall be final and there shall be no further right of appeal except for issuance of a writ of certiorari ordered by a majority of the Supreme Court which may affirm, modify or make such other changes in said decision as it deems proper. The Supreme Court and intermediate appellate court decisions shall be in such form as the Supreme Court shall specify by rule and the Court of Criminal Appeals decisions shall be in such form as it shall specify by rule, until otherwise provided by statute. The Supreme Court shall appoint a Clerk of the Supreme Court, who shall serve at the pleasure of the Supreme Court and who shall perform the duties prescribed by law and rules of the Supreme Court. The Clerk of the Supreme Court in office on the effective date of this Article shall continue in office for the duration of his elective term.

Section 6. Administrative Authority - Director and Staff

Except with reference to the Senate sitting as a Court of Impeachment and the Court on the Judiciary, general administrative authority over all courts in this State, including the temporary assignment of any judge to a court other than that for which he was selected, is hereby vested in the Supreme Court and shall be exercised by the Chief Justice in accordance with its rules. The Supreme Court shall appoint an administrative director and staff, who shall serve at its pleasure to assist the Chief Justice in his administrative duties and to assist the Court on the Judiciary.

Section 7. District Courts - Jurisdiction - Courts Abolished - Transfer of Jurisdiction, Files Etc

(a) The State shall be divided by the Legislature into judicial districts, each consisting of an entire county or of contiguous counties. There shall be one District Court for each judicial district, which shall have such number of District Judges, Associate District Judges and Special Judges as may be prescribed by statute. The District Court shall have unlimited original jurisdiction of all justiciable matters, except as otherwise provided in this Article, and such powers of review of administrative action as may be provided by statute. Existing electing districts for all who are or who become District Judges and Associate District Judges under the terms of this Article shall remain as they are constituted for the offices formerly held by such persons on the effective date of this Article, until changed by statute. The Legislature may at any time delegate authority to the Supreme Court to designate by court rule the division of the State into districts and the number of judges.

(b) All Courts in the State of Oklahoma, except those specifically provided for in this Article, are hereby abolished at midnight on the day preceding the effective date of this Article and their jurisdiction, functions, powers and duties are transferred to the respective District Courts, and, until otherwise provided by statute, all non-judicial functions vested in such courts are transferred to the District Courts and Judges thereof. No person shall file a declaration of candidacy for any such court abolished herein on or after July 1, 1968.

(c) Each court into which jurisdiction of other courts is transferred shall succeed to and assume jurisdiction of all causes, matters and proceedings then pending, with full power and authority to dispose of them and to carry into execution or otherwise to give effect to all orders, judgments and decrees theretofore entered by the predecessor courts.

(d) The files, books, papers, records, documents, monies, securities and other property in the possession, custody, or control of the court hereby abolished, or in the possession, custody or control of any officer thereof, are transferred to the District Court; and thereafter all proceedings in all court shall be matters of record.

(e) In the event a transfer or transition has not been provided for by law, the Supreme Court shall by rule provide for the orderly transfer or transition.

Section 8. Classes of District Court Judges - Selection - Terms - Jurisdiction – Qualifications

(a) The Judges of the District Court shall be District Judges, Associate District Judges, and Special Judges. Each District Judge, each Associate District Judge, and each Special Judge shall be selected according to the provisions of this Article.

(b) Superior Court Judges shall become District Court Judges on the effective date of this Article.

(c) Common Pleas, County, Children's and Juvenile Court Judges shall become Associate District Judges in the following manner: Those Judges whose terms expire after the effective date of this Article shall become Associate District Judges on the effective date of this Article. Those Judges whose terms expire on or before the effective date of this Article, shall be subject to selection, in a manner provided by law, as Associate District Judges for a term expiring the day preceding the second Monday in January, 1971, and the selectees shall become Associate District Judges on the effective date of this Article.

(d) There shall be at least one Associate District Judge for each County in the State. The number of District Judges, including Superior Court Judges who become District Judges, and Associate District Judges shall continue at the number held over under this Article until changed by statute. The District Judges and Associate District Judges shall exercise all jurisdiction in the District Court except as otherwise provided by law. The District Courts, or any Judges thereof, shall have the power to issue any writs, remedial or otherwise necessary or proper to carry into effect their orders, judgments, or decrees.

(e) The appointment of any Judge to any Court abolished by this Article made after its adoption shall be for a period ending on the day preceding the effective day of this Article.

(f) The terms of District Judges and Associate District Judges shall be for four years commencing on the second Monday of January in 1971 and vacancies shall be filled in the manner provided by law.

(g) Each District Judge shall have had prior to election or appointment, a minimum of four years' experience as a licensed practicing attorney, or as a judge of a court of record, or both, within the State of Oklahoma; shall be a qualified elector of the respective district; and shall have such additional qualifications as may be prescribed by statute. Each Associate District Judge shall be an attorney licensed to practice in the State of Oklahoma and an elector in the County at the time of filing; and they shall have such additional qualifications as prescribed by statute. Both District Judges and Associate District Judges shall continue to be licensed attorneys while in office.

(h) The District Judges in each judicial administrative district shall appoint special judges to serve at their pleasure. The District Judges may appoint a non-lawyer as a special judge if no qualified licensed attorney is available. The jurisdiction of Special Judges shall be limited as may be prescribed by statute. The formula used for the number of special judges to be allowed to each judicial administrative district shall be set by the Legislature. All judges of special sessions courts shall become Special Judges for the remainder of their terms.

(i) District Judges, Associate District Judges and Special Judges may hold court anywhere in this State authorized by rule of the Supreme Court.

Section 9. Election of District Judges and Associate District Judges

District Judges and Associate District Judges shall be elected by the voters of the several respective districts or counties at a nonpartisan election in the manner provided by statute.

Section 10. Judicial Administrative Districts

(a) The State shall be divided into Judicial Administrative Districts, by statute, each consisting of one or more District Court Judicial Districts.

(b) The District Judges and Associate District Judges in each Judicial Administrative District shall select one of the District Judges to serve at their pleasure as Presiding Judge of such Judicial Administrative District. Subject to the authority of the Supreme Court, the Presiding Judge shall have general administrative authority over the Judicial Administrative District, including authority to provide for divisions, general or specialized, and for appropriate times and places of holding court subject to law.

Section 11. Salaries and Expenses - Retirement

(a) Judges and Supreme Court Justices shall receive for their services salaries provided by statute. The salaries of Judges and Justices shall not be diminished, but may be increased during their respective terms of office. Judicial officers may be paid such actual and necessary expenses as may be provided by statute. All basic salaries and expenses, or any portion thereof, of judges of District Courts shall be paid by the State unless otherwise provided by Statute, with such additional salaries as may be provided by statute to be paid by the respective districts or counties.

(b) No Justices or Judges, except those of Municipal Courts, shall engage in the practice of law nor hold any other office or position of profit under the United States or this State or any municipal corporation or political subdivision of this State, nor shall hold office in any political party. Provided that the Judges of the Court on the Judiciary, the Court of Tax Review and the Court of Bank Review and the Judges of any other such Special Courts may serve in such capacities in addition to their other judicial office. Compensation for service in the National Guard or the armed forces of the United States for such periods of time as may be determined by rules of the Supreme Court shall not be deemed "profit."

(c) Notwithstanding the provisions of this Article relating to terms of office, the Legislature may provide by statute for a maximum age qualification for election or appointment to office and for the retirement of Justices and Judges automatically at a prescribed age or after a certain number of years of service, or both. The compensation, age of retirement and procedure for retirement shall be prescribed by statute. Any retired Justice or Judge may, in the discretion of the Supreme Court, be assigned to Judicial service. The compensation for such service shall be that to which the Justice or Judge is entitled in accordance with benefits as provided by statute.

Section 12. Continuing Provisions

Except to the extent inconsistent with the provisions of this Article, all provisions of law and rules of court in force on the effective date of this Article shall continue in effect until superseded in a manner authorized by law.

Section 13. Savings Clause

In the event the abolition of any court or office hereunder is held by any court of competent jurisdiction to not take effect upon the effective date of this Article, then such court or office shall be abolished and terminated at the expiration of the term of the officer holding such office with the same provisions applying thereto, as if abolished on the effective date of this Article.

Section 14. Effective Dates - Implementing Acts

This Judicial Article shall become effective on January 13, 1969; except those provisions expressly authorizing or directing a different date; and except those provisions relating to the Supreme Court, the Court of Criminal Appeals, intermediate appellate courts and the Justices and Judges of such Courts, which shall become effective immediately upon the adoption of this Judicial Article. On or after the first Tuesday after the first Monday in January, 1968, the Legislature shall enact the necessary and appropriate laws to implement and place in operation the provisions of this Article.

Section 15. Jury trials – Verdicts

In all jury trials the jury shall return a general verdict, and no law in force nor any law hereafter enacted, shall require the court to direct the jury to make findings of particular questions of fact, but the court may, in its discretion, direct such special findings.

Section 16. Repealed

ARTICLE VIIA: COURT ON THE JUDICIARY

Section 1. Removal of Judges from Office - Compulsory Retirement – Causes

(a) In addition to other methods and causes prescribed by the Constitution and laws, the judges of any court, exercising judicial power under the provisions of Article VII, or under any other provision, of the Constitution of Oklahoma, shall be subject to removal from office, or to compulsory retirement from office, for causes herein specified, by proceedings in the Court on the Judiciary.

(b) Cause for removal from office shall be: Gross neglect of duty; corruption in office; habitual drunkenness; commission while in office of any offense involving moral turpitude; gross partiality in office; oppression in office; or other grounds as may be specified hereafter by the legislature.

(c) Cause for compulsory retirement from office, with or without compensation, shall be mental or physical disability preventing the proper performance of official duty, or incompetence to perform the duties of the office.

Section 2. Creation of Court on the Judiciary - Trial and Appellate Divisions - Jurisdiction – Membership

(a) There is created a Court on the Judiciary, hereinafter referred to as the Court, divided into a Trial Division and an Appellate Division. The Court is vested, subject to the provisions of this Article, with sole and exclusive jurisdiction to hear and determine causes arising thereunder.

(b) The Trial Division shall be composed of nine (9) members, eight (8) of whom shall be the district judges senior in service, but under sixty (60) years of age, with no two (2) from the same Supreme Court Judicial District (in case of equal seniority, the eldest in years to serve), and one (1) active member of the

Oklahoma Bar Association, chosen by its Executive Council or other body exercising similar powers.

(c) The Appellate Division shall be composed of two (2) members of the Supreme Court, chosen by that court; one (1) member of the Court of Criminal Appeals, chosen by that court; one (1) active member of the Oklahoma Bar Association, chosen by its Executive Council or other body exercising similar powers; and five (5) district judges, senior in service but under sixty-five (65) years of age; except that no more than one (1) district judge from any Supreme Court Judicial District shall serve. In the event of equal seniority, the eldest in years shall serve. If any district judge is qualified for both divisions, he shall serve on the Appellate Division and the next in qualification shall serve on the Trial Division.

(d) Within thirty (30) days after the adoption of this amendment, and thereafter prior to the first day in February of each odd-numbered year, the Chief Justice of the Supreme Court, the Presiding Judge of the Court of Criminal Appeals and the President of the Bar Association shall certify to the Secretary of State the names of the judges who are chosen, respectively, by the said courts and by the Oklahoma Bar Association. The Secretary of State shall determine the district judges who hold membership on the Trial Division and the Appellate Division. Promptly thereafter he shall notify the members of the respective divisions to meet at the State Capitol on a day certain, within thirty (30) days, for purposes of organization and of making or amending rules of procedure.

(e) Members of the courts so designated shall serve until March First of the odd-numbered year next after the year in which they are named. The attainment of the age limit specified shall not terminate their service during the term.

Section 3. Presiding judge - Rules - Meetings - Clerk – Powers

(a) Subject to the provisions of this Article, each division of the Court shall select its presiding judge, and shall be judge of the qualifications and the disqualification of its own members and shall make and publish its own rules of procedure. Each division shall meet on call of its presiding judge or three (3) of its members; a majority of the authorized membership of either division of the court shall constitute a quorum for the exercise of any or all of the jurisdiction of that division, regardless of whether or not vacancies exist in the membership of that division.

(b) The Clerk of the Supreme Court shall be the clerk of the court. He shall perform his duties under the direction of the Court or of the presiding judges.

(c) In the exercise of its jurisdiction, the Court is vested with full judicial power and authority, including the power to summon witnesses to appear and testify under oath and to compel the production of books, papers, documents, records and other evidential objects; to issue all manner of judicial and remedial process and writs, legal or equitable; to provide for discovery procedures in advance of trial; to make rules governing procedure; to grant full immunity from prosecution or punishment when deemed necessary and proper in order to compel the giving of testimony under oath or the production of books, papers, documents, records or other evidential objects. The specific enumeration of powers herein shall not derogate from the existence of other judicial power and authority in the Court, or from the exercise thereof in aid of its jurisdiction.

Section 4. Invoking Jurisdiction by Petition - Hearing

(a) The jurisdiction of the Trial Division of the Court may be invoked by a petition, filed either by the Supreme Court or the Chief Justice thereof; by the Governor; by the Attorney General; or by the Executive Secretary of the Oklahoma Bar Association when directed so to do by a vote of a majority of all members of its Executive Council; or by Resolution of the House of Delegates or by Resolution of the House of Representatives of the State of Oklahoma. The petition shall state the name of the respondent; the grounds upon which his removal from office or compulsory retirement from office is sought; and such other matters as may be specified by the rules of the Trial Division. It shall be subject to amendment by order of either division of the Court.

(b) Immediately upon the filing of the petition, the Clerk shall notify the presiding officer of the Trial Division, and the respondent named therein, in accordance with the rules of the Trial Division. The presiding judge of the Trial Division shall secure from the Executive Council of the Oklahoma Bar Association a panel of five (5) active members of the Association from which the presiding judge shall designate the prosecutor, and any necessary assistant, to conduct the proceeding against the respondent.

(c) The Trial Division or the presiding judge shall set the matter for hearing, not less than sixty (60) days after notice of the filing of the petition shall have been given the respondent. In all procedural matters not covered by rule of the Trial Division, the provisions of the Code of Civil Procedure, or of the common law of Oklahoma, shall be followed, so far as they may be applicable.

(d) Pending the determination of the proceedings, the Trial Division in its discretion may suspend the respondent from the exercise of his office. After full hearing, the Trial Division shall render such judgment as the facts may justify. No judgment shall extend further than:

(1) to removal of the respondent from office, with or without disqualification to hold any public office of honor, trust, or profit under this State, or

(2) to compulsory retirement from office; but such a proceeding, regardless of result, shall not bar or prejudice any other proceeding, civil or criminal, authorized by law. A judicial officer who is a member of the retirement compensation system prescribed by this Article and is compulsory retired shall receive the retirement compensation to which his term of service entitled him. If he is not qualified for full retirement compensation, he may receive such compensation as the Court may decree, in proportion to time served and in accordance with principles of justice and equity, alike as to amount, commencement of payment, terms of payment, or other relevant conditions or limitations.

Section 5. Appeal to Appellate Division

(a) From any judgment of the Trial Division, the respondent or the prosecutor may appeal to the Appellate Division, by filing a notice of appeal with the Clerk of the Supreme Court, within ten days after entry of the judgment. The notice shall be served upon the opposite party in the manner prescribed by the rules of the Appellate Division.

(b) The preparation and certification of the record upon appeal and all proceedings upon the appeal, not prescribed by this action, shall be governed by the rules of the Appellate Division.

(c) The review in the Appellate Division shall be an equity appeal, as to both law and fact. The Appellate Division may affirm, modify or reverse the judgment of the Trial Division, or enter a new judgment, as justice may require.

(d) If justice requires, the Appellate Division may hear additional evidence upon the appeal, upon a showing to the satisfaction of the Division that the additional evidence is material and that there were good reasons for failure to present it to the Trial Division.

Section 6. Established Rules to Apply - Judge Pro Tem – Compensation

(a) In all proceedings before the Court the established rules for disqualification of judges for interest, prejudice or partiality shall apply. No district judge shall sit in a matter in which the respondent is a judge of a court within his district court judicial district. In the event of the disqualification or failure to act of a member of the Court, a judge pro tem to sit in his place shall be named by the authority appointing him, if he is a district judge, the qualified district judge from his Supreme Court judicial district, next in seniority, shall serve as judge pro tem.

(b) Members of the Court shall serve without compensation, but shall receive the allowance for expense permitted district judges serving outside their districts.

(c) The prosecutors shall receive such fair and just compensation as the respective division of the Court shall award for service before that division.

(d) The Legislature shall appropriate such sums as may be necessary to carry out the provisions of this Article.

Section 7. Exclusive Jurisdiction

No other court shall have jurisdiction to restrict or control or review the orders of the Appellate Division of the Court on the Judiciary and no court except the Appellate Division shall have jurisdiction to restrict, control or review the orders of the Trial Division. District and Superior Courts shall, on direction of the Division of the Court on the Judiciary, aid in carrying out its procedure and mandates.

ARTICLE VIIB: SELECTION OF JUSTICES AND JUDGES

Section 1. Governing Provisions – Definitions

(a) The provisions of this Article shall govern the selection and tenure of all Justices of the Supreme Court and Judges of the Court of Criminal Appeals of the State of Oklahoma, to which the provisions hereof may be extended as hereinafter provided, other provisions of the Constitution or statutes of the State of Oklahoma to the contrary notwithstanding, and the provisions of Article VII as proposed by House Joint Resolution No. 508 of the First Session of the Thirty-first Oklahoma Legislature to the contrary notwithstanding.

(b) As used in this Section, "Judicial Office" means the offices of Justice of the Supreme Court and Judges of the Court of Criminal Appeals and "Judicial Officer" means a Justice or Judge of each such court, excluding retired or supernumerary Justices or Judges.

Section 2. Declaration of Candidacy – Election

At the general election next before his term expires, any Judicial Officer may seek retention in office by filing with the Secretary of State, not less than sixty (60) days before the date of such election, a declaration of candidacy to succeed himself. Thereupon, at such election, there shall be submitted to the qualified electors of the State, on a separate ballot, without party designation, this question:

"Shall (Here insert name of Justice or Judge) of (Here insert the title of the court) be retained in Office?

_____ YES
_____ NO

The question shall be decided by a majority of those voting thereon. If the decision is "yes" the Judicial Officer shall be retained in office for the next ensuing six (6) year term. If the decision is "no," or if no declaration of candidacy is filed, the office shall be vacant upon expiration of the term then being served, and the former Judicial Officer shall not be eligible for appointment to succeed himself. Retention in office may be sought for successive terms without limit as to number, except for retirement as may be provided by the Legislature for a maximum retirement age.

Section 3. Judicial Nominating Commission a) There is established as a part of the Judicial Department a Judicial Nominating Commission of fifteen (15) members, to consist of:

(1) six members to be appointed by the Governor, which shall include at least one from each congressional district established by the Statutes of Oklahoma and existing at the date of the adoption of this Article, none of whom shall be admitted to practice law in the State of Oklahoma or have any immediate family member who has been admitted to the practice of law in the State of Oklahoma or any other state;

(2) six members, which shall include at least one from each congressional district established by the Statutes of Oklahoma and existing at the date of the adoption of this Article who are, however, members of the Oklahoma Bar Association and who have been elected by the other active members of their district under procedures adopted by the Board of Governors of the Oklahoma Bar Association, until changed by statute; and

(3) Three members at large who shall not have been admitted to the practice of law in the State of Oklahoma or any other State or have any immediate family member who has been admitted to the practice of law in the State of Oklahoma or any other state but who shall be a resident of the State of Oklahoma, one to be selected by not less than eight members of the Nominating Commission. In the event eight members of the Commission cannot agree upon the member at large within thirty (30) days of the initial organization of the Commission or within thirty (30) days of a vacancy in the member at large position, the Governor shall make the appointment of the member at large; one to be selected by the President Pro Tempore of the Senate; and one to be selected by the Speaker of the House of Representatives. No more than two members at large shall belong to any one political party.

The Commission shall elect one of its members to serve as chair for a term of one (1) year.

The six lay members of the Commission who are appointed by the Governor shall be appointed within ninety (90) days from the date that this Article becomes effective. Two members shall be appointed for a term of two (2) years, two members for a term of four (4) years, and two members for a term of six (6) years. The Oklahoma Bar Association shall hold its election and certify to the Secretary of State its members within ninety (90) days from the effective date of this Article, two of whom shall be elected for a term of two (2) years, two for a term of four (4) years, and two for a term of six (6) years. Thereafter all of the members of the Commission, whether elected or appointed, shall serve for a term of six (6) years, except that the member at large shall serve for a term of two (2) years.

(b) Vacancies arising during the term of any lay commissioner, other than the member at large, shall be filled by appointment by the Governor for the remainder of his or her term. Vacancies of any lawyer commissioner shall be filled by the Board of Governors of the Oklahoma Bar Association for the remainder of his or her term.

(c) In the event of vacancy in the member at large position, the said vacancy shall be filled in the same manner as the original selection.

(d) Of those Commissioners named by the Governor, not more than three shall belong to any one political party.

(e) The concurrence of the majority of Commissioners in office at the time shall be sufficient to decide any question, unless otherwise provided herein. The Commission shall have jurisdiction to determine whether the qualifications of nominees to hold Judicial Office have been met and to determine the existence of vacancies on the Commission.

(f) No Commissioner, while a member of the Commission, shall hold any other public office by election or appointment or any official position in a political party and he or she shall not be eligible, while a member of the Commission and for five (5) years thereafter, for nomination as a Judicial Officer.

(g) Commissioners shall serve without compensation but the Legislature shall provide funds to reimburse them for their necessary travel and lodging expenses while performing their duties as such Commissioners.

(h) No Commissioner shall be permitted to succeed himself or herself.

(i) As used herein, the words "Oklahoma Bar Association" shall include any successor thereof and any future form of the organized Bar of this State.

Section 4. Vacancy in Judicial Office – Filling

When a vacancy in any Judicial Office, however arising, occurs or is certain to occur, the Judicial Nominating Commission shall choose and submit to the Governor and the Chief Justice of the Supreme Court three (3) nominees, each of whom has previously notified the Commission in writing that he will serve as a Judicial Officer if appointed. The Governor shall appoint one (1) of the nominees to fill the vacancy, but if he fails to do so within sixty (60) days the Chief Justice of the Supreme Court shall appoint one (1) of the nominees, the appointment to be certified by the Secretary of State.

Section 5. Terms and Election

Each Judicial Officer elected before or after the adoption of this Article shall, unless removed for cause, serve out the term for which he is elected and those Judicial Officers serving at the date of the adoption of this Article, whose Judicial Office comes under the provision of this Article on the date of the expiration of said term, shall be deemed to have been appointed as provided herein and eligible to file a declaration of candidacy to succeed themselves as provided in this Article. If retained in office, the term of each such Judicial Officer shall be six (6) years commencing the second Monday in January following such election.

The term and election of each Judicial Officer appointed to fill a vacancy after the adoption of this Article shall be as follows: If such appointed officer has served or will have served twelve (12) months on or before the next general election following appointment, such officer may file for election for the remainder of the term for which such officer was appointed, or for a six (6) year term, whichever is applicable, within the time and in the manner elected Judicial Officers file their candidacy under this Article. If such appointed officer has not served or will not have served twelve (12) months on or before the next general election following appointment, such officer shall continue in office until the second general election following appointment and may file for election for the remainder of the term or for a six (6) year term, whichever is applicable, as herein provided.

Section 6. Political Activity Prohibited .

No Judicial Officer appointed or retained in office under the provisions hereof shall make, directly or indirectly, any contribution to or hold office in a political party or organization.

Section 7. Effective Date

This proposed amendment to the Constitution of the State of Oklahoma as set forth herein shall be effective upon adoption and shall become operative only and in the event the amendment of Article VII of the Constitution proposed by House Joint Resolution No. 508, of the First Session of the Thirty-first Oklahoma Legislature, repealing the previously existing Article VII of the Oklahoma Constitution and adopting in lieu thereof a new Article VII of the Constitution is approved by the people.

ARTICLE VIII: IMPEACHMENT AND REMOVAL FROM OFFICE

Section 1. Officers Subject to Impeachment - Grounds - Suspension from Office upon Felony Conviction - Reinstatement - Temporary Judges

The Governor and other elective state officers, including the Justices of the Supreme Court, shall be liable and subject to impeachment for wilful neglect of duty, corruption in office, habitual drunkenness, incompetency, or any offense involving moral turpitude committed while in office. All elected state officers, including Justices of the Supreme Court and Judges of the Court of Criminal Appeals, shall be automatically suspended from office upon their being declared guilty of a felony by a court of competent jurisdiction and their pay and allowances, otherwise payable to such official, shall be withheld during the period of such suspension. In the event such verdict of guilty is reversed by a court of competent jurisdiction on appeal, such accumulated pay and allowances which have been withheld shall be paid to such official and he shall be automatically reinstated in office to serve the remaining part of the term for which he was elected. Such official shall not be entitled to any pay or allowances for a period of time after the term of office would otherwise have expired and he shall not be entitled to reinstatement in office after the expiration of the term for which he was elected. Whenever any Justice of the Supreme Court or Judge of the Court of Criminal Appeals is suspended by reasons of this section, the Governor shall be authorized to appoint a temporary Justice or Judge to serve during the period of such suspension and such temporary Justice or Judge shall be paid for his services the compensation allowed for such regular Justice or Judge.

Section 2. Removal of Officers Not Subject to Impeachment
All elective officers, not liable to impeachment, shall be subject to removal from office in such manner and for such causes as may be provided by law.

Section 3. Presiding Officer in Case of Impeachment -
Presentation of Impeachment

When sitting as a Court of Impeachment, the Senate shall be
presided over by the Chief Justice, or if he is absent or
disqualified, then one of the Associate Justices of the Supreme
Court, to be selected by it, except in cases where all the
members of said court are absent or disqualified, or in cases of
impeachment of any Justice of the Supreme Court, then the
Senate shall elect one of its own members as a presiding officer
for such purpose. The House of Representatives shall present all
impeachments.

Section 4. Oath or Affirmation - Number Concurring
When the Senate is sitting as a Court of Impeachment, the
Senators shall be on oath, or affirmation, impartially to try the
party impeached, and no person shall be convicted without the
concurrence of two-thirds of the Senators present.

Section 5. Judgment of Impeachment

Judgment of impeachment shall not extend beyond removal from
office, but this shall not prevent punishment of any such officer
on charges growing out of the same matter by the courts of the
State.

Section 6. Necessary Laws to Be Passed

The Legislature shall pass such laws as are necessary for
carrying into effect the provisions of this article.

ARTICLE IX: CORPORATIONS

General:

Section 1. Corporation - Company - Charter – License

As used in this article, the term "corporation" or "company" shall include all associations and joint stock companies having any power or privileges, not possessed by individuals, and exclude all municipal corporations and public institutions owned or controlled by the State; the term "charter" shall mean the charter of incorporation, by or under which any corporation is formed. The term "license" shall mean the authority under which all foreign corporations are permitted to transact business in this State.

Railroad, Transportation, Transmission and Public Service Corporations:

Section 2. Rights as to Construction of Lines

Every railroad, oil pipe, car, express, telephone or telegraph corporation or association organized or authorized to do a transportation or transmission business under the laws of this State for such purpose, shall, each respectively, have the right to construct and operate its line between any points in this State, and as such to connect at the State line with like lines; and every such company shall have the right with its road or line, to intersect, connect with, or cross any railroad or such line.

Section 3. Receipt of Cars, Tonnage and Passengers from Other Lines

Every railroad, car, or express company, shall each respectively receive and transport without delay or discrimination each other's cars, loaded or empty, tonnage, and passengers, under such rules and regulations as may be prescribed by law or any commission created by this Constitution or by act of the

Legislature, for that purpose.

Section 4. Oil pipe Line Companies - Regulation - Duties
All oil pipe companies shall be subject to the reasonable control
and regulation of the Corporation Commission, and shall receive
and transport each other's tonnage, or oils, or commodities,
under such rules and regulations as shall be prescribed by law, or
such commission.

Section 5. Telegraph and Telephone Companies - Transmission
of Messages - Physical Connections to Lines

All telephone and telegraph lines, operated for hire, shall each
respectively, receive and transmit each other's messages without
delay or discrimination, and make physical connections with each
other's lines, under such rules and regulations as shall be
prescribed by law, or by any commission created by this
Constitution, or any act of the Legislature, for that purpose.

Section 6. Railroads as Public Highways - Offices - Meetings -
Reports – Enforcement

Railroads heretofore constructed, or which may hereafter be
constructed in this State, are hereby declared public highways.
Every railroad or other public service corporation organized or
doing business in this State, under the laws or authority thereof,
shall have and maintain a public office or place in this State, for
the transaction of its business, where transfers of stock shall be
made, and where shall be kept, for inspection by the
stockholders of such corporation, books, in which shall be
recorded the amount of capital stock subscribed, the names of
the owners of stock, the amounts owned by them, respectively;
the amount of stock paid, and by whom; the transfer of said
stock, with the date of transfer; the amount of its assets and
liabilities, and the names and places of residence of its officers,
and such other matters required by law or by order of the
Corporation Commission. The directors of every railroad
company, or other public service corporation, shall hold at least

one meeting annually in this State, public notice of which shall be given thirty days previously, and the president or superintendent of every railroad company and other public service corporation organized or doing business in this State, under the laws of this State, or the authority thereof, shall report annually under oath, and make such other reports as may be required by law or order of the Corporation Commission, to said Commission, their acts and doings, which report shall include such matters relating to railroads and other public service corporations as may be prescribed by law. The Legislature shall pass all necessary laws enforcing, by suitable penalties, all the provisions of this section.

Section 7. Movable Property as Personal Property - Liability of Property to Execution

The rolling stock and all other movable property belonging to any railroad, transportation, transmission, or other public service corporation in this State, shall be considered personal property, and its real and personal property, or any part thereof, shall be liable to execution and sale in the same manner as the property of individuals; and the Legislature shall pass no laws exempting any such property from execution and sale.

Section 8. Consolidation of Public Service Corporations - Common Officer

No public service corporation, or the lessees, purchasers, or managers thereof, shall consolidate the stock, property, or franchises, of such corporation with, or lease or purchase the works or franchises of, or in any way control, any other public service corporation owning or having under its control a parallel or competing line; except by enactment of the Legislature upon the recommendation of the Corporation Commission: Provided, however, That the Legislature shall never enact any law permitting any public service corporation, the lessees, purchasers, or managers thereof when such public service corporation is organized under the laws of any other State, or of the United States, to consolidate the stock, property, or franchises, of such corporation with, or lease, or purchase, the works of, franchises of, or in any way control, any other public service corporation, organized under the laws of any other State, or of the United States, owning or having under its control in this State a parallel or competing line; nor shall any officer of such corporation act as an officer of any other corporation owning or controlling a parallel or competing line.

Section 9. Sales and Leases - Additional Restrictions on Consolidation

Upon the consent of the Corporation Commission in writing first had and obtained, any foreign or domestic railroad transportation or transmission company or corporation may lease, sell, or otherwise dispose of its property and franchises to, or may lease, buy, or otherwise acquire and operate the property and franchises of any like Company or Corporation; provided, that the Legislature may impose additional limitations or restrictions upon the rights of any railroad company or transmission company to consolidate.

Section 10. Street Railroads - Consent to Construction and Operation

No law shall be passed by the Legislature granting the right to construct and operate a street railroad within any city, town, or village, or upon any public highway, without first acquiring the consent of the local authorities having control of the street or highway proposed to be occupied by such street railroad.

Section 11. Acceptance of Provisions of Constitution

No railroad, transportation, transmission, or other public service corporation in existence at the time of the adoption of this Constitution, shall have the benefit of any future legislation, except on condition of complete acceptance of all the provisions of this Constitution, applicable to railroads, transportation companies, transmission companies, and other public service corporations: Provided, That nothing herein shall be construed as validating any charter which may be invalid, or waiving any of the conditions contained in any charter.

Section 12. Transportation of Railroad's Own Commodities

No railroad company shall transport, within this State, any article or commodity manufactured, mined, or produced by it, or under its authority, or which it may own, in whole or in part, or in which it may have any interest, direct or indirect, except such articles or commodities as may be necessary and intended for its use in the conduct of its business as a common carrier.

Section 13. Free Transportation of Passengers

No railroad corporation or transportation company, or transmission company shall, directly or indirectly, issue or give any free frank or free ticket, free pass or other free transportation, for any use, within this State, except to its employees and their families, its officers, agents, surgeons, physicians, and attorneys at law; to ministers of religion, traveling secretaries for railroad Young Men's Christian Associations, inmates of hospitals and charitable and eleemosynary institutions and persons exclusively engaged in charitable and eleemosynary work; to indigent, destitute and homeless persons, and to such persons when transported by charitable societies or hospitals, and the necessary agents employed in such transportations; to inmates of the National Homes, or State Homes for Disabled Volunteer Soldiers, and of Soldiers' and Sailors' Homes, including those about to enter and those returning home after discharge, and boards of managers of such Homes; to members of volunteer fire departments and their equipage, while traveling as such; to necessary caretakers of live stock, poultry, and fruit; to employees of sleeping cars, of express cars, and to linemen of telegraph and telephone companies; to Railway Mail Service employees, postoffice inspectors, customs inspectors, and immigration inspectors; to newsboys on trains, baggage agents, witnesses attending any legal investigation in which the railroad company or transportation company is interested, persons injured in wrecks, and physicians and nurses attending such persons: Provided, That this provision shall not be construed to prohibit the interchange of passes for the officers, agents, and employees of common carriers and their families; nor to prohibit any common carriers from carrying passengers free with the object of providing relief in cases of general epidemic, pestilence, or other calamitous visitation; nor to prevent them from transporting, free of charge, to their places of employment persons entering their service, and the interchange of passes to that end; and any railroad, transportation, or transmission company or any person, other than the persons excepted in this provision, who grants or uses any such free frank, free ticket, free pass, or free transportation within this State, shall be deemed guilty of a crime, and the Legislature shall provide proper penalties for the violation of any provision of this section by the railroad or transportation or transmission company, or by any individual: Provided, That nothing herein shall prevent the Legislature from extending these provisions so as to exclude such free transportations or franks from other persons.

Section 14. Repealed

Corporation Commission:

Section 15. Creation - Terms of Office – Vacancies

A Corporation Commission is hereby created, to be composed of three persons, who shall be elected by the people at a general election for State officers, and their terms of office shall be six years: Provided, Corporation Commissioners first elected under this Constitution shall hold office as follows: One shall serve until the second Monday in January, nineteen hundred and nine; one until the second Monday in January, nineteen hundred and eleven; and one until the second Monday in January nineteen hundred and thirteen; their terms to be decided by lot immediately after they shall have qualified. In case of a vacancy in said office, the Governor of the State shall fill such vacancy by appointment until the next general election, when a successor shall be elected to fill out any unexpired term.

Section 16. Qualifications of Commissioners

The qualifications of such commissioners shall be as follows: To be resident citizens of this State for over two years next preceding the election, and qualified voters under the Constitution and laws, and not less than thirty years of age; nor shall such commissioners, or either of them, be, directly or indirectly, interested in any railroad, street railway, traction line, canal, steam boat, pipe line, car line, sleeping car line, car association, express line, telephone or telegraph line, operated for hire, in this State, or out of it, or any stock, bond, mortgage, security, or earnings of any such railroad, street railway, traction line, canal, steam boat, pipe line, car line, sleeping car line, car association, express line, telephone or telegraph line, compress or elevator companies; and if such Commissioner shall voluntarily become so interested, his office shall become vacant; and if any Corporation Commissioner shall become so interested otherwise than voluntarily, he shall, within a reasonable time, divest himself of such interest; and failing to do this, his office shall become vacant. Nor shall any such commissioner hold any other office under the government of the United States, or of this State, or any other state government, and shall not, while such Commissioner, engage in any occupation or business inconsistent with his duties as such commissioner.

Section 17. Oath of Office - Additional Oath

Before entering upon the duties of his office, each of said commissioners shall take and subscribe to the oath of office as prescribed in this Constitution and shall, in addition thereto, swear that he is not, directly or indirectly, interested in any railroad, street railway, traction line, canal, steam boat, pipe line, car line, sleeping car line, car association, express line, telephone or telegraph line, nor in the bonds, stocks, mortgages, securities, contract or earnings of any railroad, street railway, traction line, canal, steam boat, pipe line, car line, sleeping car line, car association, express line, telephone or telegraph line; and that he will, to the best of his ability, faithfully and justly execute and enforce the provisions of this Constitution, and all the laws of this State concerning railroads, street railways, traction lines, canals, steam boats, pipe lines, car lines, sleeping car lines, car associations, express lines, telephone and telegraph lines, compress and elevator companies, and all other corporations over which said Commission has jurisdiction, which oath shall be filed with the Secretary of State.

Section 18. Powers and Duties - Notice before Taking Action - Process for Witnesses - Authority of Legislature - Municipal Powers

The Commission shall have the power and authority and be charged with the duty of supervising, regulating and controlling all transportation and transmission companies doing business in this State, in all matters relating to the performance of their public duties and their charges therefore, and of correcting abuses and preventing unjust discrimination and extortion by such companies; and to that end the Commission shall, from time to time, prescribe and enforce against such companies, in the manner hereinafter authorized, such rates, charges, classifications of traffic, and rules and regulations, and shall require them to establish and maintain all such public service, facilities, and conveniences as may be reasonable and just, which said rates, charges, classifications, rules, regulations, and requirements, the Commission may, from time to time, alter or amend. All rates, charges, classifications, rules and regulations adopted, or acted upon, by any such company, inconsistent with those prescribed by the commission, within the scope of its authority, shall be unlawful and void. The commission shall also have the right, at all times, to inspect the books and papers of all transportation and transmission companies doing business in this State, and to require from such companies, from time to time, special reports and statements, under oath, concerning their business; it shall keep itself fully informed of the physical condition of all the railroads of the State, as to the manner in which they are operated, with reference to the security and accommodation of the public, and shall, from time to time, make and enforce such requirements, rules, and regulations as may be necessary to prevent unjust or unreasonable discrimination and extortion by any transportation or transmission company in favor of, or against any person, locality, community, connecting line, or kind of traffic, in the matter of car service, train or boat schedule, efficiency of transportation, transmission, or otherwise, in connection with the public duties of such company. Before the Commission shall prescribe or fix any rate, charge or classification of traffic, and before it shall make any order, rule, regulation, or requirement directed against any one or more companies by name, the company or companies to be affected by such rate, charge, classification, order, rule, regulation, or requirement, shall first be given, by the Commission, at least ten days' notice of the time and place, when and where the contemplated action in the premises will be considered and disposed of, and shall be afforded a reasonable opportunity to introduce evidence and to be heard thereon, to the end that justice may be done, and shall have process to enforce the attendance of witnesses; and before said Commission shall make or prescribe any general order, rule, regulation, or requirement, not directed against any specific company or companies by name, the contemplated general order, rule, regulation, or requirement shall first be published one time in substance in one or more of the newspapers of general circulation published in the county in which the Capitol of this State may be located, together with the notice of the time and place, when and where the Commission will hear any objections which may be urged by any person interested, against the proposed general order, rule, regulation, or requirement; and every such general order, rule, regulation, or requirement, made by the Commission, shall be published at length, in the next annual report of the Commission. The authority of the Commission (subject to review on appeal as hereinafter provided) to prescribe rates, charges, and classifications of traffic, for transportation and transmission companies, shall, subject to regulation by law, be paramount; but its authority to prescribe any other rules, regulations or requirements for corporations or other persons shall be subject to the superior authority of the Legislature to legislate thereon by general laws: Provided, However, That nothing in this section shall impair the rights which have heretofore been, or may hereafter be, conferred by law upon the authorities of any city, town or county to prescribe rules, regulations, or rates of charges to be observed by any public service corporation in connection with any services performed by it under a municipal or county franchise granted by such city, town, or county, so far as such services may be wholly within the limits of the city, town, or county granting the franchise. Upon the request of the parties interested, it shall be the duty of the Commission, as far as possible, to effect, by mediation, the adjustment of claims, and the settlement of controversies, between transportation or transmission companies and their patrons or employees.

Section 18a. Organization - Quorum - Necessary Vote

A. The salary of Corporation Commissioners shall be set by the Legislature and may be increased at any time during the term of their office. The purpose of this provision is to assure that all Corporation Commissioners are paid equal salaries for their service, without regard to the time of their appointment or election.

B. The Corporation Commission shall organize by electing one of its members chairman and appointing a secretary, whose salary shall be fixed by the Legislature. A majority of said Commission shall constitute a quorum, and the concurrence of the majority of said Commission shall be necessary to decide any question.

Section 18b. Company Defined

As used in this article, the term "Company" shall include associations and joint stock companies having any power or privileges not possessed by individuals, and include all corporations except municipal corporations and public institutions owned or controlled by the State.

Section 19. Powers of Court of Record - Additional Powers - Failure or Refusal to Obey Orders

In all matters pertaining to the public visitation, regulation, or control of corporations, and within the jurisdiction of the Commission, it shall have the powers and authority of a court of record, to administer oaths, to compel the attendance of witnesses, and the production of papers, to punish for contempt any person guilty of disrespectful or disorderly conduct in the presence of the Commission while in session, and to enforce compliance with any of its lawful orders or requirements by adjudging, and by enforcing its own appropriate process, against the delinquent or offending party or company (after it shall have been first duly cited, proceeded against by due process of law before the Commission sitting as a court, and afforded opportunity to introduce evidence and to be heard, as well against the validity, justness, or reasonableness of the order or requirement alleged to have been violated, as against the liability of the company for the alleged violation), such fines or other penalties as may be prescribed or authorized by this Constitution or by law. The Commission may be vested with such additional powers, and charged with such other duties (not inconsistent with this Constitution) as may be prescribed by law, in connection with the visitation, regulation, or control of corporations, or with the prescribing and enforcing of rates and charges to be observed in the conduct of any business where the State has the right to prescribe the rates and charges in connection therewith, or with the assessment of the property of corporations, or the appraisement of their franchises, for taxation, or with the investigation of the subject of taxation generally. Any corporation failing or refusing to obey any valid order or requirement of the Commission, within reasonable time, not less than ten days, as shall be fixed in the order, may be fined by the Commission (proceeding by due process of law as aforesaid) such sum, not exceeding five hundred dollars, as the Commission may deem proper, or such sum, in excess of five hundred dollars, as may be prescribed or authorized by law; and each day's continuance of such failure or refusal, after due service upon such corporation of the order or requirement of the Commission, shall be a separate offense: Provided, That should the operation of such order or requirement be suspended, pending any appeal therefrom, the period of such suspension shall not be computed against the company in the matter of its liability to fines or penalties.

Section 20. Appeals to Supreme Court - Other Courts to Have no Jurisdiction - Mandamus and Prohibition

From any action of the Corporation Commission prescribing rates, charges, services, practices, rules or regulations of any public utility or public service corporation, or any individual, person, firm, corporation, receiver or trustee engaged in the public utility business, an appeal may be taken by any party affected, or by any person deeming himself aggrieved by any such action, or by the State, directly to the Supreme Court of the State of Oklahoma, in the manner and in the same time in which appeals may be taken to the Supreme Court from the District Courts, except that such an appeal shall be of right, and the Supreme Court may provide by rule for proceedings in the matter of appeals in any particular in which the existing rules of law are inapplicable. If such appeal be taken by the public utility or public service corporation affected by any such action, the State of Oklahoma shall be made the appellee, but in other appeals hereunder, the public utility or public service corporation affected shall be made the appellee.

An appeal from an order of the Corporation Commission affecting the rates, charges, services, practices, rules or regulations of public utilities, or public service corporations, shall be to the Supreme Court only, and in all appeals to which the State is a party it shall be represented by the Attorney for the Corporation Commission, and the Attorney General, or his duly authorized representative.

The Supreme Court's review of appealable orders of the Corporation Commission shall be judicial only, and in all appeals involving an asserted violation of any right of the parties under the Constitution of the United States or the Constitution of the State of Oklahoma, the Court shall exercise its own independent judgment as to both the law and the facts. In all other appeals from orders of the Corporation Commission the review by the Supreme Court shall not extend further than to determine whether the Commission has regularly pursued its authority, and whether the findings and conclusions of the Commission are sustained by the law and substantial evidence. Upon review, the Supreme Court shall enter judgment, either affirming or reversing the order of the Commission appealed from.

No court of this State, except the Supreme Court, shall have jurisdiction to review, affirm, reverse, or remand any action of the Corporation Commission with respect to the rates, charges, services, practices, rules or regulations of public utilites, or of public service corporations, or to suspend or delay the execution or operation thereof, or to enjoin, reverse, or interfere with the Corporation Commission in the performance of its official duties; provided, however, that writs of mandamus or prohibition shall lie from the Supreme Court to the Corporation Commission in all cases where such writs respectively would lie to any inferior court or officer.

Section 21. Supersedeas - Security - Accounts - Refunds - Precedence of Appeals

Upon the giving of notice of appeal from an order of the Corporation Commission, the Commission, if requested, shall suspend the effectiveness of the order complained of until the final disposition of the order appealed, and fix the amount of suspending or supersedeas bond. Such suspending or supersedeas bond shall be approved and filed with the Corporation Commission (or approved, on review, by the

Supreme Court), and made payable to the State of Oklahoma; provided, however, that in all cases involving orders of the Corporation Commission affecting rates or charges, the suspending or supersedeas bond must be sufficient in amount and security to insure the prompt refunding, by the appealing party, to the parties entitled thereto, of all rates or charges which such appealing party may collect or receive, pending the appeal, in excess of those authorized by the order appealed from, in event such order is, by such court, affirmed on appeal. The Corporation Commission, upon the execution of such suspending or supersedeas bond, shall forthwith require the appealing party, under penalty of immediate enforcement (pending the appeal and notwithstanding any supersedeas), of the order appealed from, to keep such accounts, and make to the Corporation Commission, from time to time, such reports, verified by oath, as may, in the judgment of the Corporation Commission, suffice to show the amounts being charged or received by the appealing party, pending the appeal, in excess of the charge allowed by the order or action of the Corporation Commission appealed from, together with the names and addresses of the persons to whom such overcharges may be refundable, in case such charges made by the appealing party, pending the appeal, be not sustained on such appeal; and the Corporation Commission shall also, from time to time, require such appealing party, under like penalty, to give additional security, or to increase such suspending bond, whenever, in the opinion of the Corporation Commission, the same may be necessary to secure the prompt refunding of the overcharges aforesaid. Upon the final decision of the appeal, all amounts which the appealing party may have collected, pending the appeal, in excess of that authorized by such final decision, shall be promptly refunded by the appealing party to the parties entitled thereto, in such manner and through such method of distribution, as may be prescribed by the Corporation Commission, or by law. All such appeals, affecting the rates, charges, practices, rules or regulations of any public utility, or of any public service corporation, or any individual, person, firm, corporation, receiver or trustee engaged in the public utility business, shall have precedence upon the docket of the Supreme

Court, irrespective of its place of session, next after habeas corpus cases, to the end that a plain, speedy and efficient remedy may be afforded the parties to such appeals.

Section 22. Statement of Reasons for Action - Cause Heard on Record - Certification of Facts and Evidence - New or Additional Evidence

The Corporation Commission shall, whenever an appeal is taken therefrom, file with the record of the case, and as a part thereof, a written statement of the reasons upon which the action appealed from was based, and such statement shall be read and considered by the Supreme Court, upon disposing of the appeal. In no case of appeal from an order of the Corporation Commission shall any new or additional evidence be introduced in the Supreme Court, but the cause shall be heard on the record made before the Corporation Commission, and the Chairman of the Commission, under the seal of the Commission, shall certify to the Supreme Court all the facts upon which the action appealed from was based, and which may be essential for the prompt decision of the appeal, together with all evidence introduced before said Corporation Commission, as may be selected, specified or required to be certified, by any party in interest, as well as such other evidence, so introduced before the Commission as the Chairman may deem proper to certify; provided, however, that in any appeal from an order of the Corporation Commission in which a party thereto asserts the violation of any right under the Constitution of the United States or the Constitution of the State of Oklahoma, the Supreme Court shall require the Commission to take and receive such additional evidence as is necessary to judicially determine the rights of the parties and report the same to the Court, in such manner as the Court may prescribe, for its consideration before the appeal is finally decided.

Section 23. Repealed

Section 24. Rights of Action Not Affected - Questioning Action of Commission

The right of any person, firm, corporation, receiver or trustee to institute and prosecute in the ordinary courts of justice, any action, suit or motion against any public utility, or public service corporation, or any individual, person, firm, corporation, receiver or trustee, engaged in the public utility business, shall not be extinguished or impaired by reason of any fine or other penalty which the Corporation Commission may impose or be authorized to impose upon such public utility, public service corporation, or any individual, person, firm, corporation, receiver or trustee engaged in the public utility business, because of its breach of any public duty or because of its failure to comply with any order or requirement of the Corporation Commission; but in no such proceeding by any person, firm, corporation, receiver or trustee, against such public utility, public service corporation, or any individual, person, firm, corporation, receiver or trustee engaged in the public utility business, nor in any collateral proceeding, shall the reasonableness, justness, or validity of any rate, charge, service, practice, rule, regulation or requirement, theretofore prescribed by the Corporation Commission, within the scope of its authority, and then in force, be questioned.

Section 25. Reports and Recommendations

The Commission shall make annual reports to the Governor of its proceedings, in which reports it shall recommend, from time to time, such new or additional legislation in reference to its powers or duties, or the creation, supervision, regulation or control of corporations, or to the subject of taxation, as it may deem wise or expedient, or as may be required by law.

Section 26. Railway Depots and Depot Buildings

It shall be the duty of each and every railway company, subject to the provisions herein, to provide and maintain adequate, comfortable, and clean depots, and depot buildings, at its several stations, for the accommodation of passengers, and said depot buildings shall be kept well lighted and warmed for the comfort and accommodation of the traveling public; and all such roads shall keep and maintain adequate and suitable freight depots and buildings for the receiving, handling, storing, and delivering of all freight handled by such roads.

Section 27. Railroad Crossings at Grade

In case any railroad company shall hereafter seek to cross at grade with its track or tracks, the track or tracks of another railroad, the railroad seeking to cross at grade, within a reasonable time, shall be compelled to interlock or protect such crossings by safety devices, to be designated by the Commission, and all costs of appliance, together with the expenses of putting them in, shall be borne equally by each company: Provided, That this act shall not apply to crossings of sidetracks.

Section 28. Inspection of Books and Papers - Examination of Officers and Agents

The commissioners, or either of them, or such persons as they may employ therefore, shall have the right, at such times as they may deem necessary, to inspect the books and papers of any railroad company or other public service corporation, and to examine, under oath, any officer, agent, or employee of such corporations in relation to the business and affairs of the same. If any railroad company or other public service corporation shall refuse to permit the commissioners, or either of them, or any person authorized thereto, to examine its books and papers, such railroad company or other public service corporation shall, until otherwise provided by law, for each offense, pay to the State of Oklahoma not less than one hundred and twenty-five dollars, nor more than five hundred dollars, for each day it shall so fail or refuse, and the officer or other person so refusing shall be punished as the law shall prescribe.

Section 29. Record of Financial Transactions

The Commission shall ascertain, and enter of record, the same to be a public record, as early as practicable, the amount of money expended in construction and equipment per mile of every railroad and other public service corporation in Oklahoma, the amount of money expended to procure the right of way, and the amount of money it would require to reconstruct the roadbed, track, depots, and transportation facilities, and to replace all the physical properties belonging to the railroad or other public service corporation. It shall also ascertain the outstanding bonds, debentures, and indebtedness, and the amount, respectively, thereof, when issued, and rate of interest, when due, for what purposes issued, how used, to whom issued, to whom sold, and the price in cash, property, or labor, if any, received therefore, what became of the proceeds, by whom the indebtedness is held, the amount purporting to be due thereon, the floating indebtedness of the company, to whom due, and his address, the credits due on it, the property on hand belonging to the railroad company or other public service corporation, and the judicial or other sales of said road, its property or franchises, and the amounts purporting to have been paid, and in what manner paid therefore. The Commission shall also ascertain the amounts paid for salaries to the officers of the railroad, or other public service corporation, and the wages paid its employees. For the purpose in this section named, the Commission may employ experts to assist them when needed, and from time to time, as the information required by this section is obtained, it shall communicate the same to the Attorney General by report, and file a duplicate thereof with the State Examiner and inspector for public use, and said information shall be printed, from time to time, in the annual report of the Commission.

Section 30. Greater Charge for Less Distance

No transportation or transmission company shall charge or receive any greater compensation, in the aggregate, for transporting the same class of passengers or property, or for transmitting the same class of messages, over a shorter than a longer distance, along the same line and in the same direction - the shorter being included in the longer distance; but this section shall not be construed as authorizing any such company to charge or receive as great compensation for a shorter as for a longer distance. The Commission may, from time to time, authorize any such company to disregard the foregoing provisions of this section, by charging such rates as the Commission may prescribe as just and equitable between such company and the public, to or from any junctional or competitive points or localities, or where the competition of points located without this State may make necessary the prescribing of special rates for the protection of the commerce of this State; but this section shall not apply to mileage tickets, or to any special excursion, or commutation rates, or to special rates for services rendered to this State, or to the United States, or in the interest of some public object, when such tickets or rates shall have been prescribed or authorized by the Commission.

Section 31. Foreign Corporations - Eminent Domain - Restrictions on Exercise

No railroad, oil pipe line, telephone, telegraph, express, or car corporation organized under the laws of any other state, or of the United States, and doing business or proposing to do business in the State of Oklahoma, shall be allowed to exercise the right of eminent domain, unless it shall become a body corporate pursuant to the laws of this state; or unless such corporation shall comply with such limitations and restrictions as may be prescribed by the Corporation Commission, and file with the commission its written acceptance of such requirements and procure from the commission a certificate entitling it to exercise such right.

Section 32. Through Rates - Investigation - Notice - Application to Interstate Commerce Commission

The said Commission shall have power, and it is hereby made its duty, to investigate all through freight or passenger rates on railroads in this State, and when the same are, in the opinion of the Commission, excessive or levied or laid in violation of the Interstate Commerce law, or the rules and regulations of the Interstate Commerce Commission, the proper officials of the railroads are to be notified of the facts and requested to reduce them or make the proper corrections, as the case may be. When the rates are not changed, or the proper corrections are not made according to the request of the Commission, it shall be the duty of the latter to notify the Interstate Commerce Commission and to make proper application to it for relief, and the Attorney General or such other persons as may be designated by law shall represent the Commission in all such matters.

Section 33. Switches to Mines, Mills, Elevators and Industries
Any person, firm, or corporation owning or operating any coal, lead, iron, or zinc mine, or any saw mill, grain elevator, or other industry, whenever the Commission shall reasonably determine that the amount of business is sufficient to justify the same, near or within a reasonable distance of any track, may, at the expense of such person, firm, or corporation, build and keep in repair a switch leading from such railroad to such mine, saw mill, elevator or other industry; such railroad company shall be required to furnish the switch stand and frog and other necessary material for making connection, with such side track or spur under such reasonable terms, conditions and regulations as the said Commission may prescribe, and shall make connection therewith. The party owning such mine, saw mill, elevator or other industry shall pay the actual cost thereof. If any railroad company, after proper demand therefore is made, shall refuse to furnish said material for making said connection and put the same in place, or after the building of such switch, shall fail or refuse to operate the same, such railroad company failing and refusing for a reasonable time, shall forfeit and pay to the party or corporation

aggrieved, the sum of five hundred dollars for each and every offense, to be recovered by civil action in any court of competent jurisdiction; and every day of such refusal on the part of the railroad company to operate such switch as aforesaid, after such demand is made, shall be deemed a separate offense.

Construction of Laws - Power of Legislature:

Section 34. Definitions - Avoidance of Conflicts with U. S. Constitution

As used in this Article, the term "transportation company" shall include any company, corporation, trustee, receiver or any other person owning, leasing or operating for hire a railroad, street railway, canal, steamboat line, and also any freight car company, car corporation, or company, trustee or persons in any way engaged in such business as a common carrier over a route acquired in whole or in part under the right of eminent domain, or under any grant from the Government of the United States; the term "rate" shall be construed to mean rate of charge for any service rendered, or to be rendered; the terms "rate," "charge" and "regulation" shall include joint rates, joint charges and joint regulations, respectively; the term "transmission company" shall include any company, receiver or other person owning, leasing or operating for hire any telegraph or telephone line; the term "freight" shall be construed to mean any property transported or received for transportation by any transportation company. The term "public service corporation" shall include all transportation and transmission companies, all gas, electric, heat, light and power companies, and all persons, firms, corporations, receivers or trustees engaged in said businesses, and all persons, firms, corporations, receivers or trustees authorized to exercise the right of eminent domain or having a franchise to use or occupy any right of way, street, alley or public highway, whether along, over or under the same, in a manner not permitted to the general public, and all persons, firms, corporations, receivers and trustees engaged in any business which is a public utility or a public service corporation, at the present time or which may hereafter be declared to be a public utility or a public service corporation. The term "person" as used in this Article shall include individuals, partnerships, and corporations in the singular as well as plural number; the term "bond" shall mean all certificates or written evidence of indebtedness issued by any corporation and secured by mortgage or trust deed. The term "frank" shall mean any writing or token issued by or under authority of a transmission company, entitling the holder to any service from such company free of charge.

The provisions of this Article shall always be so restricted in their application as not to conflict with any of the provisions of the Constitution of the United States, and as if the necessary limitations upon their interpretation had been herein expressed in each case.

Section 35. Power of Legislature

After the second Monday in January, nineteen hundred and nine, the Legislature may, by law, from time to time, alter, amend, revise, or repeal sections from eighteen to thirty-four, inclusive, of this article, or any of them, or any amendments thereof: Provided, That no amendment made under authority of this section shall contravene the provisions of any part of this Constitution other than the said sections last above referred to or any such amendments thereof.

Section 36. Common Law Doctrine Abrogated - Liability for Acts of Receivers - Power of Legislature

The common law doctrine of the fellow-servant, so far as it affects the liability of the master for injuries to his servant, resulting from the acts or omissions of any other servant or servants of the common master, is abrogated as to every employee of every railroad company and every street railway company or inter-urban railway company, and of every person, firm, or corporation engaged in mining in this State; and every such employee shall have the same right to recover for every injury suffered by him for the acts or omissions of any other employee or employees of the common master that a servant would have if such acts or omissions were those of the master himself in the performance of a non-assignable duty; and when death, whether instantaneous or not, results to such employee from any injury for which he could have recovered under the above provisions, had not death occurred, then his legal or personal representative, surviving consort or relatives, or any trustee, curator, committee or guardian of such consort or relatives, shall have the same rights and remedies with respect thereto, as if death had been caused by the negligence of the master. And every railroad company and every street railway company or inter-urban railway company, and every person, firm, or corporation engaged in underground mining in this State shall be liable under this section, for the acts of his or its receivers. Nothing contained in this section shall restrict the power of the Legislature to extend to the employees of any person, firm, or corporation, the rights and remedies herein provided for.

Fares:

Section 37. Repealed

Private Corporations:

Section 38. Creation or Licensing - Necessity of General Law

No private corporation shall be created nor foreign corporation licensed to conduct business in the State, except by general law.

Section 39. Restrictions on Issuance of Stock

No corporation shall issue stock except for money, labor done, or property actually received, at a stated value thereof, and the Legislature shall prescribe the necessary regulations to prevent the issue of fictitious stock or indebtedness.

Section 40. Influencing Elections or Official Duty

No corporation organized or doing business in this State shall be permitted to influence elections or official duty by contributions of money or anything of value.

Section 41. Banks and Trust Companies - Restriction on Controlling Other Stock

No trust company, or bank or banking company shall own, hold, or control, in any manner whatever, the stock of any other trust company or bank or banking company, except such stock as may be pledged in good faith to secure bona fide indebtedness, acquired upon foreclosure, execution sale, or otherwise for the satisfaction of debt; and such stock shall be disposed of in the time and manner hereinbefore provided.

Section 42. Arbitration of Differences with Employees
Every license issued or charter granted to a mining or public service corporation, foreign or domestic, shall contain a stipulation that such corporation will submit any difference it may have with employees in reference to labor, to arbitration, as shall be provided by law.

Section 43. Foreign Corporations - Designation of Resident Agent - Service - Place of Suit

Every foreign corporation shall, before being licensed to do business in the State, designate an agent residing in the State; and service of summons or legal notice may be had on such designated agent and such other agents as now are or may hereafter be provided for by law. Suit may be maintained against a foreign corporation in the county where an agent of such corporation may be found, or in the county of the residence of plaintiff, or in the county where the cause of action may arise.

Section 44. Foreign Corporations Subject to Same Restrictions and Requirements as Domestic Corporations

No foreign corporation shall be authorized to carry on in this State any business which a domestic corporation is prohibited form doing, or be relieved from compliance with any of the requirements made of a similar domestic corporation by the Constitution or laws of the State. Nothing in this article, however, shall restrict or limit the power of the Legislature to impose conditions under which foreign corporations may be licensed to do business in this State.

Section 45. Monopoly or Destruction of Competition - Discrimination Prohibited

Until otherwise provided by law, no person, firm, association, or corporation engaged in the production, manufacture, distribution, or sale of any commodity of general use, shall, for the purpose of creating a monopoly or destroying competition in trade, discriminate between different persons, associations, or corporations, or different sections, communities or cities of the State, by selling such commodity at a lower rate in one section, community, or city than in another, after making due allowance for the difference, if any, in the grade, quantity, or quality, and in the actual cost of transportation from the point of production or manufacture.

Section 46. Grants of Special or Exclusive Privileges

All existing charters or grants of special or exclusive privileges under which a bona fide organization shall not have taken place and business commenced in good faith at the time this Constitution becomes effective, shall thereafter have no validity.

Section 47. Power to Alter, Amend or Repeal Charters or Franchises

The Legislature shall have power to alter, amend, annul, revoke, or repeal any charter of incorporation or franchise now existing and subject to be altered, amended, annulled, revoked, or repealed at the time of the adoption of this Constitution, or any that may be hereafter created, whenever in its opinion it may be injurious to the citizens of this State, in such manner, however, that no injustice shall be done to the incorporators.

Section 48. Penalties and Regulations

The Legislature shall provide such penalties and regulations as may be necessary for the proper enforcement of the provisions of this article.

ARTICLE X: REVENUE AND TAXATION

In General:

Section 1. Fiscal Year

The fiscal year shall commence on the first day of July in each year, unless otherwise provided by law.

Section 2. Tax to Defray State Expenses

The Legislature shall provide by law for an annual tax sufficient, with other resources, to defray the estimated ordinary expenses of the State for each fiscal year.

Section 3. Tax to Pay Deficiency

Whenever the expenses of any fiscal year shall exceed the income, the Legislature may provide for levying a tax for the ensuing fiscal year, which, with other resources, shall be sufficient to pay the deficiency, as well as the estimated ordinary expenses of the State for the ensuing year.

Section 4. Levy to Pay State Debt

For the purpose of paying the State debt, if any, the Legislature shall provide for levying a tax, annually, sufficient to pay the annual interest and principal of such debt within twenty-five years from the final passage of the law creating the debt.

Section 5. Surrender of Power of Taxation - Uniformity of Taxes

A. Except as otherwise provided by this section, the power of taxation shall never be surrendered, suspended, or contracted away.

B. Taxes shall be uniform upon the same class of subjects.

C. The Legislature is hereby authorized to enact laws providing for the abatement of tax assessments, or portions thereof, if:

1. Collection of the tax liability and interest and penalties accruing thereto would reasonably result in the taxpayer declaring bankruptcy;

2. The tax is uncollectible due to insolvency of the taxpayer resulting from factors beyond control of the taxpayer or for other similar cause beyond the control of the taxpayer;

3. The tax liability is attributable to actions of a person other than the taxpayer and it would be inequitable to hold the taxpayer liable for the tax liability; or

4. In cases of nonpayment of trust fund taxes, the taxes were not collected by the taxpayer from its customer and the taxpayer had a good faith belief that collection of the taxes was not required.

Section 6. Property Exempt from Taxation - Exemptions under Territorial Law - Storm Shelters - Exemption of Certain Property Determined by Special Election

A. Except as otherwise provided in subsection B of this section, all property used for free public libraries, free museums, public cemeteries, property used exclusively for nonprofit schools and colleges, and all property used exclusively for religious and charitable purposes, and all property of the United States except property for which a federal agency obtains title through foreclosure, voluntary or involuntary liquidation or bankruptcy unless the taxation of such property is prohibited by federal law; all property of this state, and of counties and of municipalities of this state; household goods of the heads of families, tools, implements, and livestock employed in the support of the family, not exceeding One Hundred Dollars ($100.00) in value, and all growing crops, shall be exempt from taxation: Provided, that all property not herein specified now exempt from taxation under the laws of the Territory of Oklahoma, shall be exempt from taxation until otherwise provided by law.

All property owned by the Murrow Indian Orphan Home, located in Coal County, and all property owned by the Whitaker Orphan Home, located in Mayes County, so long as the same shall be used exclusively as free homes or schools for orphan children, and for poor and indigent persons, and all fraternal orphan homes, and other orphan homes, together with all their charitable funds, shall be exempt from taxation, and such property as may be exempt by reason of treaty stipulations, existing between the Indians and the United States government, or by federal laws, during the force and effect of such treaties or federal laws. The Legislature may authorize any incorporated city or town, by a majority vote of its electors voting thereon, to exempt manufacturing establishments and public utilities from municipal taxation, for a period not exceeding five (5) years, as an inducement to their location.

Up to one hundred (100) square feet of a storm shelter designed for protection and safety from tornadoes or tornadic winds and installed or added to an improvement to real property after January 1, 2002, shall be exempt from taxation. A storm shelter shall include, but not be limited to, a safe room built as part of and within an improvement to real property. If title to property with an exempt storm shelter is transferred, changed or conveyed to another person, such storm shelter shall be assessed for that year based on the fair cash value as set forth in Section 8 of this article.

B. The board of county commissioners of any county may call a special election to determine whether or not household goods of the heads of families and livestock employed in support of the family located within the county shall be exempt from ad valorem taxation. Such an election shall also be called by the board upon petition signed by not less than twenty-five percent (25%) of the registered voters of the county. Upon passage of the question, the exemption provided for in this subsection shall become effective on January 1 of the following year.

Section 6A. Intangible Personal Property Exempt from Ad Valorem or Other Tax

Beginning January 1, 2013, intangible personal property shall not be subject to ad valorem tax or to any other tax in lieu of ad valorem tax within this State.

Section 6A. Tangible Personal Property Moving Through State – Situs

A. All property consigned to a consignee in this State from outside this State to be forwarded to a point outside this State, which is entitled under the tariffs, rules, and regulations approved by the Interstate Commerce Commission to be forwarded at through rates from the point of origin to the point of destination, if not detained within this State for a period of more than ninety (90) days, shall be deemed to be property moving in interstate commerce, and no such property shall be subject to taxation in this State; provided, that goods, wares and merchandise, whether or not moving on through rates, shall be deemed to move in interstate commerce, and not subject to taxation in this State if not detained more than nine (9) months where such goods, wares and merchandise are so held for assembly, storage, manufacturing, processing or fabricating purposes; provided, further, that personal property consigned for sale within this State must be assessed as any other personal property.

B. The Legislature shall enact laws governing the procedures for making application to the county assessor for purposes of the exemption authorized by this section, including the time as of which the application must be filed and information to be included with the application.

Section 6B. Qualifying Manufacturing Concern--Ad Valorem Tax Exemption

A. For the purpose of inducing any manufacturing concern to locate or expand manufacturing facilities within any county of this state, a qualifying manufacturing concern shall be exempt from the levy of any ad valorem taxes upon new, expanded or acquired manufacturing facilities for a period of five (5) years.

B. For purposes of this section, a "qualifying manufacturing concern" means a concern that:

1. Is not engaged in business in this state or does not have property subject to ad valorem tax in this state and constructs a manufacturing facility in this state or acquires an existing facility that has been unoccupied for a period of twelve (12) months prior to acquisition; or

2. Is engaged in business in this state or has property subject to ad valorem tax in this state and constructs a manufacturing facility in this state at a different location from present facilities and continues to operate all of its facilities or acquires an existing facility that has been unoccupied for a period of twelve (12) months prior to acquisition and continues to operate all of its facilities.

C. The exemption allowed by this section shall apply to expansions of existing facilities. Provided, however that any exemption shall be limited to the increase in ad valorem taxes directly attributable to the expansion.

D. The Legislature shall define the term "manufacturing facility" for purposes of the ad valorem tax exemption provided by this section in order to promote full employment of labor resources within the state; provided, however, that a manufacturing facility that qualifies for the ad valorem tax exemption provided by this section, pursuant to the definition of "manufacturing facility" then applicable, shall be eligible for the exemption without regard to subsequent changes in the definition of the term "manufacturing facility."

E. The Legislature shall enact laws to carry out the provisions of this section and to provide for the reimbursement to common schools, county governments, cities and towns, emergency medical services districts, vocational-technical schools, junior colleges, county health departments and libraries for revenues lost to such entities as a result of the exemption provided by this section.

F. The assessed valuation of property exempt from taxation by virtue of this section shall be added to the assessed valuation of taxable property in computing the limit on indebtedness of political subdivisions contained in Section 26 of this article.

G. Pursuant to an affirmative vote of a majority of the eligible voters of the county at an election for such purpose which may be called by the county commissioners of each county, after the expiration of the period prescribed by this section for the exemption, a county may retain not to exceed twenty-five percent (25%) of the increased ad valorem taxes derived from the levy imposed by the county upon the taxable value of property previously exempt pursuant to this section. The revenue retained by the county pursuant to this subsection may be used by the county as an economic development incentive to attract additional investment which will result in additional employment in the county. Only ad valorem tax revenue derived from ten (10) mills of the total ad valorem tax levy imposed by the county may be used for this purpose. The ad valorem tax revenue derived from the levy imposed by any other taxing jurisdiction shall be apportioned as otherwise required by law. The provisions of this subsection shall be applicable to qualified manufacturing concerns exempt prior to the adoption of the amendment contained in this subsection and which become taxable, either by expiration of the exemption period or for other reasons, on or after the date as of which the provisions of this subsection become law and to qualified manufacturing concerns which are exempt for the first time on or after the date of the adoption of the amendment contained in this subsection and which subsequently become taxable.

Section 6C. Tax Relief for Historic preservation, Reinvestment, or Enterprise Areas--Economic Stagnation or Decline--Use of Local Taxes and Fees for Public Investments--Development or Redevelopment of Unproductive, Etc. Areas

A. The Legislature, by law, may grant incorporated cities, towns, or counties the ability to provide incentives, exemptions and other forms of relief from taxation for historic preservation, reinvestment, or enterprise areas that are exhibiting economic stagnation or decline. Relief from taxes imposed by other local taxing jurisdictions shall only be allowed by contractual arrangement with the municipal or county governing body. The law shall require public hearings before such relief may be granted and shall provide for the local initiative power and referendum of the people. The Legislature may set limitations on the cumulative incentives and relief provided pursuant to the provisions of this section, the time period for the exemptions, the geographical area of the jurisdiction covered, the percentage of the tax base of the jurisdiction eligible for the relief programs, and threshold limits of investment credit and jobs created.

B. The Legislature, by law, may authorize that the cities, towns, or counties may specifically use local taxes and local fees, in whole or in part, for specific public investments, assistance in development financing, or as a specific revenue source for other public entities in the area in which the improvements take place and may direct the apportionment of the taxes and fees specified in this subsection for the purposes specified in this section. A direction of apportionment may be prospective and may continue for one or more years, and apportioned tax increments may be pledged beyond the current fiscal year to the repayment of indebtedness of other public entities, notwithstanding the provisions of Section 26 of Article X of the Oklahoma Constitution, or other constitutional provisions. The Legislature may establish for this subsection, the same procedures and limitations authorized in subsection A of this section.

C. The Legislature, by law, may authorize any city, town, or county to plan, finance and carry out the development or redevelopment of areas determined by the governing body of such city, town, or county to be unproductive, undeveloped, underdeveloped or blighted. The authority of the county shall be limited to the unincorporated areas of such county but any city, town or county may by agreement jointly plan, finance or carry out a development plan with any other public or private entity for one or more development projects within their respective boundaries.

D. Any city, town, or county may exercise the provisions of this section separately or in combination with powers granted by any other laws of this state.

Section 7. Assessments for Local Improvements

The Legislature may authorize county and municipal corporations to levy and collect assessments for local improvements upon property benefited thereby, homesteads included, without regard to a cash valuation.

Section 8. Valuation of Property for Taxation - Limit on Percentage of Fair Cash Value - Approval by Voters

A. Except as otherwise provided in Article X of this Constitution, beginning January 1, 1997, all property which may be taxed ad valorem shall be assessed for taxation as follows:

1. Tangible personal property shall not be assessed for taxation at less than ten percent (10%) nor more than fifteen percent (15%) of its fair cash value, estimated at the price it would bring at a fair voluntary sale;

2. Real property shall not be assessed for ad valorem taxation at a value less than eleven percent (11%) nor greater than thirteen and one-half percent (13.5%) of its fair cash value for the highest and best use for which such property was actually used, or was previously classified for use, during the calendar year next preceding the first day of January on which the assessment is made. The transfer of property without a change in its use classification shall not require a reassessment based exclusively upon the sale value of such property. In connection with the foregoing, the Legislature shall be empowered to enact laws defining classifications of use for the purpose of applying standards to facilitate uniform assessment procedures in this state; and

3. All other property which is assessed by the State Board of Equalization shall be assessed for ad valorem taxation at the percentage of its fair cash value, estimated at the price it would bring at a fair voluntary sale, at which it was assessed on January 1, 1996.

B. Beginning January 1, 1997, the percentage at which real or tangible personal property is assessed within a county shall not be increased except upon approval by a majority of the registered voters of the county, voting at an election called for that purpose by a majority of the county commissioners, or upon a petition initiated by not less than ten percent (10%) of the registered voters of the county based on the total number of votes cast at the last general election for the county office receiving the highest number of votes at the election. In no event shall the percentage be increased by more than one percentage point per year or increase in excess of the limitations set forth in paragraphs 1 and 2 of subsection A of this section. The percentage at which real or tangible personal property is assessed within a county may be decreased, within the limitations set forth in paragraphs 1 and 2 of subsection A of this section, without approval of the voters of the county.

C. Any officer or other person authorized to assess values or subjects for taxation, who shall commit any wilful error in the performance of the duties of the office, shall be deemed guilty of malfeasance, and upon conviction thereof shall forfeit the office and be otherwise punished as may be provided by law.

Section 8A. Approval of Exemption of Household Goods of Heads of Families and Livestock Employed in Support of Family - Adjusted Millage Rate - Computation Procedure - Maximum Rate

(a) If a county approves an exemption of household goods of the heads of families and livestock employed in support of the family from taxation pursuant to the provisions of subsection (b) of Section 6 of this article, the millage rate levied against the net taxable valuation of all property of each taxing jurisdiction located within such county levying ad valorem taxes for a general fund or a building fund shall be adjusted pursuant to the provisions of subsection (b) of this section to compensate for the potential loss of revenue to the taxing jurisdiction directly attributable to the exemption of all such property. For purposes of this section, "taxing jurisdiction" shall include, but not be limited to, counties, cities, towns, common school districts, vocational-technical school districts and any other unit of government authorized to collect ad valorem taxes from millage levied against the taxable value of property.

(b) The adjusted millage rate for a general fund or building fund of each taxing jurisdiction located within a county which exempts household goods of the heads of families and livestock employed in support of the family from ad valorem taxation pursuant to the provisions of subsection (b) of Section 6 of this Article shall be computed, for each taxing jurisdiction, by dividing the net taxable valuation of all property for the year preceding the year in which the exemption of such property becomes effective by the difference between the net taxable valuation of all property for the year preceding the year in which the exemption of such property becomes effective and the net taxable valuation of the household goods of the heads of families and livestock employed in support of the family for the year preceding the year in which the exemption of such property becomes effective. The resulting quotient shall be the millage adjustment factor, and shall be multiplied by the millage rate which would otherwise have been applied for the year in which the exemption of such property becomes effective to derive the adjusted millage rate, which shall be levied against the net taxable valuation of all property, other than the exempt property, within the jurisdiction for the year in which the exemption of household goods of the heads of families and livestock employed in support of the family becomes effective; provided, such adjusted millage rate may be increased or decreased in the manner provided by the provisions of this Article.

(c) If a county approves an exemption of household goods of the heads of families and livestock employed in support of the family from ad valorem taxation pursuant to the provisions of subsection (b) of Section 6 of this article, the maximum allowable millage for any millage levied by any taxing jurisdiction located within such county for a general fund or building fund, as prescribed by Sections 9, 9A, 9B, 9C, 9D, 10, 10A, 10B and 35 of this article or as otherwise authorized by Section 36 of Article V of the Oklahoma Constitution, shall be adjusted by multiplying such millage by the millage adjustment factor as specified in subsection (b) of this section. The resulting product shall be the adjusted maximum allowable millage for that particular millage levied by such taxing jurisdiction for a general fund or building fund.

(d) If approved by the people, this section will become effective January 1, 1993.

Section 8B. Limit on Percentage of Fair Cash Value of Real Property

Despite any provision to the contrary, on and after January 1, 2013, the fair cash value of any parcel of locally assessed real property shall not increase by more than five percent (5%) in any taxable year; provided, if such property qualified for a homestead exemption or is classified as agricultural land, any increase to the fair cash value of such locally assessed real property in a taxable year shall be limited to three percent (3%). The provisions of this section shall not apply in any year when title to the property is transferred, changed, or conveyed to another person or when improvements have been made to the property. If title to the property is transferred, changed, or conveyed to another person, the property shall be assessed for that year based on the fair cash value as set forth in Section 8 of Article X of this Constitution. If any improvements are made to the property, the increased value to the property as a result of the improvement shall be assessed for that year based on the fair cash value as set forth in Section 8 of Article X of this Constitution. The provisions of this section shall not apply to any personal property which may be taxed ad valorem or any property which may be valued or assessed by the State Board of Equalization.

The Legislature shall enact any laws necessary to implement the provisions of this section.

Section 8C. Limit on Fair Cash Value on Homestead

A. Despite any provision to the contrary, beginning January 1, 2005, the fair cash value, as determined by law, on each homestead of an individual head of household whose gross household income from all sources for the preceding calendar year did not exceed an amount as provided in subsection B of this section, and which individual head of household is sixty-five (65) years of age or older, shall not exceed the fair cash value placed upon the property during the first year in which the individual head of household was sixty-five (65) years of age or older and had gross household income from all sources which did not exceed an amount as provided in subsection B of this section. Subject to the limitations of this section, the fair cash value shall not exceed such amount as long as the individual head of household who is sixty-five (65) years of age or older owns and occupies the property and as long as the gross household income from all sources does not exceed an amount as provided in subsection B of this section. If any improvements are made to the property, the fair cash value of the improvements shall be assessed in accordance with law by the county assessor and added to the assessed value of the property.

Once the fair cash value of the improvements has been added to the fair cash value of the property, the total fair cash value shall not exceed the revised valuation of the property so long as the individual head of household who is sixty-five (65) years of age or older owns and occupies the property and so long as the gross household income from all sources does not exceed an amount as provided in subsection B of this section. For any individual head of household who is sixty-five (65) years of age or older prior to January 1, 1997, and has gross household income from all sources of Twenty-five Thousand Dollars ($25,000.00) or less in calendar year 1996, the fair cash value of the real property shall be the fair cash value placed upon the property on January 1, 1997. If the individual head of household ceases to own and occupy the property or if the gross household income from all sources exceeds an amount as provided in subsection B of this section, the fair cash value of the property shall be determined as if the provisions of Section 8 of Article X of the Constitution of the State of Oklahoma or any other provisions relating to a limitation on the fair cash value of locally assessed real property had been in effect during the time the property was valued pursuant to the provisions of this section.

B. The income threshold for the gross household income from all sources for an individual head of household under this section shall not exceed the amount determined by the United States Department of Housing and Urban Development to be the estimated median income for the preceding year for the county or metropolitan statistical area which includes such county. The Oklahoma Tax Commission shall provide such information to each county assessor each year as soon as such information becomes available.

Section 8E. Homestead Exemption - Military Service Disability

A. Despite any provision to the contrary, beginning January 1, 2006, each head of household who has been honorably discharged from active service in any branch of the Armed Forces of the United States or Oklahoma National Guard and who has been certified by the United States Department of Veterans Affairs or its successor to have a one hundred percent (100%) permanent disability sustained through military action or accident or resulting from disease contracted while in such active service or the surviving spouse of such head of household shall be entitled to claim an exemption for the full amount of the fair cash value of the homestead.

B. In order to be eligible for the exemption authorized by this section, the individual shall be required to prove residency within the State of Oklahoma and must have previously qualified for the homestead exemption authorized by law or be eligible for the homestead exemption pursuant to law.

C. If a homestead otherwise eligible for the exemption authorized by this section is transferred on or after January 1 of a calendar year, another homestead property acquired by the qualifying head of household or by the surviving spouse of such qualifying head of household shall be exempt to the same extent as the homestead property previously owned by such person or persons for the year during which the new homestead is acquired and, subject to the requirements of this section, for each year thereafter.

Section 8F.

A. Despite any provision to the contrary, and except as otherwise provided by subsection D of this section, beginning January 1, 2015, the surviving spouse of the head of household who is determined by the United States Department of Defense or any branch of the United States military to have died while in the line of duty shall be entitled to claim an exemption for the full amount of the fair cash value of the homestead until such surviving spouse remarries.

B. In order to be eligible for the exemption authorized by this section, the surviving spouse shall be required to prove residency within the State of Oklahoma and must have previously qualified for the homestead exemption authorized by law or be eligible for the homestead exemption pursuant to law.

C. If a homestead otherwise eligible for the exemption authorized by this section is transferred on or after January 1 of a calendar year, another homestead property acquired by the surviving spouse shall be exempt to the same extent as the homestead property previously owned by such person for the year during which the new homestead is acquired and, subject to the requirements of this section, for each year thereafter.

D. The provisions of this section shall be applicable for the 2014 calendar year with respect to an existing homestead property owned by the surviving spouse of a person previously determined to have died while in the line of duty by the United States Department of Defense or applicable branch of the United States military.

Section 9. Amount of Ad Valorem Tax

(a) Except as herein otherwise provided, the total taxes for all purposes on an ad valorem basis shall not exceed, in any taxable year, fifteen (15) mills on the dollar, no less than five (5) mills of which is hereby apportioned for school district purposes, the remainder to be apportioned between county, city, town and school district, by the County Excise Board, until such time as a regular apportionment thereof is otherwise provided for by the Legislature.

No ad valorem tax shall be levied for State purposes, nor shall any part of the proceeds of any ad valorem tax levy upon any kind of property in this State be used for State purposes.

(b) A tax of four (4) mills on the dollar valuation of all taxable property in the county shall be levied annually in each county of the State for school purposes and, until otherwise provided by law, the proceeds thereof shall be apportioned to the school districts of the county by the County Treasurer on the basis of the legal average daily attendance for the preceding school year as certified by the State Board of Education. Provided that in case a school district lies in more than one county, such district shall be deemed a school district of the county having the greater part of the area comprising such district, unless otherwise provided by law, and shall be entitled to participate in the proceeds of such tax on the same basis as districts lying wholly within such county but revenue from such tax on the assessed valuation of the district in other counties shall, when collected, be transmitted to the County Treasurer of such county having the greater part of the area comprising the district, unless otherwise provided by law, and be apportioned as hereinbefore provided for the proceeds of such tax on the assessed valuation of such county. Not to exceed seventy-five per centum (75%) of the amount received by a school district from the proceeds of such county levy in any year shall be required to finance the State guaranteed program of such district.

(c) Upon certification of a need therefore by the board of education of any school district an additional tax of not to exceed fifteen (15) mills on the dollar valuation of all taxable property in the district shall be levied for the benefit of the schools of such district.

(d) In addition to the levies hereinbefore authorized, any school district may make an emergency levy for the benefit of the schools of such district, in an amount not to exceed five (5) mills on the dollar valuation of the taxable property in such district when approved by a majority of the electors of the district voting on the question at an election called for such purpose. This emergency levy shall provide only sufficient additional revenue to meet the needs of the district each fiscal year as determined by the board of such district and must be approved by a majority of the electors voting on said question at such an election for each fiscal year.

(d-1) In addition to the levies hereinbefore authorized, any school district may make a local support levy for the benefit of the schools of such district, in an amount not to exceed ten (10) mills on the dollar valuation of the taxable property in such district, when approved by a majority of the ad valorem taxpaying voters voting on said question at an election for each fiscal year called for such purposes. This local support levy shall provide only sufficient additional revenue to meet the needs of the district for each such fiscal year as determined by the board of such district; provided, an elector desiring to vote upon such local support levy must present an ad valorem tax receipt for the year immediately preceding before being issued a ballot, or sign a sworn affidavit certifying the fact of such payment.

(d-2) A school district may upon approval by a majority of the electors of the district voting on the question make the ad valorem levy for emergency levy and local support levy under (d) and (d-1) of this section permanent. If the question is approved, the levies, in the amount approved as required by this section, shall be made each fiscal year thereafter until such time as a majority of the electors of the district voting on the question rescind the making of the levy permanent. An election on such question shall be held at such time as a petition is signed by ten percent (10%) of the school district electors or a recommendation by the board of education of the school district is made asking that the levies be made each fiscal year.

(e) The amount of revenue from school district ad valorem taxes levied under (a) and (c) of this Section which any school district may be required to use to finance its State guaranteed program shall not be in excess of its share, based upon its relative taxpaying ability as may be defined by law, of an amount equivalent to the net proceeds from a fifteen (15) mill tax levy on the aggregate net assessed valuation of the State; but until such relative taxpaying ability is defined by the Legislature, the amount of revenue from such taxes which any school district may be required to use to finance its State guaranteed program shall not be in excess of the net proceeds from an ad valorem tax levy of fifteen (15) mills on the dollar net assessed valuation of the district. No part of the proceeds from any ad valorem levy for emergency levy and local support levy under (d) and (d-1) of this Section shall be required to finance the State guaranteed program of such district.

Nothing in the amendments to the Constitution incorporated herein shall be construed to amend, alter or supersede the present application of Article XII-A, Sections 1 and 2 of the Oklahoma Constitution.

Section 9A. Additional County Ad Valorem Tax Levy for Department of Health

For the purpose of maintaining or aiding in maintaining a department of health within any county of the State, an additional levy not to exceed two and one- half mills on the dollar of the assessed valuation of the county may be levied annually, when such levy is approved by a majority of the qualified ad valorem tax paying voters of the county, voting on the question at an election called for such purpose by the Board of County Commissioners, or by initiative petition by voters of a county. A maximum levy of two and one-half mills may be made for such purpose after such approval until repealed by a majority of the qualified ad valorem tax paying voters of the county, voting on the question at an election called for such purpose by the Board of County Commissioners, or by initiative petition by voters of a county. Such department of health may be maintained jointly or in conjunction with one or more counties, cities, towns or school districts, or any combination thereof, and shall be maintained as now or hereafter provided by law. Nothing herein shall prohibit other levies or the use of other public funds for such department of health.

Section 9B. Technology Center School Districts for Technology Center Schools--Tax Levies

A. Technology center school districts for technology center schools may be established and a levy of not to exceed five (5) mills on the dollar valuation of the taxable property in any technology center school district so established may be made annually, for the district, when the levy is approved by a majority of the electors of the technology center school district, voting on the question at an election called for that purpose. The levy shall be in addition to all other levies authorized by this Constitution, and when approved, shall be made each fiscal year thereafter until repealed by a majority of the electors of the technology center school district, voting on the question at an election called for that purpose. Any technology center school district so established shall be considered as a school district for the purposes of Sections 10 and 26 of this Article. The administrative control and direction of the technology center school district shall be vested in a school board which shall be constituted and empowered as provided for by law for school boards of independent school districts. Provisions of other subsections of this section notwithstanding, in any case where a college technology center school district recognized pursuant to Section 4423 of Title 70 of the Oklahoma Statutes and established by vote of the people after December 31, 1968, overlaps and includes territory which is included within the district of a technology center school established as prescribed by the State Board of Career and Technology Education pursuant to Section 14-108 of Title 70 of the Oklahoma Statutes, except as otherwise provided herein, only the levies made by the college technology center school district shall be applied to said overlap territory, provided that incentive levies may be applied to the overlap area by either the college technology center school district or technology center school district and revenues from the overlap area collected pursuant to any incentive levy so made shall be apportioned one-half to the college technology center school district making the levy and one-half to the overlapped technology center school district; provided, only one district shall make an incentive levy in such overlap territory during any given time period. In any case where a college technology center school district recognized pursuant to Section 4420 or 4420.1 of Title 70 of the Oklahoma Statutes overlaps and includes territory which is included within the district of a technology center school established as prescribed by the State Board of Career and Technology Education pursuant to Section 14-108 of Title 70 of the Oklahoma Statutes, said overlap territory shall be subject to all levies of both kinds of districts that are approved by a majority of the electors.

B. In addition to any other levies authorized by this section, a technology center school district may make a local incentive levy for the benefit of the technology center school district in an amount not to exceed five (5) mills on the dollar valuation of the taxable property in the technology center school district when approved by a majority of those registered voters of the technology center school district voting on the question at an election called for that purpose. Except as otherwise provided, this levy, when approved, shall be made each fiscal year thereafter until repealed by a majority of the electors of the technology center school district voting on the question at an election called for that purpose. A technology center school district which has previously failed to approve a local incentive levy at two consecutive elections held between January 1, 1994 and May 31, 1994 may make a local incentive levy for the benefit of the technology center school district only if approved by a majority of the registered voters of the technology center school district voting on said question at such an election for each fiscal year. If a majority of voters approve the local incentive levy for three (3) consecutive years, the levy approved on the third year shall be made each fiscal year thereafter until repealed by a majority of the electors of the technology center school district voting on the question at an election called for that purpose.

C. Upon the establishment of technology center school districts, such districts are authorized to become indebted separate and apart from the indebtedness of any school district included in the technology center school district up to five percent (5%) of the net valuation of taxable property within the technology center school district for capital improvements, including purchasing sites and constructing, purchasing, improving, and equipping real property and buildings when the indebtedness is approved by a majority of the electors of the technology center school district voting on the question in an election called for that purpose.

D. Until otherwise provided for by law, technology center school districts and the government thereof shall be established in accordance with criteria and procedures prescribed by the State Board of Career and Technology Education.

E. The Legislature may alter, amend, delete, or add to the provisions of this section by law.

Section 9C. Emergency Medical Service Districts

(a) The board of county commissioners, or boards if more than one county is involved, may call a special election to determine whether or not an ambulance service district shall be formed. An election shall also be called by the board or boards involved upon petition signed by not less than ten percent (10%) of the registered voters of the area affected. Said area may embrace a county, a part thereof, or more than one county or parts thereof, and in the event the area covers only a part or parts of one or more counties, the area must follow school district boundary lines. All registered voters in such area shall be entitled to vote, as to whether or not such district shall be formed, and at the same time and in the same question authorize a tax levy not to exceed three (3) mills for the purpose of providing funds for the purpose of support, organization, operation and maintenance of district ambulance services, known as emergency medical service districts and hereinafter referred to as "districts." If the formation of the district and the mill levy is approved by a majority of the votes cast, a special annual recurring ad valorem tax levy of not more than three (3) mills on the dollar of the assessed valuation of all taxable property in the district shall be levied. The number of mills shall be set forth in the election proclamation, and may be increased in a later election, not to exceed a total levy of three (3) mills. This special levy shall be in addition to all other levies and when authorized shall be made each fiscal year thereafter.

Each district which is herein authorized, or established, shall have a board of trustees composed of not less than five members. Such trustees shall be chosen jointly by the board or boards of county commissioners, provided that such membership shall be composed of not less than one individual from each county or part thereof which is included in said district. Original members of the board of trustees shall hold office, as follows: At the first meeting of said board, board members shall draw lots to determine each trustee's original length of term in office. The number of lots to be provided shall be equal to the number of original members of the board, and lots shall be numbered sequentially from one through five, with lots in excess of the fifth lot being also numbered sequentially from one through five until all lots are numbered. Each original member or members added by an expansion area of the board shall hold office for the number of years indicated on his or her lot. Each year, as necessary, the board or boards of county commissioners shall appoint successors to such members of the board of trustees whose terms have expired, and such subsequent appointments shall be for terms of five (5) years.

Such board of trustees shall have the power and duty to promulgate and adopt such rules, procedures and contract provisions necessary to carry out the purposes and objectives of these provisions, and shall individually post such bond as required by the county commissioners, which shall not be less than Ten Thousand Dollars ($10,000.00).

The district board of trustees shall have the additional powers to hire a manager and appropriate personnel, contract, organize, maintain or otherwise operate the emergency medical services within said district and such additional powers as may be authorized by the Legislature.

(b) Any district board of trustees may issue bonds, if approved by a majority vote at a special election for such purpose. All registered voters within the designated district shall have the right to vote in said election. Such bonds shall be issued for the purpose of acquiring emergency vehicles and other equipment and maintaining and housing the same.

(c) The bonds authorized above shall not bear interest at a greater rate than that authorized by statute for the issuance of city municipal bonds. Such bonds shall be sold only at public sale after twenty (20) days' advertisement in a newspaper for publication of legal notices with circulation in the district. Any district may refund its bonds as is now provided by law for refunding municipal bonds.

(d) Any district board of trustees, upon issuing bonds as authorized in subsection (b) of this section, shall levy a special annual ad valorem tax upon the property within the district, payable annually, in a total amount not to exceed three (3) mills on the dollar, on the real and personal taxable property in such district, for the payment of principal and interest on outstanding bonds, until same are paid. However, the trustees may, from time to time, suspend the collection of such annual levy when not required for the payment of the bonds. In no event shall the real and personal taxable property in any city or town be subject to a special tax in excess of three (3) mills for the payment of bonds issued hereunder.

(e) There may also be pledged to the payment of principal and interest of the bonds herein authorized to be issued: (1) any net proceeds from operation of the district that the board of trustees of the district shall deem not necessary to the future operation and maintenance of said emergency medical service; or (2) any monies available from other funds of the district not otherwise obligated.

(f) Bonds shall be issued for designated sums with serial numbers thereon and maturing annually after three (3) years from date of issue. All bonds and interest thereon shall be paid upon maturity and no bonds shall be issued for a period longer than thirty (30) years. Any district board of trustees may in its discretion schedule the payment of principal over the thirty-year period so that when interest is added there will be approximately level annual payments of principal and interest.

(g) In the event the mill levy as set forth in the original election proclamation is less than three (3) mills, the board of trustees may request the county commissioners to call a subsequent election to consider increasing the mill levy; provided, however, the total levy authorized by subsection (a) hereof shall not exceed three (3) mills.

(h) The board of trustees of any district shall have jurisdiction over the sale or refunding of any bonds issued by the district and shall be responsible for the economical expenditure of the funds derived from the bonds.

(i) Such districts shall be empowered to charge fees for services, and accept gifts, funds or grants from sources other than the mill levy, which shall be used and accounted for in a like manner. Persons served outside the district shall be charged an amount equal to the actual costs for the service, not taking into account any income the district receives from millage or sources within the district. The board of trustees shall have legal authority to bring suits necessary to collect accounts owed and to sue and defend as necessary for the protection of the board. The State Auditor and Inspector shall conduct an annual audit of the operations of such districts.

(j) Any emergency medical service district may expand to include other counties or parts thereof, provided that an election is called by the county commissioners whose county or counties, or parts thereof, are to be added to in the established district; and provided further, that the county commissioners in the original district concur in the calling of said election. The proposed expansion area shall only be added to the original district if approved separately by a majority vote, by the voters in both the original district and in the expansion area, at an election called for that purpose. The county in which the expansion area is located shall have not less than one member on the board of trustees. Appropriate millage or other approved method of financial support shall be levied in the expansion area, when said area is added to the original district which millage shall be levied at the rate used to cover operational costs and outstanding bonded indebtedness as provided in Section 9C, (d) and (e), Article X.

(k) Any county or parts thereof may withdraw from a district provided that an election is called by the county commissioners of the county whose county or parts thereof is to be withdrawn from the district. The county or parts thereof shall be withdrawn from the district if approved by a majority vote of the voters in the county at an election called for such purpose. If the county commissioners are presented a petition signed by not less than twenty percent (20%) of all registered voters in the county, the county commissioners shall call an election. The petition for an election for a county or parts thereof to withdraw from a district and the ballot shall provide for the payment of any debt for operational costs and outstanding bonded indebtedness in proportional shares, for which the county or parts thereof would be responsible as a result of the membership of the county or parts thereof in the district.

(l) Any district may be dissolved, or the millage levy changed, by a majority vote of the registered voters voting at an election called for that purpose by the county commissioners of each county or part thereof included within the district; provided that such an election shall not be called unless either three-fifths (3/5) of the trustees of such district request the county commissioners to call such an election, or the respective county commissioners are presented a petition signed by not less than twenty percent (20%) of all registered voters in the district.

(m) In the event a district is dissolved, any mill levy used to support, organize, operate and maintain the emergency medical service district shall cease, provided that such mill levy shall not cease until all outstanding emergency medical service bonds of that district are retired and all other debts incurred by the emergency medical service district have been satisfied.

(n) All elections called under the provisions hereof shall be conducted by the county election board or boards of each county or counties involved, upon receipt of an election proclamation, issued by a majority of the board or boards of county commissioners in the area affected. In the event more than one county is involved, said proclamation must be a joint proclamation from a majority of the board of county commissioners of each county involved. Said proclamation shall be published in one issue of a newspaper of general circulation in each county involved in the area affected at least ten (10) days prior to said election, and said proclamation shall set forth the purpose of the election, and the date thereof. The county election board or boards shall certify the results of an election to the board or boards issuing such proclamation.

(o) The board of any district shall have capacity to sue and be sued. Provided, however, the board shall enjoy immunity from civil suit for actions or omissions arising from the operation of the district, so long as, and to the same extent as, municipalities and counties within the state enjoy such immunity.

(p) In lieu of proceeding to establish a district as outlined hereinabove through the county commissioners, the governing body of any incorporated city or town may proceed to form a district, join an existing district or join with other incorporated cities or towns in forming a district. In such case, said governing body shall be considered as being substituted as to the powers and duties of said county commissioners as set forth hereinabove; provided, further, said city or town shall be considered as being substituted as to the powers and duties of a district formed, as set forth hereinabove. All rights, duties, privileges and obligations of the residents and voters in such city or town shall be the same as those outlined for the district as set forth above.

Section 9D. Solid Waste Management Services

A. The board of county commissioners of any county may call a special election to determine whether or not the board shall provide solid waste management services for the county. An election shall also be called by the board upon petition signed by not less than ten percent (10%) of the registered voters of the county. All registered voters in such county shall be entitled to vote, as to whether or not such services shall be provided, and at the same time and in the same question authorize a tax levy of not to exceed three (3) mills for the purpose of providing funds for the purpose of support, organization, operation and maintenance of such services. If the provision of the services and the mill levy is approved by a majority of the votes cast, a special annual recurring ad valorem tax levy of not more than three (3) mills on the dollar of the assessed valuation of all taxable property in the county shall be levied. The number of mills shall be set forth in the election proclamation, and may be increased in a later election, not to exceed a total levy of three (3) mills. This special levy shall be in addition to all other levies and when authorized shall be made each fiscal year thereafter.

B. Upon passage of the question, the board of county commissioners shall provide solid waste management services for county residents and businesses. The board may provide for one or more disposal facilities and for solid waste collection services. The board may purchase landfill sites, construct and operate landfills and transfer stations and other solid waste disposal and handling facilities. The board shall provide a solid waste disposal and collection system for the county, using the funds available from the millage levy and any service charges the board may assess. The board may purchase, operate, and maintain vehicles for curbside or roadside solid waste collection. In rural areas where curbside collection services may not be economically feasible, the board may construct and operate transfer stations for area-wide collection and transfer of solid waste to ultimate disposal sites.

C. The board of county commissioners of a county in which the question has passed shall have the power and duty to promulgate and adopt such rules, procedures and contract provisions necessary to implement the purposes and objectives of this section. The board of county commissioners shall have the additional powers to hire a manager and appropriate personnel, contract, organize, maintain or otherwise operate the solid waste management services within said county and such additional powers as may be authorized by the Legislature.

D. Two or more counties in which the question has passed may enter into agreements with each other to provide solid waste management services in all counties involved in the most economical fashion, including agreements to provide collection and disposal services for each other where areas in one county may be more economically served by facilities located in another county.

E. In addition to other powers provided for pursuant to the provisions of this section, the board of county commissioners of any county in which the question has passed may issue bonds, if approved by a majority vote at a special election for such purpose. All registered voters within the county shall have the right to vote in said election. Such bonds may be issued for the purpose of:

1. acquiring vehicles, equipment and other necessary items;

2. purchasing landfill sites;

3. constructing landfills, transfer stations, or other facilities for solid waste management, disposal, and recycling; and

4. operating and maintaining all of the above listed items. Landfill sites, equipment and other items, no longer needed, shall be disposed of as provided for by law for the sale of county-owned property.

F. The bonds authorized, pursuant to the provisions of subsection
E of this section shall not bear interest at a greater rate than that authorized by statute for the issuance of city municipal bonds. Such bonds shall be sold only at public sale after twenty (20) days' advertisement in a newspaper of general circulation in the county. Any county may refund its bonds as is now provided by law for refunding municipal bonds.

G. Any board of county commissioners, upon issuing bonds as authorized in subsection E of this section, shall levy a special annual ad valorem tax upon the property within the county, payable annually, in a total amount not to exceed three (3) mills on the dollar, on the real and personal taxable property in such county, for the payment of principal and interest on outstanding bonds, until same are paid. However, the board may suspend, from time to time, the collection of such annual levy when not required for the payment of the bonds.

H. There may also be pledged to the payment of principal and interest of the bonds authorized to be issued:

1. any net proceeds from operation of the county solid waste management services that the board of county commissioners shall deem not necessary to the future operation, maintenance or closure of said solid waste management services and facilities;

or

2. any monies available from other funds of the county not otherwise obligated.

I. Bonds shall be issued for designated sums with interest payable semiannually and with the principal maturing annually beginning not more than three (3) years from date of issue. All bonds and interest thereon shall be paid upon maturity and no bonds shall be issued for a period longer than thirty (30) years. Any board of county commissioners may in its discretion schedule the payment of principal over the period of maturity of the bond issue, so that when interest is added there will be approximately level annual payments of principal and interest.

J. In the event the mill levy as provided for in the original election proclamation is less than three (3) mills, the board of county commissioners may call a subsequent election to consider increasing the mill levy; provided, however, the total levy authorized by subsection A of this section shall not exceed three (3) mills.

K. The board of county commissioners shall have jurisdiction over the sale or refunding of any bonds issued by the county pursuant to the provisions hereof, and shall be responsible for the economical expenditure of the funds derived from the bonds.

L. The board of county commissioners shall be empowered to charge fees for services, and accept gifts, funds or grants from sources other than the mill levy, which shall be used and accounted for in a like manner. Persons served outside the county shall be charged an amount equal to the actual costs for providing the service, not taking into account any income the county receives from millage or sources within the county. The board shall have legal authority to bring such suits necessary to collect accounts owed and to sue and defend as necessary for the protection of the board. The State Auditor and Inspector shall conduct an annual audit of the solid waste management operations of such counties.

Any county may cease providing solid waste management services, or cause the millage levy authorized by subsection G of this section to be changed, by a majority vote of the registered voters voting at an election called for that purpose by the board of county commissioners. Such an election shall not be called unless either two-thirds (2/3) of the board members vote to call such an election, or the board is presented a petition signed by not less than twenty percent (20%) of all registered voters in the county.

If a county ceases to provide solid waste management services, any mill levy used to support, organize, operate and maintain the services and facilities shall cease, provided that such mill levy shall not cease until all outstanding solid waste management services bonds of that county are retired, all other debts incurred by the county in providing solid waste management services have been satisfied, and all facilities have been properly closed as provided for by law.

All elections called pursuant to the provisions of this section shall be conducted by the county election board of each county involved, upon receipt of an election proclamation, issued by the board of county commissioners in the county affected. Said proclamation shall be published in one issue of a newspaper of general circulation in the county at least ten (10) days prior to said election. The proclamation shall set forth the purpose of the election, and the date thereof. The county election board shall certify the results of the election to the board issuing the proclamation.

Section 10. Increased Rate for Public Buildings or for Building Fund for School Districts - - Permanent Levy

A. For the purpose of erecting public buildings in counties or cities, or for the purpose of raising money for a building fund for a school district which may be used for erecting, remodeling or repairing school buildings, and for purchasing furniture, the rates of taxation herein limited may be increased, when the rate of such increase and the purpose for which it is intended shall have been submitted to a vote of the people, and a majority of the qualified voters of such county, city, or school district, voting at such election, shall vote therefore: Provided, that such increase shall not exceed five (5) mills on the dollar of the assessed value of the taxable property in such county, city, or school district.

B. A school district may upon approval by a majority of the electors of the district voting on the question make the ad valorem levy for a building fund under subsection A of this section permanent. If the question is approved, the levy in the amount approved as required by this section, shall be made each fiscal year thereafter until such time as a majority of the electors of the district voting on the question rescind the making of the levy permanent. An election on such question shall be held at such time as a petition is signed by ten percent (10%) of the school district electors or a recommendation by the board of education of the school district is made asking that the levies be made each fiscal year.

Section 10A. Tax Levy for Cooperative County Libraries and Joint city-County Libraries

To provide funds for the purpose of establishing and maintaining or aiding in establishing and maintaining public libraries and library services, a special annual recurring ad valorem tax shall be levied when such levy is approved by a majority vote of the qualified electors of the county voting on the question at an election called for that purpose by the Board of County Commissioners, either upon its own initiative or upon petition initiated by not less than ten percent (10%) of the qualified electors of the county based on the total number of votes cast at the last general election for the county office receiving the highest number of votes at such an election.

Except as provided in this section, in a county having less than one hundred fifty thousand (150,000) population, according to the most recent Federal Decennial Census, the special annual recurring ad valorem tax levy shall be not less than one (1) mill nor more than four (4) mills on the dollar of the assessed valuation of all taxable property in the county. In a county having more than one hundred fifty thousand (150,000) population or in a multi-county library system with a county having more than one hundred fifty thousand (150,000) population, according to the most recent Federal Decennial Census, the special annual recurring ad valorem tax levy for each such county shall be not less than one (1) mill nor more than six (6) mill on the dollar of the assessed valuation of all taxable property in the county. This special levy shall be in addition to all other levies and when authorized shall be made each fiscal year thereafter until such authority shall be canceled by a majority vote of the qualified electors of the county voting on the question at an election called for that purpose by the Board of County Commissioners upon petition initiated by not less than twenty percent (20%) of the qualified electors of the county based on the total numbers of votes cast at the last general election for the county office receiving the highest number of votes at such an election. The proceeds of such levy shall be used by the county for creation, development, operation and maintenance of such public libraries and library services as are authorized by the Legislature. Nothing herein shall prohibit other levies for public libraries and library services or the use of other public funds for such purposes. All expenditures of the proceeds of such levies shall be made in accordance with laws heretofore or hereafter enacted concerning such libraries and library services. The provisions hereof shall be self-executing.

Section 10B. Municipal-Owned Hospitals - Operation and Maintenance - Tax levy

For the purpose of operating and maintaining municipal-owned hospitals in cities, the rates of taxation herein limited may be increased, when the rate of such increase and the purpose of which it is intended shall have been submitted to a vote of the people, and a majority of the qualified voters of such city, voting at such election, shall vote therefore: Provided, that such increase shall not exceed five (5) mills on the dollar of the assessed value of the taxable property in such city.

Section 11. Officer Receiving Interest, Profit or Perquisites
The receiving, directly or indirectly, by any officer of the State, or of any county, city, or town, or member or officer of the Legislature, of any interest, profit, or perquisites, arising from the use or loan of public funds in his hands, or moneys to be raised through his agency for State, city, town, district, or county purposes shall be deemed a felony. Said offense shall be punished as may be prescribed by law, a part of which punishment shall be disqualification to hold office.

Section 12. Special Forms of Taxation - Amounts - Reference to Federal Taxation

The Legislature shall have power to provide for the levy and collection of license, franchise, gross revenue, excise, income, collateral and direct inheritance, legacy, and succession taxes; also graduated income taxes, graduated collateral and direct inheritance taxes, graduated legacy and succession taxes; also stamp, registration, production or other specific taxes.
In the exercise of the powers provided for in this section, and notwithstanding any other provision of this Constitution, the Legislature may, with or without exceptions, modifications, or adjustments, define the amount on, in respect to, or by which any such tax or taxes are imposed or measured (a) by reference to any provisions of the laws (including administrative regulations, determinations, and interpretations) of the United States, as such laws may be or become effective at any time or from time to time; (b) by reference to any amount or amounts finally ascertained in determining amounts subject to taxation by the United States; or (c) by reference to any amount or amounts of tax finally ascertained to be payable to the United States.

Section 12a. Common School Taxes on Property of Public Service Corporations

All taxes collected for the maintenance of the common schools of this State, and which are levied upon the property of any railroad company, pipe line company, telegraph company, or upon the property of any public service corporation which operates in more than one county in this State, shall be paid into the Common School Fund and distributed as are other Common School Funds of this State.

Section 13. Independence of State Taxation
The State may select its subjects of taxation, and levy and collect its revenues independent of the counties, cities, or other municipal subdivisions.

Section 14. Levy and Collection by General Laws and for Public Purposes - Assumption of Debts

A. Except as otherwise provided by this section, taxes shall be levied and collected by general laws, and for public purposes only, except that taxes may be levied when necessary to carry into effect Section thirty-one of the Bill of Rights. Except as required by the Enabling Act, the State shall not assume the debt of any county, municipal corporation, or political subdivision of the State, unless such debt shall have been contracted to defend itself in time of war, to repel invasion, or to suppress insurrection.

B. Subject to requirements imposed by law, use of public facilities of institutions within The Oklahoma State System of Higher Education shall be authorized by this section if the use is made in connection with a project involving the research or development of a technology, whether or not the technology is protected pursuant to federal or state law governing intellectual property, the results of which have potential economic value for a business enterprise or private business entity involved in the project with the institution.

Section 15. Pledge or Loan of Credit - Donation - Exceptions

A. Except as provided by this section, the credit of the State shall not be given, pledged, or loaned to any individual, company, corporation, or association, municipality, or political subdivision of the State, nor shall the State become an owner or stockholder in, nor make donation by gift, subscription to stock, by tax, or otherwise, to any company, association, or corporation.

B. Pursuant to authority of and subject to requirements of law and according to professional norms established nationally in similar activities, the Oklahoma Center for the Advancement of Science and Technology or its successor may be authorized to use public funds not exceeding one percent (1%) of total state appropriations for the current fiscal year to promote economic development through grants or loans to individuals, companies, corporations or associations. Pursuant to authority of and subject to requirements of law and according to professional norms established nationally in similar activities, the Oklahoma Center for the Advancement of Science and Technology or its successor may be authorized to use public funds in order to promote economic development by purchase or ownership of stock or to make other investments in private enterprises and to receive income from such investments which are involved with research or patents from projects involving Oklahoma colleges or universities. The Oklahoma Center for the Advancement of Science and Technology or its successor may only use public funds for the purposes authorized in this subsection if a statute specifically authorizing such use is approved by an affirmative vote of at least two-thirds (2/3) of the members elected to the Senate and to the House of Representatives upon final passage of such measure in each of the respective houses and with the approval of the Governor.

C. The Legislature shall only authorize use of public funds by the Oklahoma Center for the Advancement of Science and Technology or its successor as permitted by this section for promotion of economic development by creation of new employment, enhancement of existing employment or by the addition of economic value to goods, services or resources within the State authorized by subsection B herein.

D. The Legislature shall establish procedures to review and evaluate the extent to which the purposes of any statute authorizing use of public funds by the Oklahoma Center for the Advancement of Science and Technology are achieved.

E. Bonds issued by the board of education of any school district or public institutions of higher education may be guaranteed by the corpus of the permanent school fund, provided:

1. As to bonds issued by the board of education such bonds must be approved by election of the school district upon the question of issuing such bonds;

2. As to bonds issued by an institution within The Oklahoma State System of Higher Education such bonds are issued in accordance with all applicable provisions of law; and

3. Provisions shall be made by the Legislature to guarantee prompt reimbursement to the corpus of the permanent school fund for any payment from the fund on behalf of a school district or on behalf of an institution within The Oklahoma State System of Higher Education. The reimbursement shall include a reasonable rate of interest. The provisions of this paragraph regarding use of the permanent school fund for guarantee of bonds issued by an institution within The Oklahoma State System of Higher Education shall not be self- executing and the Legislature shall provide by law the procedure pursuant to which such obligations may be guaranteed and the procedures for repayments, if any, required to be made to the permanent school fund.

F. Subject to requirements imposed by law, the governing boards of institutions within The Oklahoma State System of Higher Education and employees of those institutions may have an ownership interest in a technology, whether or not the technology is protected pursuant to federal or state law governing intellectual property, and may have an ownership interest in a business enterprise or private business entity, if the ownership interest is acquired as a result of research or development of a technology involving the authorized use of facilities, equipment, or services of such institutions.

Section 16. Borrowing Money - Specification of Purpose – Use

All laws authorizing the borrowing of money by and on behalf of the State, county, or other political subdivision of the State, shall specify the purpose for which the money is to be used, and the money so borrowed shall be used for no other purpose.

Section 17. Aid to Corporations, Etc., by Counties, Cities, Towns, Etc

The Legislature shall not authorize any county or subdivision thereof, city, town, or incorporated district, to become a stockholder in any company, association, or corporation, or to obtain or appropriate money for, or levy any tax for, or to loan its credit to any corporation, association, or individual.

Section 18. Aid to Corporations, Etc., by Counties, Cities, Towns, Etc

Repealed

Section 19. Specification of Purpose of Tax - Devotion to Another Purpose

Every act enacted by the Legislature, and every ordinance and resolution passed by any county, city, town, or municipal board or local legislative body, levying a tax shall specify distinctly the purpose for which said tax is levied, and no tax levied and collected for one purpose shall ever be devoted to another purpose.

Section 20. Taxes for County, City, Town or Municipal Purposes

The Legislature shall not impose taxes for the purpose of any county, city, town, or other municipal corporation, but may, by general laws, confer on the proper authorities thereof, respectively, the power to assess and collect such taxes.

Section 21. State Board of Equalization - Assessment Levels

A. There shall be a State Board of Equalization consisting of the Governor, State Auditor, State Treasurer, Lieutenant Governor, Attorney General, State Inspector and Examiner and President of the Board of Agriculture. The duty of said Board shall be to adjust and equalize the valuation of real and personal property of the several counties in the state, and it shall perform such other duties as may be prescribed by law, and they shall assess all railroad and public service corporation property.

B. Should the Offices of State Examiner and Inspector and State Auditor be consolidated in the Office of State Auditor and Inspector, the State Auditor shall be replaced as a member of the State Board of Equalization by the State Auditor and Inspector and the Superintendent of Public Instruction shall be added as a member thereof. Should the offices not be so consolidated, the membership shall remain the same as provided in subsection A of this section and the Superintendent of Public Instruction shall not be added to the membership.

Section 22. Classification of Property

Nothing in this Constitution shall be held, or construed, to prevent the classification of property for purposes of taxation; and the valuation of different classes by different means or methods.

Public Indebtedness:

Section 23. Balanced Budget – Procedures

The state shall never create or authorize the creation of any debt or obligation, or fund or pay any deficit, against the state, or any department, institution or agency thereof, regardless of its form or the source of money from which it is to be paid, except as may be provided in this section and in Sections 24 and 25 of Article X of the Constitution of the State of Oklahoma.

To ensure a balanced annual budget, pursuant to the limitations contained in the foregoing, procedures are herewith established as follows:

1. Not more than forty-five (45) days or less than thirty-five (35) days prior to the convening of each regular session of the Legislature, the State Board of Equalization shall certify the total amount of revenue which accrued during the last preceding fiscal year to the General Revenue Fund and to each Special Revenue Fund appropriated directly by the Legislature, and shall further certify amounts available for appropriation which shall be based on a determination, in accordance with the procedure hereinafter provided, of the revenues to be received by the state under the laws in effect at the time such determination is made, for the next ensuing fiscal year, showing separately the revenues to accrue to the credit of each such fund of the state appropriated directly by the Legislature.

Amounts certified as available for appropriation from each fund, as hereinbefore provided, shall be ninety-five percent (95%) of an itemized estimate made by the State Board of Equalization, which shall include all sources of revenue to each fund for the next ensuing fiscal year; provided, however, appropriated federal funds shall be certified for the full amount of the estimate. Said estimate shall consider any increase or decline in revenues that would result from predictable changes in the economy. Legislative appropriations for any fiscal year, except for special appropriations provided for in paragraph 6, 7 or 8 shall be limited to a sum not to exceed the total amount appropriated from all funds in the preceding fiscal year, plus twelve percent (12%), adjusted for inflation for the previous calendar year. Said limit shall be adjusted for funds not previously appropriated. The limit on the growth of appropriations shall be certified to by the State Board of Equalization.

2. Such certification shall be filed with the Governor, the President and President Pro Tempore of the Senate, and the Speaker of the House of Representatives. The Legislature shall not pass or enact any bill, act or measure making an appropriation of money for any purpose until such certification is made and filed, unless the State Board of Equalization has failed to file said certification at the time of convening of said Legislature. In such event, it shall be the duty of the Legislature to make such certification pursuant to the provisions of this section. All appropriations made in excess of such certification shall be null and void; provided, however, that the Legislature may at any regular session or special session, called for that purpose, enact laws to provide for additional revenues or a reduction in revenues, other than ad valorem taxes, or transferring the existing revenues or unappropriated cash on hand from one fund to another, or making provisions for appropriating funds not previously appropriated directly by the Legislature. Whereupon, it shall be the duty of the State Board of Equalization to make a determination of the revenues that will accrue under such laws and ninety-five percent (95%) of the amount of any increase or decrease resulting, for any reason, from such changes in laws shall be added to or deducted from the amount previously certified available for appropriation from each respective fund, as the case may be. The State Board of Equalization shall file the amount of such adjusted certification, or additional certification for funds not previously appropriated directly by the Legislature, with the Governor, with the President and President Pro Tempore of the Senate, and the Speaker of the House of Representatives, and such adjusted amount shall be the maximum amount which can be appropriated for all purposes from any such fund for the fiscal year being certified.

3. The State Board of Equalization shall meet within five (5) days after the monthly apportionment in February of each year, and at that time may adjust the certification, based upon the most current information available, and determine the amount of funds available for appropriation for that legislative session. At said meeting the Board shall determine the limit on the growth of appropriations as provided for in this section.

4. Surplus funds or monies shall be any amount accruing to the General Revenue Fund of the State of Oklahoma over and above the itemized estimate made by the State Board of Equalization.

5. Beginning July 1, 1985, all such surplus funds or monies accruing after said date shall be placed in a Constitutional Reserve Fund by the State Treasurer until such time that the amount of said Fund equals ten percent (10%) of the General Revenue Fund certification for the preceding fiscal year. Appropriations made from said Fund shall be considered special appropriations.

6.

a. Up to three-eighths (3/8) of the balance at the beginning of the current fiscal year in the Constitutional Reserve Fund may be appropriated for the forthcoming fiscal year, when the certification by the State Board of Equalization for said forthcoming fiscal year General Revenue Fund is less than that of the current fiscal year certification. In no event shall the amount of monies appropriated from the Constitutional Reserve Fund be in excess of the difference between the two said certifications.

b.

(1) In years when the provisions of subparagraph a of this paragraph are not applicable and the balance at the beginning of the current fiscal year in the Constitutional Reserve Fund is equal to or greater than Eighty Million Dollars ($80,000,000.00), up to Ten Million Dollars ($10,000,000.00) may be expended for the purpose of providing incentives to support retention of at-risk manufacturing establishments in this state in order to retain employment for residents of this state. Such incentives shall be paid by the Oklahoma Tax Commission upon a unanimous finding by the Governor, the Speaker of the House of Representatives and the President Pro Tempore of the Senate that:

(a) such incentives have been recommended by an independent committee created by the Legislature for such purposes as provided herein pursuant to criteria set out by law,

(b) the incentive will result in a substantial benefit to this state, and

(c) payment of the incentive would be in accordance with the provisions of this subparagraph and laws enacted to implement provisions of this subparagraph.

(2) The independent committee will be composed of not less than seven (7) people appointed or otherwise determined pursuant to laws enacted by the Legislature providing for membership on the committee. The committee shall make recommendations to the Governor, the Speaker of the House of Representatives and the President Pro Tempore of the Senate for the awarding of incentives. Such recommendations shall give priority to establishments which:

(a) are at greater risk of losing jobs because the plant is no longer competitive or leaving the state and thereby causing the loss of more employment in this state than other eligible recipients, and

(b) provide the largest economic impact to the state.

(3) For any fiscal year, the incentives shall not exceed ten percent (10%) of the amount invested by an establishment in capital assets to be utilized in this state. Incentives may only be paid pursuant to an investment contract between the establishment and a state agency designated by law, which provides for a specified amount of investment in a capital asset to be made by the establishment over a period of not to exceed five (5) years. No incentive payment shall be made prior to the actual investment by the establishment. The contract shall make payment of any incentives in any fiscal year contingent on the balance at the beginning of such fiscal year in the Constitutional Reserve Fund being equal to or greater than Eighty Million Dollars ($80,000,000.00) and on the certification by the State Board of Equalization for such fiscal year of the amount available for appropriation from the General Revenue Fund being greater than the amount certified for the preceding fiscal year. Investment contracts authorized by this subparagraph shall provide that if any incentive payment is payable during a fiscal year in which either the balance at the beginning of the fiscal year in the Constitutional Reserve Fund is not equal to or greater than Eighty Million Dollars ($80,000,000.00) or when the certification by the State Board of Equalization for such fiscal year General Revenue Fund is less than that of the immediately prior fiscal year certification, then any incentive payments which would have been payable during such fiscal year shall be payable in the first fiscal year when funds are available pursuant to the provisions of division (1) of this subparagraph. In the event that the amount of incentives payable under investment contracts authorized by this subparagraph is greater than the amounts available for payment under this subparagraph in a fiscal year, then no new contracts may be authorized during such year and incentive payments which are made shall be reduced pro rata as necessary to apply all available funds to incentive payments which are payable in such year.

(4) The Legislature is authorized to enact laws necessary to implement the provisions of this section.

7. Up to three-eighths (3/8) of the balance at the beginning of the current fiscal year in the Constitutional Reserve Fund may be appropriated for the current fiscal year if the State Board of Equalization determines that a revenue failure has occurred with respect to the General Revenue Fund of the State Treasury. In no event shall the amount of monies appropriated from the Constitutional Reserve Fund pursuant to this paragraph be in excess of the amount of the projected revenue failure in the General Revenue Fund, which total amount shall be computed by the State Board of Equalization, for the entire fiscal year. Monies appropriated to any state governmental entity from the Constitutional Reserve Fund pursuant to this paragraph may only be made in order to ensure that the monies actually received by the entity for the then current fiscal year are equal to or less than, but not in excess of, the total appropriation amount for such entity in effect at the beginning of the then current fiscal year.

8. Up to one-quarter (1/4) of the balance at the beginning of the current fiscal year in the Constitutional Reserve Fund may be appropriated, upon a declaration by the Governor that emergency conditions exist, with concurrence of the Legislature by a two-thirds (2/3) vote of the House of Representatives and Senate for the appropriation; or said one-quarter (1/4) could be appropriated upon a joint declaration of emergency conditions by the Speaker of the House of Representatives and the President Pro Tempore of the Senate, with a concurrence of a three-fourths (3/4) vote of the House of Representatives and Senate.

9. That portion of every appropriation, at the end of each fiscal year, in excess of actual revenues collected and allocated thereto, as hereinafter provided, shall be null and void. Revenues deposited in the State Treasury to the credit of the General Revenue Fund or of any special fund (which derives its revenue in whole or in part from state taxes or fees) shall, except as to principal and interest on the public debt, be allocated monthly to each department, institution, board, commission or special appropriation on a percentage basis, in that ratio that the total appropriation for such department, institution, board, commission or special appropriation from each fund for that fiscal year bears to the total of all appropriations from each fund for that fiscal year, and no warrant shall be issued in excess of said allocation. Any department, institution or agency of the state operating on revenues derived from any law or laws which allocate the revenues thereof to such department, institution or agency shall not incur obligations in excess of the unencumbered balance of cash on hand. Nothing in this section shall prevent, under such conditions and limitations as shall be prescribed by law, the governing board of an institution of higher education within The Oklahoma State System of Higher Education from contracting with a president of such institution of higher education for periods extending more than one (1) year, but not to exceed three (3) years beyond the fiscal year in which the contract is signed.

10. The Legislature shall provide a method whereby appropriations shall be divided and set up on a monthly, quarterly or semiannual basis within each fiscal year to prevent obligations being incurred in excess of the revenue to be collected, and notwithstanding other provisions of this Constitution, the Legislature shall provide that all appropriations shall be reduced to bring them within revenues actually collected, but all such reductions shall apply to each department, institution, board, commission or special appropriation made by the State Legislature in the ratio that its total appropriation for that fiscal year bears to the total of all appropriations from that fund for that fiscal year; provided, however, that the Governor may in his discretion issue deficiency certificates to the State Treasurer for the benefit of any department, institution or agency of the state, if the amount of such deficiency certificates be within the limit of the current appropriation for that department, institution or agency, whereupon the State Treasurer shall issue warrants to the extent of such certificates for the payment of such claims as may be authorized by the Governor, and such warrants shall become a part of the public debt and shall be paid out of any money appropriated by the Legislature and made lawfully available therefore; provided further, that in no event shall said deficiency certificates exceed in the aggregate the sum of Five Hundred Thousand Dollars ($500,000.00) in any fiscal year.

Section 23a. Surplus Accruing to General Revenue Fund - Payment of Bonded Indebtedness - Investments - Appropriation of Surplus

Any surplus which has accrued or may hereafter accrue to the General Revenue Fund of the State of Oklahoma during any fiscal year shall be placed monthly in a sinking fund in the State Treasury to be used solely for the purpose of paying the principal and interest of the outstanding and unpaid bonded indebtedness of the State of Oklahoma. The monies and securities heretofore credited to the Surplus Accounts of the State Funding Bond Funds of 1935, 1939, and 1941 also shall be placed in said Sinking Fund. The State Treasurer shall be the custodian of said Sinking Fund and shall apply the monies and securities placed to the credit of said fund to the payment of the principal and interest of the state's bonded indebtedness. The State Treasurer with the approval of the Governor and Attorney General shall have the authority to invest the monies in said sinking fund in bonds or securities of the United States of America, and the State Treasurer with the approval of the Governor and Attorney General may sell said securities to provide funds to meet maturing State bonds and coupons. The provisions of this section shall be self-executing. When the monies credited to said sinking fund together with the monies set aside to pay said bonded indebtedness, pursuant to the statutes authorizing the issuance of said bonds, are sufficient to pay all outstanding bonds and coupons heretofore issued by the State of Oklahoma, it shall no longer be necessary to credit surplus funds to the Sinking Fund herein created. The sufficiency of said monies to fully pay the State's bonded indebtedness shall be determined by the Governor, State Treasurer, and Attorney General. After such determination any surplus monies thereafter to the credit of the State General Revenue Fund shall be subject to appropriation by the Legislature.

Section 23b. Contracts for Incarceration of State Inmates with Counties and Municipalities

A. The state is hereby authorized to enter into contracts for the incarceration of state prisoners with counties, municipalities, or any combination thereof authorized by law. The term of such a contract shall not exceed fifteen (15) years.

B. Any county, municipality or combination thereof authorized by law that builds a new jail or provides for capital improvements to an existing jail to enter into a contract authorized by subsection A of this section may provide for financing of the project by any means authorized by the provisions of this Constitution or state law.

Section 24. Debts in Case of Invasion, Insurrection, or War

In addition to the above limited power to contract debts, the State may contract debts to repel invasion, suppress insurrection or to defend the State in war; but the money arising from the contracting of such debts shall be applied to the purpose for which it was raised, or to repay such debts, and to no other purpose whatever.

Section 25. Authorization of Debt - Annual Tax - Submission to Voters - Final Passage

Except the debts specified in sections twenty-three and twenty-four of this article, no debts shall be hereafter contracted by or on behalf of this State, unless such debt shall be authorized by law for some work or object, to be distinctly specified therein; and such law shall impose and provide for the collection of a direct annual tax to pay, and sufficient to pay, the interest on such debt as it falls due, and also to pay and discharge the principal of such debt within twenty-five years from the time of the contracting thereof. No such law shall take effect until it shall, at a general election, have been submitted to the people and have received a majority of all the votes cast for and against it at such election. On the final passage of such bill in either House of the Legislature, the question shall be taken by yeas and nays, to be duly entered on the journals thereof, and shall be: "Shall this bill pass, and ought the same to receive the sanction of the people?"

Section 26. Indebtedness of Political Subdivisions - Assent of Voters - Annual Tax- Computation of Amount of Indebtedness

(a) Except as herein otherwise provided, no county, city, town, township, school district, or other political corporation, or subdivision of the state, shall be allowed to become indebted, in any manner, or for any purpose, to an amount exceeding, in any year, the income and revenue provided for such year without the assent of three-fifths of the voters thereof, voting at an election, to be held for that purpose, nor, in cases requiring such assent, shall any indebtedness be allowed to be incurred to an amount, including existing indebtedness, in the aggregate exceeding five percent (5%) of the valuation of the taxable property therein, to be ascertained from the last assessment for state and county purposes previous to the incurring of such indebtedness: Provided, that if a school district has an absolute need therefore, such district may, with the assent of three-fifths of the voters thereof voting at an election to be held for that purpose, incur indebtedness to an amount, including existing indebtedness, in the aggregate exceeding five percent (5%) but not exceeding ten percent (10%) of the valuation of the taxable property therein, to be ascertained from the last assessment for state and county purposes previous to the incurring of such indebtedness, for the purpose of acquiring or improving school sites, constructing, repairing, remodeling or equipping buildings, or acquiring school furniture, fixtures or equipment; and such assent to such indebtedness shall be deemed to be a sufficient showing of such absolute need, unless otherwise provided by law. Provided further, that if a city or town has an absolute need therefore, such city or town may, with the assent of three-fifths of the voters thereof voting at an election to be held for that purpose, incur indebtedness to an amount, including existing indebtedness, in the aggregate exceeding five percent (5%) but not exceeding ten percent (10%) of the valuation of the taxable property therein, to be ascertained from the last assessment for state and county purposes previous to the incurring of such indebtedness, and such assent to such indebtedness shall be deemed to be a sufficient showing of such absolute need unless otherwise provided by law. Provided, further, that any county, city, town, school district, or other political corporation, or subdivision of the state, incurring any indebtedness requiring the assent of the voters as aforesaid, shall, before or at the time of doing so, provide for the collection of an annual tax sufficient to pay the interest on such indebtedness as it falls due, and also to constitute a sinking fund for the payment of the principal thereof within twenty-five (25) years from the time of contracting the same, and provided further that nothing in this section shall prevent, under such conditions and limitations as shall be prescribed by law, any school district from contracting with:

(1) certificated personnel for periods extending one (1) year beyond the current fiscal year; or

(2) a school superintendent for periods extending more than one

(1) year, but not to exceed three :(3) years beyond the current fiscal year.

(b) If a county approves an exemption of household goods of the heads of families and livestock employed in support of the family from ad valorem taxation pursuant to the provisions of subsection (b) of Section 6 of this article, the percentage limitations on indebtedness as specified in subsection (a) of this section for political subdivisions or political corporations located in any such county shall be adjusted by multiplying the percentage levels specified in subsection (a) of this section by the millage adjustment factor as specified in subsection (b) of Section 8A of this article.

(c) If approved by the people, the amendment to this section shall become effective January 1, 1993.

Section 27. Indebtedness for Purchase, Construction or Repair of Public Utilities

Any incorporated city or town in this state may, by a majority of the voters of such city or town, voting at an election to be held for that purpose, be allowed to become indebted in a larger amount than that specified in Section 26, for the purpose of purchasing or constructing public utilities, or for repairing the same, to be owned exclusively by such city or town, or for the purpose of constructing, reconstructing, improving or repairing streets or bridges. Provided, that any such city or town incurring any such indebtedness requiring the assent of the voters as aforesaid, shall have the power to provide for, and, before or at the time of incurring such indebtedness, shall provide for the collection of an annual tax in addition to the other taxes provided for by this Constitution, sufficient to pay the interest on such indebtedness as it falls due, and also to constitute a sinking fund for the payment of the principal thereof within twenty-five years from the time of contracting the same.

Section 27A. Municipal Water and Water Facilities – Financing

Any incorporated city or town in Oklahoma may individually or jointly, after approval of the proposition by a majority of the qualified electors voting in an election in each of said cities and towns, contract and pledge revenues for a term of years with other cities or towns, the State of Oklahoma, the United States of America, or any other governmental subdivision or agency of any of them, for the purpose of purchasing water, constructing, acquiring, or operating water facilities, or purchasing or leasing reservoir space. Any one or more incorporated cities and towns in Oklahoma may after approval of the proposition by a majority of the qualified electors voting in an election in each of said cities and towns issue bonds payable over a period not to exceed thirty (30) years and secured by revenues derived from the sale of water for the joint construction, acquisition, repair, extension or improvement of said water facilities; and thereafter enact ordinances giving effect to the provisions of this section. This section shall be independent and shall not be limited by or limit other existing provisions of the Constitution relating to municipal water or the financing thereof, nor shall it be exclusive as to other agencies of the State of Oklahoma authorized by law to incur indebtedness, Section 27 of Article X of the Constitution which pertains to incurring of tax secured indebtedness by cities and towns for public utilities is hereby amended to permit joint ownership by cities and towns of water facilities.

Section 27B. Political Subdivisions - Public Utilities Financing – Indebtedness

A. Any incorporated city or town may borrow money or issue bonds, notes or other evidences of indebtedness, which debt shall be payable from and secured by revenues over a term of years, for the purpose of financing the purchase, construction, or improvement of any public utility or combination of public utilities which shall be owned exclusively by such city or town in the following manner:

1. The governing body of a city or town shall submit the question of financing the purchase or construction of a public utility or combination of public utilities to the qualified voters at an election if:

a. the public utility or combination of public utilities has not been voted on by the voters of the city or town at any time during a ten-year period preceding the date of the election, or
b. the public utility or combination of public utilities does not come within the terms of paragraph 3 of this subsection;

2. If the question of financing the purchase or construction of a public utility or combination of public utilities has been approved by a majority vote of the qualified voters voting on the question at an election, or if improvements to a public utility or combination of public utilities pursuant to paragraph 3 of this subsection are authorized, the governing body of a city or town may borrow money or issue bonds, notes or other evidences of indebtedness, which debt shall be payable from and secured by revenues over a term of years, upon an affirmative vote of at least three-fourths (3/4) of all the members of such governing body;

3. Any additions, extensions, reconstruction, maintenance, repairs or other improvement to any public utility or combination of public utilities of a city or town may be financed by the city or town if the original financing of the purchase or construction of the public utility was approved by a majority vote of the qualified voters voting on the question at an election, or if the public utility or combination of public utilities acquired by the city or town was financed originally by bonds or other debt of a public trust of which the city or town is a beneficiary, excluding an industrial trust. Any such bonds or other debt originally issued by a public trust of which the city or town is a beneficiary, excluding an industrial trust, may be refunded by the governing body of the city or town in the manner provided in paragraph 2 of this subsection.

B. Nothing in this section shall allow an indebtedness of the city or town, other than revenues pledged from the utility involved.

C. The revenue indebtedness or contractual obligations of any city or town incurred pursuant to this section shall be a limited obligation payable from and secured by a lien and charge on revenues or funds so pledged for their payment by the governing body of the city or town, and shall not constitute an indebtedness of the city or town for the purpose of any constitutional or statutory limitation.

D. This section shall be independent and shall not be limited by or limit other provisions of the Oklahoma Constitution or statutes relating to financing public utilities or indebtedness of a city or town, nor shall it be exclusive as to other agencies of this state authorized by law to incur indebtedness. As used in this section, the words "public utility" shall have the same meaning as the words "public utilities" in Section 27 of Article X of the Constitution.

E. Notwithstanding any provision to the contrary, the provisions of this section shall not apply to the purchase of any utility regulated by the Oklahoma Corporation Commission or to the purchase of any facility or property of any such utility, unless the purchase is made with the agreement and consent of the utility, including its agreement and consent as to a specific price to be paid in connection with the purchase.

Section 28. Revenue for Sinking Fund - Uses to Which Applied

Counties, townships, school districts, cities, and towns shall levy sufficient additional revenue to create a sinking fund to be used, first, for the payment of interest coupons as they fall due; second, for the payment of bonds as they fall due; third, for the payments of such parts of judgments as such municipality may, by law, be required to pay.

Section 29. Bonds and Evidence of Indebtedness - Certificates as to Compliance with Law

No bond or evidence of indebtedness of this State shall be valid unless the same shall have endorsed thereon a certificate, signed by the Auditor and Attorney General of the State, showing that the bond or evidence of debt is issued pursuant to law and is within the debt limit. No bond or evidence of debt of any county, or bond of any township or any other political subdivision of any county, shall be valid unless the same have endorsed thereon a certificate signed by the County Clerk, or other officer authorized by law to sign such certificate, and the County Attorney of the county, stating that said bond, or evidence of debt, is issued pursuant to law, and that said issue is within the debt limit.

Section 30. System of Accounting

The Legislature shall require all money collected by taxation, or by fees, fines, and public charges of every kind, to be accounted for by a system of accounting that shall be uniform for each class of accounts, State and local, which shall be prescribed and audited by authority of the State.

Section 31. Indebtedness for Construction, Equipment, Etc., of State Buildings - Use of Part of Cigarette Tax for Payment

The Legislature of the State of Oklahoma is hereby authorized to enact a law whereby the State may become indebted in an amount not to exceed Thirty-six Million Dollars ($36,000,000.00) for the purpose of constructing, equipping, remodeling and repairing any and all buildings of the State, including those of its educational, recreational, penal and eleemosynary establishments; and such laws shall provide that two cents (2¢) of the tax on each package of cigarettes authorized by 68 O.S. 1941, Par. 586 to 586p, as amended and supplemented to the effective date of this Section, or so much of said tax as may be necessary, shall be pledged and used for the sole purpose of paying the interest on such debt as it falls due, and also to pay and discharge the principal of such debt within twenty-five (25) years from the time of the contracting thereof; provided, that if said tax is not sufficient to so pay and discharge said interest and principal, the Legislature shall impose and provide for the collection of an additional tax, other than an ad valorem tax, sufficient to pay and discharge said interest and principal.

Section 32. State Public Common School Building Equalization Fund

For the purpose of providing buildings for school districts, there is hereby established a State Public Common School Building Equalization Fund in which shall be deposited:

(1) such monies as may be designated or provided for such purpose by the Legislature, other than ad valorem taxes, and

(2) the proceeds of all property that shall fall to the State by escheat and penalties for unlawful holding of real estate by corporations; provided, that if such disposition and use of money from any such sources shall be declared invalid, the validity of other provisions of this section shall not be affected thereby. The State Public Common School Building Equalization Fund shall be administered by the State Board of Education, until otherwise provided by the Legislature. Such Fund shall be used to aid school districts in acquiring buildings, under such regulations as may be prescribed by the administering agency, unless otherwise provided by law, and the amount paid therefrom to or for any school district shall be determined by a formula established by the Legislature. The administering agency is authorized to accept grants-in-aid from the federal government for building purposes.

Section 33. Indebtedness for Construction of Buildings and other Capital Improvements - Restrictions - Term - Sources of Payment

The Legislature of the State of Oklahoma is hereby authorized to enact a law whereby the State may become indebted in an amount not to exceed Fifteen Million Dollars ($15,000,000.00) for the purpose of constructing any buildings and other capital improvements and for equipping, remodeling, modernizing and repairing any and all existing buildings and capital improvements at the constituent institutions of the Oklahoma State System of Higher Education and other State institutions. No part of any of said monies shall be, directly or indirectly, allocated to or used by the Oklahoma Educational Television Authority for any purpose whatsoever. Such law shall provide for the payment and discharge of the principal of such debt within twenty-seven (27) years and shall further provide for the payment and discharge of the principal and interest on such indebtedness from one or more of the following sources of State income as follows:

(1) Any remainder available from the two cents (2¢) of the tax on each package of cigarettes as heretofore provided and defined in Article X, Section 31 of the Constitution of the State of Oklahoma, after the annual requirements for principal and interest on the indebtedness created pursuant to said Section have been fully met, until such indebtedness created by said Section has been fully paid and retired, and thereafter, the full amount of said two cents (2¢) of the cigarette tax so provided, or so much thereof as may be required, until the indebtedness herein authorized to be created is fully paid and retired;

(2) An additional three cents (3¢) of the tax now imposed, or which may hereafter be imposed, on each package of cigarettes containing more than twenty (20) cigarettes, or so much of said additional three cents (3¢) as may be necessary; (3) Any funds available in the Public Building Fund of the State, not otherwise encumbered, or funds available in other funds of the State not created or realized from ad valorem tax sources; (4) The proceeds of any tax which the Legislature may impose and collect for the purpose of paying the principal and interest on the indebtedness herein authorized to be created, if the funds available for use and pledge under (1), (2), and (3) above should be insufficient; provided, that the Legislature shall never impose or collect an ad valorem tax for the purpose of paying any part of the principal or interest on the indebtedness herein authorized to be incurred.

Section 33A. State Industrial Finance Authority

The Legislature of the State of Oklahoma is hereby authorized to enact legislation creating a State Industrial Finance Authority, to be composed of the State Treasurer (who shall be an ex officio, non-voting member) and seven members, appointed by the Governor for overlapping terms, one of whom shall be the Director of the Department of Economic Development representing the State at large, and one each from the present six Congressional Districts, at least five of whom shall have had at least fifteen (15) years experience in banking, mortgage loans, or financial management, and the remaining member shall have demonstrated outstanding ability in business or industry, which Authority shall be, and is hereby, authorized to issue and sell State Industrial Finance Bonds in such amounts as shall be needed from time to time for the purposes herein provided, not to exceed in the aggregate Ninety Million Dollars ($90,000,000.00) outstanding at any one time, said bonds to be payable in full within thirty (30) years from their date, the proceeds whereof shall be deposited in the State Treasury in a fund known as a State Industrial Revolving Loan Fund to be loaned, and re-loaned, by said Authority only to Oklahoma incorporated industrial development agencies (whether profit or nonprofit) in Oklahoma communities, which agencies shall first have been approved and qualified by said Authority, such loans to be secured either by first or second mortgage on the land, buildings and facilities of such industrial properties, whether existing or to be constructed, held for sale or lease to approved responsible industrial firms on such terms as will amortize such loans within a period of twenty-five (25) years or less, but in no event shall the state's participation exceed thirty-three and one-third percent (33 1/3 %) of the total cost or value of such industrial properties when such loan is secured by a second mortgage on such industrial properties and sixty-six and two-thirds percent (66 2/3 %) of the total cost or value of such industrial properties when such loan is secured by a first mortgage on such industrial properties. Provided, however that up to one-half of such monies in said fund may be used by said Authority to purchase federally guaranteed SBA loans or loans of similar federal programs for investment purposes. All bonds representing the state indebtedness herein authorized to be created by the State Industrial Finance Authority shall be backed by the full faith and credit of the State of Oklahoma and there shall be pledged to the payment of principal and interest of the bonds herein authorized to be issued:

(1) The net proceeds from repayment of loans and interest received thereon;

(2) any moneys available from other funds of the State not otherwise obligated; and

(3) the proceeds of any tax, other than ad valorem, which may be imposed for such purpose in the event funds available for use and pledge under (1) and (2) should be insufficient. The Legislature shall enact appropriate and needful legislation pertaining to procedure, terms and necessary covenants for issuance of the bonds herein authorized and establishing such safeguards and regulations governing the lending of such funds as in its wisdom may be necessary to the vitalization of this Section, and helpful in carrying out the purpose and intent hereof; to aid and assist with Oklahoma's industrial development. The additional bonds as authorized herein shall only be sold as needed in increments not to exceed Ten Million Dollars ($10,000,000.00).

Section 34. Indebtedness for Capital Improvements to Institutions of Higher Education - School and Hospital for Mentally Retarded Children

The Legislature of the State of Oklahoma is hereby authorized to enact a law or laws whereby the State may become indebted in an amount not to exceed Thirty Five Million, Five Hundred Thousand Dollars ($35,500,000.00) for the purpose of constructing new buildings and other capital improvements and for equipping, remodeling, modernizing and repairing any and all existing buildings and capital improvements at the constituent institutions of the Oklahoma State System of Higher Education, provided that Five Million Dollars ($5,000,000.00) shall be used to construct and equip a School and Hospital for Mentally Retarded Children in Northeastern Oklahoma, out of said monies such law or laws shall provide for the payment and discharge of the principal of such debt, together with principal and interest on such indebtedness, from one or more of the following sources of State income as follows:

1. Any remainder of revenue available from the revenues lawfully levied and collected by the State of Oklahoma on the sale of cigarettes not already committed to other obligations of the State of Oklahoma;

2. Allocations by the Legislature of the State of Oklahoma from any monies in the general revenue fund of the State not otherwise obligated, committed or appropriated; and

3. The proceeds of any tax which the Legislature may impose and collect for the purpose of paying the principal and interest on the indebtedness herein authorized to be created, authority hereby being granted to the Legislature to so impose and collect such tax, if necessary.

Such law or laws hereby authorized to be enacted by the Legislature of the State of Oklahoma may provided for the issuance of bonds evidencing the indebtedness herein authorized and provide that such bonds may be issued in one or more series, may bear such date or dates, may mature at such time or times, may be in such denomination or denominations, may be in such form, coupon or registered, may carry such registration or conversion provisions, may be executed in such manner, may be payable in such medium or payment at such place or places, may be subject to such terms of redemption, with or without premium, and may bear such rate or rates of interest as the legislature may deem expedient and may contain any and all provisions which the Legislature may deem necessary or expedient to make such bonds marketable as general obligations of the State of Oklahoma with the full faith and credit of the State pledged thereto. Within the limit of indebtedness herein authorized the Legislature in its discretion may authorize the issuance of such bonds and the incurring of the authorized indebtedness in fractional amounts of the total indebtedness hereby authorized to be incurred from time to time and at one or more Sessions of the Legislature.

Section 35. Municipal and County Levy for Securing and Developing Industry

(a) Any incorporated town and any county may issue, by and with the consent of the majority of the registered voters of said municipality or county voting on the question at an election held for the purpose, bonds in sums provided by such majority at such election for economic development or community development purposes, as may be defined by law, within or near the said municipality or county holding the election.

(b) Such bonds shall bear interest at a rate as set by law and shall be sold in a manner prescribed by law.

(c) To provide for the payment of all such bonds outstanding, principal, and interest as they mature, the municipality or county may:

(1) levy a special tax, payable annually, in a total amount not to exceed five (5) mills on the dollar, in addition to the legal rate permitted, on the real and personal taxable property therein; provided, however, that in no event shall the real and personal taxable property in any city or town be subject to a special tax in excess of five (5) mills for bonds issued hereunder;

(2) levy a special sales tax, payable as may be prescribed by law, in a total amount not to exceed one cent ($0.01) on the dollar, in addition to the legal rate permitted, upon the sale of tangible personal property and services, not otherwise exempted by law;

(3) apportion revenues pursuant to Section 6C of Article X of the Constitution, in a manner prescribed by law; or

(4) implement any combination of paragraphs (1) through (3) of this subsection.

Provided, however, that the source or sources of revenue and the irrevocable pledge thereof shall be set forth in the ballot.

(d) Such bonds shall be issued under terms prescribed by law.

(e)

(1) The governing body of the municipality or the county commissioners of the county shall exercise jurisdiction over the sale or exchange of any such bonds voted by the electors at an election held for that purpose and shall expend economically the funds so provided.

(2) In the expenditure and use of proceeds from the sale of said bonds, the said governing body is hereby authorized and directed to coordinate its industrial development plans and projects insofar as practicable with similar plans and projects of local industrial development agencies and the Oklahoma Industrial Finance Authority, as set forth in Section 34 of Article X of the Constitution, so as to supplement funds to be derived from these and other sources, including federal aid available to economically depressed areas, if any; and to the extent that federal requirements shall require subordination of liens securing loans from the Oklahoma Industrial Finance Authority or from other sources, as a condition to the obtaining of such federal aid, the same is hereby approved and authorized.

(f) The election on the issuance of such bonds shall be held at such time as the governing body of the municipality may designate by ordinance, or as the county commissioners of the county may designate by order, which ordinance or order shall state the sum total of issue, the dates of maturities thereof, and shall fix the date of election so that it shall not occur earlier than thirty (30) days after the passage of the said ordinance or the granting of said order. All elections called pursuant to this section shall be conducted by the appropriate county election board or boards pursuant to the general election laws of the state. The said election shall be held and conducted, the vote thereof canvassed, and the result thereof declared under the law and in the manner now or hereafter provided for municipal elections when the election is held by a municipality, and in the manner now or hereafter provided for county elections when the election is held by a county, so far as the same may be applicable, except as herein otherwise provided. Notice of the election shall be given by the mayor of the municipality or by the county commissioners of the county by advertisement weekly for at least four times in some newspaper having a bona fide circulation in the said municipality or county, with the last publication to be not less than ten (10) days prior to the date of the said election. Only registered voters of the said municipality or county shall have a right to vote at the said election. The result of the said election shall be proclaimed by the mayor of the municipality or by the county commissioners of the county, and the result as proclaimed shall be conclusive, unless attacked in the courts within thirty (30) days after the date of such proclamation.

(g) The tax levies or revenue apportionment associated with bonds issued pursuant to this section and the pledge thereof, may not be revoked during the term of such bonds; provided, however, the municipality or county may, from time to time, suspend the collection of such levy or apportioned revenues when not required for the payment of its bonds.

(h) The Legislature may provide by law for the creation of regional economic development districts, comprised of two or more municipalities or counties, or a combination of one or more municipalities and counties, and may specify the terms and conditions under which the bonds authorized in this section may be issued by municipalities and counties located within such districts. The provisions of paragraph (f) of this section shall not apply to any bonds issued in accordance with this paragraph unless such provisions are made expressly applicable by law.

Section 36. Indebtedness for Capital Improvements - University Medical Center

The Legislature of the State of Oklahoma is hereby authorized to enact a law or laws whereby the State may become indebted in an amount not to exceed Seven Million Dollars ($7,000,000.00) for the purpose of constructing new buildings and other capital improvements and for equipping, remodeling, modernizing and repairing any and all existing buildings and capital improvements at University of Oklahoma Medical Center, and such law or laws shall provide for the payment and discharge of the principal of such debt, together with principal and interest on such indebtedness, from one or more of the following sources of State income as follows:

1. Any remainder of revenue available from the revenues lawfully levied and collected by the State of Oklahoma on the sale of cigarettes not already committed to other obligations of the State of Oklahoma;

2. Allocations by the Legislature of the State of Oklahoma from any monies in the general revenue fund of the State not otherwise obligated, committed or appropriated; and

3. The proceeds of any tax which the Legislature may impose and collect for the purpose of paying the principal and interest on the indebtedness herein authorized to be created, authority hereby being granted to the Legislature to so impose and collect such tax, if necessary.

Such law or laws hereby authorized to be enacted by the Legislature of the State of Oklahoma may provide for the issuance of bonds evidencing the indebtedness herein authorized and provide that such bonds may be issued in one or more series, may bear such date or dates, may mature at such time or times, may be in such denomination or denominations, may be in such form, coupon or registered, may carry such registration or conversion provisions, may be executed in such manner, may be payable in such medium or payment at such place or places, may be subject to such terms of redemption, with or without premium, and may bear such rate or rates of interest as the Legislature may deem expedient and may contain any and all provisions which the Legislature may deem necessary or expedient to make such bonds marketable as general obligations of the State of Oklahoma with the full faith and credit of the State pledged thereto. Within the limits of indebtedness herein authorized the Legislature in its discretion may authorize the issuance of such bonds and the incurring of the authorized indebtedness in fractional amounts of the total indebtedness hereby authorized to be incurred from time to time and at one or more sessions of the Legislature.

Section 37. Bond Issue for Capital Improvements at State Institutions

The Legislature of the State of Oklahoma is hereby authorized to enact necessary legislation whereby the State may become indebted in an amount not to exceed Fifty-Four Million Seven Hundred Fifty Thousand Dollars ($54,750,000.00) for the purpose of constructing new buildings and other capital improvements for remodeling, modernizing and repairing any and all existing buildings and capital improvements and purchase of land, equipment and furnishings necessary for such new construction or remodeling for the following departments of state government in the amounts and for the purposes indicated as follows:

Oklahoma State Regents for Higher Education for Expenditures at all Constituent Institutions - $38,500,000.00

Department of Mental Health for Expenditures at the following Institutions:

Central State Griffin Memorial Hospital, Eastern State Hospital, Western State Hospital and Taft State Hospital - $6,500,000.00

Oklahoma Public Welfare Commission for Expenditures at the following Institutions:

Pauls Valley State School, Enid State School and the Hissom Memorial Center - $1,000,000.00

State Department of Health - $2,275,000.00

Oklahoma State Library - $2,150,000.00

State Board of Public Affairs for Expenditures at the following Institutions:

Oklahoma State Penitentiary - $150,000.00

Oklahoma State Reformatory - $150,000.00

Oklahoma School for the Blind - $550,000.00

Oklahoma School for the Deaf - $550,000.00

Oklahoma Educational Television Authority - $250,000.00

Oklahoma Historical Society - $125,000.00

State Board of Health for Expenditures at the following Institutions:

Western Oklahoma Tuberculosis Sanatorium - $150,000.00

Eastern Oklahoma Tuberculosis Sanatorium - $150,000.00

Department of Public Health for the Building of Community Social Service Centers - $1,500,000.00

Purchase of Land in and about the Capital Improvement and Zoning District and Medical Center Improvement Zoning District and for Public Parks, Veterans Memorial Area and Landscaping - $750,000.00

and such legislation shall provide for the payment and discharge of the principal of such debt, together with interest on such indebtedness, from one or more of the following sources of state income as follows:

1. Any remainder of revenue available from the revenues lawfully levied and collected by the State of Oklahoma on the sale of cigarettes not already committed to other obligations of the State of Oklahoma;

2. Allocations by the Legislature of the State of Oklahoma from any monies in the general revenue fund of the state not otherwise obligated, committed or appropriated; and

3. The proceeds of any tax which the Legislature may impose and collect for the purpose of paying the principal and interest on the indebtedness herein authorized to be created, and authority is hereby granted to the Legislature to so impose and collect such tax, if necessary.

Such legislation hereby authorized to be enacted by the Legislature of the State of Oklahoma may provide for the issuance of bonds evidencing the indebtedness herein authorized and provide that such bonds may be issued in one or more series, may bear such date or dates, may mature at such time or times, may be in such denomination or denominations, may be in such form, coupon or registered, may carry such registration or conversion provisions, may be executed in such manner, may be payable in such medium or payment at such place or places, may be subject to such terms of redemption, with or without premium, and may bear such rate or rates of interest as the Legislature may deem expedient and may contain any and all provisions which the Legislature may deem necessary or expedient to make such bonds marketable as general obligations of the State of Oklahoma with the full faith and credit of the State pledged thereto. Within the limits of indebtedness herein authorized the Legislature in its discretion may authorize the issuance of such bonds and the incurring of the authorized indebtedness in fractional amounts of the total indebtedness hereby authorized to be incurred from time to time and at one or more sessions of the Legislature.

Section 38. Indebtedness for Capital Improvements at State Institutions

The Legislature of the State of Oklahoma is hereby authorized to enact necessary legislation whereby the State may become indebted in an amount not to exceed Ninety-nine Million, Eight Hundred Eight Thousand Dollars ($99,808,000.00) for the purpose of planning and constructing new buildings or additions to existing state buildings and other capital improvements for remodeling, modernizing and repairing any and all existing buildings and capital improvements and purchase of land, equipment and furnishings necessary for such new construction or remodeling for the following departments and agencies of state government in the amounts and for the purposes set forth as follows:

1. Oklahoma State Regents for Higher Education for expenditure at all constituent institutions - $34,250,000.00

2. Oklahoma State Regents for Higher Education for expenditure at the Medical Center of the University of Oklahoma - $26,870,000.00

3. Oklahoma State Regents for Higher Education for the planning and construction of a new junior college at Tulsa - $4,000,000.00

4. Oklahoma State Regents for Higher Education for the planning and construction of a new junior college at Midwest City, provided that the study of Regents for Higher Education establishes a feasibility thereof, not to exceed $1,500,000.00, otherwise for new or existing community junior colleges which meet the criteria and conditions established by the Regents for Higher Education, a total of - $2,000,000.00

5. State Department of Mental Health for expenditure at Central State Griffin Memorial Hospital, Eastern State Hospital, Western State Hospital and Taft State Hospital and for constructing and equipping community mental health centers, provided that not more than fifteen per cent (15%) of the amount may be spent on community mental health centers - $8,000,000.00

6. State Department of Health for expenditure for the administrative offices and laboratories - $4,516,000.00

7. State Department of Health for construction, remodeling and equipping Oklahoma General Hospital at Clinton, Oklahoma - $500,000.00

8. State Department of Highways for the acquisition of land and completion of streets and highways in the State Capitol Complex - $1,875,000.00

9. Oklahoma Historical Society for equipment and remodeling at the Wiley Post Building and for acquisition and improvement of historic sites - $125,000.00

10. To the State Department of Vocational Education for construction and equipping of area vocational and technical schools and technical institutes and equipment, $5,750,000.00, and for Oklahoma State University School of Technical Training (Oklahoma State Tech) at Okmulgee, $1,500,000.00 - $7,250,000.00

11. State Department of Public Welfare for expenditure at the Pauls Valley State School, Enid State School, Hissom Memorial Center, School for the Blind, School for the Deaf, Whitaker State Children's Home, Taft State Children's Home, Helena State School for Boys, Boley State School for Boys, Taft State School for Girls and Tecumseh Girls' Town - $4,375,000.00

12. State Department of Public Welfare for construction of a Juvenile Diagnostic Evaluation and Receiving Center - $1,000,000.00

13. State Department of Public Safety for construction of a plans and training building and for district headquarters - $497,000.00

14. State Military Department for the construction of headquarters, warehouse and armory buildings - $1,500,000.00 15. State Bureau of Investigation for the construction of a building near or integrated into the new headquarters facilities of the Department of Public Safety- $200,000.00

16. State Department of Corrections for construction and equipping of a reception and diagnostic center and other capital improvements at McAlester, Oklahoma, $1,000,000.00 and for constructing, renovating and equipping academic and vocational school facilities and other capital projects at Granite Reformatory, $750,000.00 and $1,750,000.00

17. State Department of Health for construction, remodeling and equipping Eastern Oklahoma Tuberculosis Sanatorium at Talihina, Oklahoma, $250,000.00, and to the Western Oklahoma Tuberculosis Sanatorium at Clinton, Oklahoma, $250,000.00, and for constructing community social service centers at Ada, Shawnee, Lawton, and other communities approved by the State Department of Health, $500,000.00, (to be used with the $1,500,000.00 heretofore authorized in Section 37 of Article X of this Constitution) - $1,000,000.00

18. Cerebral Palsy Institute - $100,000.00

and such legislation shall provide for the payment and discharge of the principal of such debt, together with interest on such indebtedness, from one or more of the following sources of state income as follows:

1. Any remainder of revenue available from the revenues lawfully levied and collected by the State of Oklahoma on the sale of cigarettes not already committed to other obligations of the State of Oklahoma;

2. Allocations by the Legislature of the State of Oklahoma from any monies in the General Revenue Fund of the State not otherwise obligated, committed or appropriated; and

3. The proceeds of any tax which the Legislature may impose and collect for the purpose of paying the principal and interest on the indebtedness herein authorized to be created, and authority is hereby granted to the Legislature to so impose and collect such tax, if necessary.

Such legislation hereby authorized to be enacted by the Legislature of the State of Oklahoma may provide for the issuance of bonds evidencing the indebtedness herein authorized and provide that such bonds may be issued in one or more series, may bear such date or dates, may mature at such time or times, may be in such denomination or denominations, may be in such form, coupon or registered, may carry such registration or conversion provisions, may be executed in such manner, may be payable in such medium of payment at such place or places, may be subject to such terms of redemption, with or without premium, and may bear such rate or rates of interest as the Legislature may deem expedient and may contain any and all provisions which the Legislature may deem necessary or expedient to make such bonds marketable as general obligations of the State of Oklahoma with the full faith and credit of the State pledged thereto. As used herein words in the singular shall be construed to include the plural, and words in the plural shall be construed to include the singular; the designation of place or location shall be considered directive and not exclusive. Within the limits of indebtedness herein authorized the Legislature in its discretion may authorize the issuance of such bonds and the incurring of the authorized indebtedness in fractional amounts of the total indebtedness hereby authorized to be incurred from time to time and at one or more Sessions of the Legislature.

Section 39. Water Resources and Sewage Treatment Programs - Funding - State Financial Assistance - State Liability

A program is hereby authorized to provide for the beneficial utilization of water resources within the State of Oklahoma through the planning, development, construction, improvement, conservation, ownership, operation and financing of water resource and sewage treatment works, facilities and projects with state monies appropriated to the State-wide Water Development Revolving Fund and monies in the Water Resources Fund. State monies appropriated to the Statewide Water Development Revolving Fund and monies in the Water Resources Fund shall be used only as authorized by the Legislature to provide for the furnishing of financial assistance to municipalities, political subdivisions and such other public entities of the state as may be designated by law as being eligible for such assistance for water resource and sewage treatment purposes. Any state liability arising from the implementation of such a program shall be limited to those monies in the Statewide Water Development Revolving Fund which have been reserved for the undertaking producing the liability. The provisions of this section shall be independent of and not be limited by the provisions of Sections 14 and 15 of Article X of the Oklahoma Constitution.

Section 39a. A. There is hereby created within the Oklahoma Water Resources Board the Water Infrastructure Credit Enhancement Reserve Fund to be used by the Oklahoma Water Resources Board solely to secure the payment of principal, interest and premiums, if any, on bonds and other financial obligations issued or incurred to provide for the financial assistance programs as authorized in Section 39 of Article X of the Oklahoma Constitution.

B. The Oklahoma Water Resources Board shall issue bonds as authorized in subsection C of this section to provide for the Water Infrastructure Credit Enhancement Reserve Fund only after the following have been used, to the extent allowed by law, to repay the bonds and other financial obligations:

1. All other pledged monies;

2. Any reserved funds required of borrowers;

3. Any reserved funds required of the Oklahoma Water Resources Board; and

4. Any surety bond payments.

C. The Oklahoma Water Resources Board is hereby authorized to issue general obligation bonds, in an amount not to exceed a cumulative total of Three Hundred Million Dollars ($300,000,000.00), for the purpose of providing for the Water Infrastructure Credit Enhancement Reserve Fund for the water resource and sewage treatment financial assistance programs for municipalities, political subdivisions and other public entities of the state provided by the Board as authorized in Section 39 of Article X of the Oklahoma Constitution.

D. The Legislature shall provide sufficient appropriations from any monies of the state not otherwise obligated, committed or appropriated to pay the principal and interest of any general obligation bond issued pursuant to this section.

E. The Legislature shall establish a method by law to provide for the issuance of the general obligation bonds authorized pursuant to this section and to provide for the administration of the Water Infrastructure Credit Enhancement Reserve Fund.

Section 40. Tobacco Settlement Endowment Trust Fund

A. There is hereby created a trust fund to be known as the " Tobacco Settlement Endowment Trust Fund."The trust fund principal shall consist of the portion of monies which are received by the State of Oklahoma on or after July 1, 2001, pursuant to any settlement with or judgment against any tobacco company or companies as provided by subsection B of this section, and any other monies that may be appropriated or otherwise directed to the trust fund by the Legislature.

B.
1. Deposits into the trust fund from monies which are received by the State of Oklahoma pursuant to any settlement with or judgment against any tobacco company or companies shall be based on the following schedule:

Fiscal Year Minimum Percentage of Payments

Ending June 30, 2002 - 50%
Ending June 30, 2003 - 55%
Ending June 30, 2004 - 60%
Ending June 30, 2005 - 65%
Ending June 30, 2006 - 70%
Ending June 30, 2007 - 75%

2. Deposits into the trust fund in subsequent fiscal years shall never be less than seventy-five percent (75%) of the payments.

3. The monies received by the State of Oklahoma pursuant to any settlement with or judgment against any tobacco company or companies after June 30, 2001, not deposited into the trust fund as provided in this section, shall be deposited into a special fund established by the Legislature solely for the purpose of receiving the payments; provided, the Legislature may, by law, direct a certain portion of such monies to the Office of the Attorney General. The special fund shall be subject to legislative appropriations.

C. There is hereby created the Board of Investors of the Tobacco Settlement Endowment Trust Fund. The Board of Investors shall have the duty of investing monies in the trust fund, subject to restrictions and limitations provided by law for and in accordance with laws applicable to the investment of monies in state retirement funds.

The Board of Investors shall consist of five (5) members as follows:

1. The State Treasurer who shall be the chair;

2. An appointee of the Governor;

3. An appointee of the Speaker of the House of Representatives;

4. An appointee of the President Pro Tempore of the Senate; and

5. An appointee of the State Auditor and Inspector.
The initial appointees shall serve staggered terms of office as provided for by law. Thereafter, appointees shall serve four-year terms of office. No more than two appointees shall be appointed from any single congressional district. All appointed members shall have demonstrated expertise in public or private investment funds management.

D. There is hereby created the Board of Directors of the Tobacco Settlement Endowment Trust Fund. The Board of Directors shall consist of seven (7) members, one appointed by each of the following appointing authorities:

1. The Governor;

2. The President Pro Tempore of the Senate;

3. The Speaker of the House of Representatives;

4. The Attorney General;

5. The State Treasurer;

6. The State Auditor and Inspector; and

7. The State Superintendent of Public Instruction.
The initial appointed members shall serve staggered terms of office as provided for by law. Thereafter, the appointed members of the Board of Directors shall serve seven-year terms of office. At least one appointee shall be appointed from each congressional district, and not more than two appointees shall be appointed from any single congressional district. Not more than four appointees shall be members of the same political party. An appointee shall have been a member of the political party to which the appointee belongs for at least one (1) year prior to the date of appointment . Appointees shall have demonstrated expertise in public or private health care or programs related to or for the benefit of children or senior adults.
The Board of Directors shall meet at least one time each calendar quarter.

E. Earnings from the trust fund, including but not limited to interest, dividends, and realized capital gains from investments of the trust fund shall be expended as provided in subsection F of this section for the following purposes:

1. Clinical and basic research and treatment efforts in Oklahoma for the purpose of enhancing efforts to prevent and combat cancer and other tobacco-related diseases;

2. Cost-effective tobacco prevention and cessation programs;

3. Programs other than those specified in paragraph 1 of this subsection designed to maintain or improve the health of Oklahomans or to enhance the provision of health care services to Oklahomans, with particular emphasis on such programs for children;

4. Programs and services for the benefit of the children of Oklahoma, with particular emphasis on common and higher education, before- and after-school and pre-school programs, substance abuse prevention and treatment programs and other programs and services designed to improve the health and quality of life of children;

5. Programs designed to enhance the health and well-being of senior adults; and

6. Authorized administrative expenses of the Office of the State Treasurer and the Board of Directors.

F. Each fiscal year, the Board of Directors may expend the amount of earnings which actually accrued to the trust fund during the preceding fiscal year. Any amount not so expended shall remain in the trust fund. The Board shall direct specific expenditures to be made for the purposes specified in subsection E of this section.

G. The Legislature may enact laws to further implement the provisions of this section.

Section 41. Oklahoma Education Lottery Trust Fund

A. There is hereby created a trust fund to be known as the "Oklahoma Education Lottery Trust Fund."The trust fund shall consist of the funds transferred to it from the Oklahoma Education Lottery.

B. Monies in the Oklahoma Education Lottery Trust Fund shall only be expended for the following educational purposes and programs:

1. Kindergarten through twelfth grade public education, including but not limited to compensation and benefits for public school teachers and support employees;

2. Early childhood development programs;

3. Tuition grants, loans and scholarships to citizens of this state to enable such citizens to attend colleges and universities located within this state which are accredited by the Oklahoma State Regents for Higher Education or to attend institutions operated under the authority of the Oklahoma Department of Career and Technology Education;

4. Construction of educational facilities for elementary school districts, independent school districts, the Oklahoma State System of Higher Education, and career and technology education;

5. Capital outlay projects for elementary school districts, independent school districts, the Oklahoma State System of Higher Education, and career and technology education;

6. Technology for public elementary school district, independent school district, state higher education, and career and technology education facilities;

7. Endowed chairs for professors at institutions of higher education operated by the Oklahoma State System of Higher Education;

8. Programs and personnel of the Oklahoma School for the Deaf and the Oklahoma School for the Blind;

9. The School Consolidation and Assistance Fund; and

10. The Teachers' Retirement System Dedicated Revenue Revolving Fund.

C. The Legislature shall appropriate funds from the Oklahoma Education Lottery Trust Fund only for the purposes specified in subsection B of this section. Even when the funds from the trust fund are used for these purposes, the Legislature shall not use funds from the trust fund to supplant or replace other state funds supporting common education, higher education, or career and technology education.

D. In order to ensure that the funds from the trust fund are used to enhance and not supplant funding for education, the State Board of Equalization shall examine and investigate appropriations from the trust fund each year. At the meeting of the State Board of Equalization held within five (5) days after the monthly apportionment in February of each year, the State Board of Equalization shall issue a finding and report which shall state whether appropriations from the trust fund were used to enhance or supplant education funding. If the State Board of Equalization finds that education funding was supplanted by funds from the trust fund, the Board shall specify the amount by which education funding was supplanted. In this event, the Legislature shall not make any appropriations for the ensuing fiscal year until an appropriation in that amount is made to replenish the trust fund.

E. The provisions of this section shall not become effective if Enrolled House Bill No. 1278 of the 1st Session of the 49th Oklahoma Legislature is not approved by the people of this state.

Section 42. Economic Development Credit Enhancement Reserve Fund - General Obligation Bonds

The Oklahoma Development Finance Authority is hereby authorized to issue general obligation bonds, in an amount not to exceed One Hundred Million Dollars ($100,000,000.00), for the purpose of providing an economic development credit enhancement reserve fund for the Authority. This fund shall be used by the Authority solely to secure the payment of principal, interest and premium, if any, on the revenue bonds and other financial obligations issued by the Authority after other pledged monies and other reserve funds are used to the extent allowable by law. The Legislature shall provide sufficient appropriations to pay the principal and interest of any general obligation bonds issued pursuant to this resolution. Further, the Legislature shall establish a method by law to provide for issuance of the bonds or portions thereof when it is necessary and to provide for administration of the economic development credit enhancement reserve fund.

Section 43. State Construction, Remodeling or Other Capital Improvements - Amount of Indebtedness - Payment and Discharge of Debt - Issuance of Bonds

The State of Oklahoma may become indebted in an amount not to exceed Three Hundred Fifty Million Dollars ($350,000,000.00) pursuant to the provisions of Enrolled House Bill No. 2428 of the 2nd Session of the 43rd Oklahoma Legislature and any amendments thereto for the purpose of constructing new buildings, remodeling, modernizing and repairing any and all existing buildings and providing other capital improvements and for the purchase of land, equipment and furnishings necessary for such new construction, remodeling or other capital improvements, including any costs of issuance associated with the indebtedness, for the following departments of state government in the amounts and for the purposes indicated as follows:

1.Oklahoma State Regents for Higher Education for expenditure as follows:

a. University of Oklahoma - Norman Campus - $22,731,000.00

b. University of Oklahoma - Health Sciences Center - $22,400,000.00

c. Oklahoma State University - Stillwater Campus - $22,328,000.00

d. Oklahoma State University - Agriculture Experiment Station - $4,000,000.00

e. Oklahoma State University - Veterinary Medicine - $5,075,000.00

f. Oklahoma State University - Technical Branch - Okmulgee - $4,118,000.00

g. Oklahoma State University - Technical Branch - Oklahoma City - $3,868,000.00

h. Oklahoma State University - College of Osteopathic Medicine - $3,750,400.00

i. University of Central Oklahoma - $7,765,106.00

j. East Central University - $5,869,000.00

k. Northeastern State University - $8,813,400.00

l. Northwestern Oklahoma State University - $2,860,000.00

m. Southeastern Oklahoma State University - $5,586,900.00

n. Southwestern Oklahoma State University - Weatherford Campus - $6,297,500.00

o. Southwestern Oklahoma State University - Sayre Campus - $300,000.00

p. Cameron University - $10,200,000.00

q. Langston University - $2,842,500.00

r. Oklahoma Panhandle State University - $2,016,500.00

s. University of Science and Arts of Oklahoma - $3,104,376.00

t. University Center at Tulsa - $15,000,000.00

u. Carl Albert State College - $3,021,000.00

v. Connors State College - $2,055,100.00

w. Eastern Oklahoma State College - $2,007,600.00

x. Murray State College - $2,045,000.00

y. Northeastern Oklahoma Agricultural and Mechanical College - $2,410,400.00

z. Northern Oklahoma College - $1,206,500.00

aa. Oklahoma City Community College- -$6,152,100.00

bb. Redlands Community College - $2,003,900.00

cc. Rogers State College - $5,035,100.00

dd. Rose State College - $6,158,600.00

ee. Seminole Junior College - $2,125,924.00

ff. Tulsa Junior College - $22,333,800.00

gg. Western Oklahoma State College - $2,500,000.00

hh. Enid Higher Education Program - $619,123.00

ii. Enid Higher Education Program - this allocation is contingent upon a $2,200,000.00 match by the local community - $1,980,877.00

jj. Ardmore Higher Education Program - $619,123.00

kk. Muskogee Higher Education Program - $619,123.00

ll. Idabel Higher Education Program - $619,123.00
mm. Tulsa Medical Center debt retirement - $6,600,000.00

nn. Food Processing Research Center - Stillwater - $14,000,000.00

oo. Natural History Museum - Norman - $15,000,000.00

2. State Department of Vocational and Technical Education for expenditure as follows:

a. Instructional equipment for area schools, including inmate training facilities - $2,300,000.00

b. Mid-Del Vo-Tech - $200,000.00

c. Okmulgee County AVTS - $3,200,000.00

d. Southwest AVTS - $1,500,000.00

e. Wes Watkins AVTS - $1,000,000.00

f. Western Oklahoma AVTS - $2,000,000.00

3. Oklahoma Water Resources Board - $5,700,000.00

4. Oklahoma Tourism and Recreation Department for the following purposes: roads, park improvements, sewage treatment, facility rehab, equipment, trails, park visitor centers, tourism information centers, Will Rogers Museum and other museums, Oklahoma Jazz Hall of Fame and Quartz Mountain Arts and Conference Center - $18,000,000.00

5. Oklahoma Historical Society - $1,700,000.00

6. Department of Human Services - $5,300,000.00

7. Department of Corrections for the following purposes: drug offender work camps and meat processing facility at Jackie Brannon - $6,500,000.00

8. State Department of Health - $7,500,000.00

9. State Department of Agriculture for purposes of dry fire hydrants and rural fire equipment - $1,000,000.00

10. Department of Central Services - $4,300,000.00

11. Oklahoma Military Department - $800,000.00

12. Oklahoma School of Science and Mathematics. Said amount shall not be used for purposes of subsection D of Section 168.3 of Title 73 of the Oklahoma Statutes - $4,500,000.00

13. Office of State Finance for expenditure for telecommunications as recommended by the State Data Processing and Telecommunications Advisory Committee - $14,000,000.00

14. Oklahoma Department of Libraries for expenditure for matching grant program for handicapped access - $500,000.00

15. Oklahoma Department of Veterans Affairs for the following purposes: New facility at Norman, computer programming-mapper system, and improvements at the facilities at Ardmore, Sulphur, Talihina, Clinton, Claremore and Okmulgee - $16,432,500.00

16. Department of Mental Health and Substance Abuse Services - $6,400,000.00

If the full amount of funding for any project specified in this section is not necessary for provision of such project, any remaining available funds shall be allocated as provided for by law.

The payment and discharge of the principal of such debt, together with principal and interest on such indebtedness, shall be paid from one or more of the following sources of state income as follows:

1. Any remainder of revenue available from the taxes lawfully levied and collected by the State of Oklahoma on the sale of cigarettes not already committed to other obligations of the State of Oklahoma;

2. Allocations by the Legislature of the State of Oklahoma from any monies in the general revenue fund of the state not otherwise obligated, committed or appropriated; and

3. The proceeds of any tax which the Legislature may impose and collect for the purpose of paying the principal and interest on the indebtedness herein authorized to be created, and authority is hereby granted to the Legislature to so impose and collect such tax, if necessary.

The bonds evidencing the indebtedness herein authorized may be issued by the Oklahoma Building Bonds Commission, the members of which shall be appointed by the Governor, the Speaker of the House of Representatives and the President Pro Tempore of the State Senate as provided for by law and may be issued in one or more series, for a term or terms not to exceed thirty (30) years from their date, and may contain any and all provisions which the Oklahoma State Legislature may deem necessary or expedient to make such bonds marketable as general obligations of the State of Oklahoma with the full faith and credit of the state pledged thereto.

The provisions of this section shall not become effective if Enrolled House Bill No. 2074 of the 2nd Session of the 43rd Oklahoma Legislature is not approved by the people of this state.

ARTICLE XI: STATE AND SCHOOL LANDS

Section 1. Acceptance of Grants and Donations - Pledge of Faith of State

The State hereby accepts all grants of land and donations of money made by the United States under the provisions of the Enabling Act, and any other Acts of Congress, for the uses and purposes and upon the conditions, and under the limitations for which the same are granted or donated; and the faith of the State is hereby pledged to preserve such lands and moneys and all moneys derived from the sale of any of said lands as a sacred trust, and to keep the same for the uses and purposes for which they were granted or donated.

Section 2. Permanent School Fund - How Constituted - Use - Reimbursement for Losses

All proceeds of the sale of public lands that have heretofore been or may be hereafter given by the United States for the use and benefit of the common schools of this State, all such per centum as may be granted by the United States on the sales of public lands, the sum of five million dollars appropriated to the State for the use and benefit of the common schools in lieu of sections sixteen and thirty-six, and other lands of the Indian Territory, the proceeds of all property that shall fall to the State by escheat, the proceeds of all gifts or donations to the State for common schools not otherwise appropriated by the terms of the gifts, and such other appropriations, gifts, or donations as shall be made by the Legislature for the benefit of the common schools, shall constitute the permanent school fund, the income from which shall be used for the maintenance of the common schools in the State. The principal shall be deemed a trust fund held by the State, and shall forever remain inviolate. It may be increased, but shall never be diminished. The State shall reimburse said permanent school fund for all losses thereof which may in any manner occur, and no portion of said fund shall be diverted for any other use or purpose.

Section 3. Interest and Income - Use and Apportionment

The interest and income of the permanent school fund, the net income from the leasing of public lands which have been or may be granted by the United States to the State for the use and benefit of the common schools, together with any revenues derived from taxes authorized to be levied for such purposes, and any other sums which may be added thereto by law, shall be used and applied each year for the benefit of the common schools of the State, and shall be, for this purpose, apportioned among and between all the several common school districts of the State in proportion to the school population of the several districts, and no part of the fund shall ever be diverted from this purpose, or used for any other purpose than the support and maintenance of common schools for the equal benefit of all the people of the State.

Section 4. Sale of Lands for Charitable, Penal, Educational and Public Purposes

All public lands set apart to the State by Congress for charitable, penal, educational, and public building purposes, and all lands taken in lieu thereof, may be sold by the State, under such rules and regulations as the Legislature may prescribe, in conformity with the regulations of the Enabling Act.

Section 5. University and College Lands - Control of Institutions - Diversion of Funds

Section thirteen in every portion of the State, which has been granted to the State, shall be preserved for the use and benefit of the University of Oklahoma and the University Preparatory School, one-third; of the normal schools now established, or hereafter to be established, one-third; and of the Agricultural and Mechanical College and Colored Agricultural and Normal University, one-third. The said lands or the proceeds thereof as above apportioned to be divided between the institutions as the Legislature may prescribe: Provided, That the said lands so reserved, or the proceeds of the sale thereof, or of any indemnity lands granted in lieu of section thirteen shall be safely kept or invested and preserved by the State as a trust, which shall never be diminished, but may be added to, and the income thereof, interest, rentals, or otherwise, only shall be used exclusively for the benefit of said educational institutions. Such educational institutions shall remain under the exclusive control of the State and no part of the proceeds arising from the sale or disposal of any lands granted for educational purposes, or the income or rentals thereof, shall be used for the support of any religious or sectarian school, college, or university, and no portion of the funds arising from the sale of sections thirteen or any indemnity lands selected in lieu thereof, either principal or interest, shall ever be diverted, either temporarily or permanently, from the purpose for which said lands were granted to the State.

Section 6. Investment of Permanent Common School and Other Educational Funds

A. The permanent common school and other educational funds may be invested in first mortgages upon good and improved farm lands within the state (and in no case shall more than fifty per centum (50%) of the reasonable valuation of the lands without improvements be loaned on any tract) and any other investments as authorized by law.

B. The Commissioners of the Land Office shall be responsible for the investment of the permanent common school and other educational funds, and public building funds solely in the best interests of the beneficiaries and:

1. For the exclusive purpose of providing maximum benefits to current and future beneficiaries, and defraying reasonable expenses of administering the trust funds;

2. With the care, skill, prudence, and diligence under the circumstances then prevailing that a prudent person acting in a like enterprise of a like character and like aim would use;

3. By diversifying the investments of the trust funds so as to minimize the risk of large losses; and

4. In accordance with the law, documents and instruments governing the administration and investment of the permanent common school and other educational funds and public building funds.

C. The Legislature shall provide by law conditions upon which the permanent common school fund, other educational funds and public building funds may be loaned or invested and shall do all things necessary for the safety of the funds and permanency of the investment.

Section 7. Grants of Commercial and Agricultural Leases in Trust Property

The Commissioners of the Land Office are authorized to grant commercial leases and agricultural leases in trust property. Commercial leases shall not exceed fifty-five (55) years. The granting of any commercial lease in excess of three (3) years shall be by public bidding at not less than fair market value. All commercial leases shall provide for fair market value throughout the term of the lease.

Agricultural leases of trust property shall be limited to a maximum of five (5) years and shall be by public bidding at not less than fair market value.

The granting of any interest in trust property at less than fair market value or not in compliance with this section is void. Any permanent improvement made on commercial trust property from and after the passage of this amendment shall revert to the trust at the end of the lease.

The Legislature shall enact the laws necessary to implement the provisions of this section and to foster the fair and equitable administration of trust property.

ARTICLE XII: HOMESTEAD AND EXEMPTIONS

Section 1. Extent and Value of Homestead - Rights of Indians

A. The homestead of any person in this State, not within any city or town, shall consist of not more than one hundred and sixty acres of land, which may be in one or more parcels, to be selected by the owner.

B. Effective November 1, 1997, the homestead of any person in this state, not within any city or town, annexed by a city or town on or after November 1, 1997, owned and occupied and used for both residential and commercial agricultural purposes shall consist of not more than one hundred sixty acres of land, which may be in one or more parcels, to be selected by the owner.

C. The homestead of any person within any city or town, owned and occupied as a residence only, or used for both residential and business purposes, shall consist of not exceeding one acre of land, to be selected by the owner.

For purposes of this subsection, at least seventy-five percent (75%) of the total square foot area of the improvements for which a homestead exemption is claimed must be used as the principal residence in order to qualify for the exemption. If more than twenty-five percent (25%) of the total square foot area of the improvements for which a homestead exemption is claimed is used for business purposes, the homestead exemption amount shall not exceed Five Thousand Dollars ($5,000).
D. Nothing in the laws of the United States, or any treaties with the Indian Tribes in the State, shall deprive any Indian or other allottee of the benefit of the homestead and exemption laws of the state.

E. Any temporary renting of the homestead shall not change the character of the same when no other homestead has been acquired.

Section 2. Exemption form Forced Sale - Consent of Spouse to Sale – Mortgages

The homestead of the family shall be, and is hereby protected from forced sale for the payment of debts, except for the purchase money therefore or a part of such purchase money, the taxes due thereon, or for work and material used in constructing improvements thereon; nor shall the owner, if married, sell the homestead without the consent of his or her spouse, given in such manner as may be prescribed by law; Provided, Nothing in this article shall prohibit any person from mortgaging his homestead, the spouse, if any, joining therein; nor prevent the sale thereof on foreclosure to satisfy any such mortgage.

Section 3. Statutes Nullified - Exemption as to Purchase Price Restricted - Encumbering Personal Exemptions - Change or Amendment of Article

After the adoption of this constitution, paragraph three of section four, and section five, of Chapter thirty-four, Statutes of Oklahoma, of 1893, shall be inoperative: Provided, That no property shall be exempt for any part of the purchase price while the same or any part thereof remains in the possession of the original vendee, or in possession of any purchaser from such vendee, with notice: And Provided Further, Nothing in this Constitution shall prevent or prohibit any person from mortgaging or encumbering his personal exemptions.

The Legislature may change or amend the terms of this article.

ARTICLE XII-A: HOMESTEAD EXEMPTION
FROM TAXATION

Section 1. Exemption from Ad Valorem Taxation Authorized

All homesteads as is or may be defined under the Laws of the State of Oklahoma for tax exemption purposes, may hereafter be exempted from all forms of ad valorem taxation by the Legislature; provided, that all assessments, levies, encumbrances and other contract obligations incurred or made prior to the taking effect of such act of the Legislature shall in no way be affected or impaired by the exercise of Legislative power as authorized by this amendment.

Section 2. Duration of Exemption - Increase of Homestead

Any act of the Legislature, which is authorized by this amendment and which provides that homesteads shall be exempted from ad valorem taxation, shall be in full force and effect for a period of not less than twenty years from the date of the taking effect of such act and for such time thereafter as the same shall remain without repeal or amendment by the Legislature, provided, that the homestead as defined in any such act of exemption may be increased at any time but not diminished.

ARTICLE XIII: EDUCATION

Section 1. Establishment and Maintenance of Public Schools
The Legislature shall establish and maintain a system of free public schools wherein all the children of the State may be educated.

Section 1a. Appropriation and Allocation of Funds for Support of Common Schools

The Legislature shall, by appropriate legislation, raise and appropriate funds for the annual support of the common schools of the State to the extent of forty-two ($42.00) dollars per capita based on total state-wide enrollment for the preceding school year. Such moneys shall be allocated to the various school districts in the manner and by a distributing agency to be designated by the Legislature; provided that nothing herein shall be construed as limiting any particular school district to the per capita amount specified herein, but the amount of state funds to which any school district may be entitled shall be determined by the distributing agency upon terms and conditions specified by the Legislature, and provided further that such funds shall be in addition to apportionments from the permanent school fund created by Article XI, Section 2, hereof.

Section 2. Institutions for Deaf, Deaf and Mute, or Blind
The Legislature shall provide for the establishment and support of institutions for the care and education of persons within the state who are deaf, deaf and mute or blind.

Section 3. Repealed

Section 4. Compulsory School Attendance

The Legislature shall provide for the compulsory attendance at some public or other school, unless other means of education are provided, of all the children in the State who are sound in mind and body, between the ages of eight and sixteen years, for at least three months in each year.

Section 5. Board of Education

The supervision of instruction in the public schools shall be vested in a Board of Education, whose powers and duties shall be prescribed by law. The Superintendent of Public Instruction shall be President of the Board. Until otherwise provided by law, the Governor, Secretary of State, and Attorney General shall be ex-officio members, and with the Superintendent, compose said Board of Education.

Section 6. Textbook System for Common Schools - Official Multiple Textbook Lists

The Legislature shall provide for a system of textbooks for the common schools of the State, and the State through appropriate legislation shall furnish such textbooks free of cost for use by all pupils therein. The Legislature shall authorize the Governor to appoint a committee composed of active educators of the State, whose duty it shall be to prepare official multiple textbook lists from which textbooks for use in such schools shall be selected by committees composed of active educators in the local school districts in a manner to be designated by the Legislature.

Section 7. Instruction in Agriculture, Horticulture, Stock Feeding and Domestic Science

The Legislature shall provide for the teaching of the elements of agriculture, horticulture, stock feeding, and domestic science in the common schools of the State.

Section 8. Board of Regents of University of Oklahoma

The government of the University of Oklahoma shall be vested in a Board of Regents consisting of seven members to be appointed by the Governor by and with the advice and consent of the Senate. The term of said members shall be for seven years, except and provided that the appointed members of the Board of Regents in office at the time of the adoption of this amendment as now provided by law shall continue in office during the term for which they were appointed, and thereafter as provided herein.

Appointments for filling vacancies occurring on said Board shall be made by the Governor with advice and consent of the Senate and said appointments to fill vacancies shall be for the residue of the term only.

Members of the Board of Regents of the University of Oklahoma shall be subject to removal from office only as provided by law for the removal of elective officers not liable to impeachment.

ARTICLE XIIIA: OKLAHOMA STATE SYSTEM
OF HIGHER EDUCATION

Section 1. Oklahoma State System of Higher Education

All institutions of higher education supported wholly or in part by direct legislative appropriations shall be integral parts of a unified system to be known as "The Oklahoma State System of Higher Education."

Section 2. Oklahoma State Regents for Higher Education - Establishment - Membership - Appointment - Terms - Vacancy - Powers as Coordinating Board of Control

There is hereby established the Oklahoma State Regents for Higher Education, consisting of nine (9) members, whose qualifications may be prescribed by law. The Board shall consist of nine (9) members appointed by the Governor, confirmed by the Senate, and who shall be removable only for cause, as provided by law for the removal of officers not subject to impeachment. Upon the taking effect of this Article, the Governor shall appoint the said Regents for terms of office as follows: one for a term of one year, one for a term of two years, one for a term of three years, one for a term of four years, one for a term of five years, one for a term of six years, one for a term of seven years, one for a term of eight years, and one for a term of nine years. Any appointment to fill a vacancy shall be for the balance of the term only. Except as above designated, the term of office of said Regents shall be nine years or until their successors are appointed and qualified. The Regents shall constitute a co-coordinating board of control for all State institutions described in Section 1 hereof, with the following specific powers:

(1) it shall prescribe standards of higher education applicable to each institution;

(2) it shall determine the functions and courses of study in each of the institutions to conform to the standards prescribed;

(3) it shall grant degrees and other forms of academic recognition for completion of the prescribed courses in all of such institutions;

(4) it shall recommend to the State Legislature the budget allocations to each institution, and;

(5) it shall have the power to recommend to the Legislature proposed fees for all of such institutions, and any such fees shall be effective only within the limits prescribed by the Legislature.

Section 3. Appropriations – Allocation

The appropriations made by the Legislature for all such institutions shall be made in consolidated form without reference to any particular institution and the Board of Regents herein created shall allocate to each institution according to its needs and functions.

Section 4. Co-Ordination of Private, Denominational and Other Institutions of Higher Learning

Private, denominational, and other institutions of higher learning may become coordinated with the State System of Higher Education under regulations set forth by the Oklahoma State Regents for Higher Education.

ARTICLE XIIIB: BOARD OF REGENTS OF OKLAHOMA COLLEGES

Section 1. Board of Regents of Oklahoma Colleges - Creation, Members, Terms, Etc.

There is hereby created a Board to be known as the Board of Regents of Oklahoma Colleges, and shall consist of nine (9) members to be appointed by the Governor, by and with the consent of the Senate. The Governor shall appoint one (1) member to serve for one (1) year, one (1) member to serve for two (2) years, one (1) member to serve for three (3) years, one (1) member to serve for four (4) years, one (1) member to serve for five (5) years, one (1) member to serve for six (6) years, one (1) member to serve for seven (7) years, one (1) member to serve for eight (8) years, and one (1) member to serve for nine (9) years. Provided that one (1) member shall come from each Congressional District and the ninth (9th) member shall be the State Superintendent of Public Instruction. Their successors shall be appointed for a term of nine (9) years, and such appointments shall be made within ninety (90) days after the term expires. Vacancies shall be filled by the Governor within ninety (90) days after the vacancy occurs. Each member of the Board, except the State Superintendent shall receive as compensation the sum of Ten ($10.00) Dollars per day, not to exceed sixty (60) days in any fiscal year while he is actually engaged in the performance of duties, and he shall also be allowed the necessary travel expenses as approved by the Board and paid in the manner provided by law. The Board shall elect a president and vice-president who shall perform such duties as the Board directs. No executive board meetings shall be held at any time unless such executive session is ordered by a unanimous vote of the Board. The personnel of the Board of Regents of the Oklahoma Colleges shall not include more than two (2) members from any one profession, vocation, or occupation. No member of the Board shall be eligible to be an officer, supervisor, president, instructor, or employee of any of the colleges set forth herein within two (2) years from the date of expiration of his term. Any member who fails to attend a board meeting more than two (2) consecutive meetings without the consent of a majority of the Board, his office shall be declared vacant by the Governor and his successor shall be appointed as provided herein.

Section 2. Powers and Duties of Board - Officers, Supervisors, Etc.

The said Board of Regents of Oklahoma Colleges shall hereafter have the supervision, management and control of the following State Colleges: Central State College at Edmond; East Central State College at Ada; Southwestern Institute of Technology at Weatherford; Southeastern State College at Durant; Northwestern State College at Alva, and the Northeastern State College at Tahlequah, and the power to make rules and regulations governing each of said institutions shall hereafter be exercised by and is hereby vested in the Board of Regents of Oklahoma Colleges created by this Act, and said Board shall appoint or hire all necessary officers, supervisors, instructors, and employees for such institutions.

Section 3. Successor to Existing Governing Boards - Records, Papers, Etc.

The Board of Regents of Oklahoma Colleges shall succeed the present governing board in the management and control of any of the institutions named in the preceding section, and such governing board shall not hereafter have the management or control of any of said institutions. All records, books, papers and information pertaining to the institutions herein designated shall be transferred to the Board of Regents of Oklahoma Colleges.

Section 4. Salaries and Expenses - Allocation of Funds for Payment

The Oklahoma State Regents for Higher Education are hereby authorized to allocate from the funds allocated for the support of its educational institutions named in this Act, funds sufficient for the payment of the per diem and expenses of the members of the Board of Regents of Oklahoma Colleges, the salaries and expenses of the clerical help of said Board; office expense, and other expenses necessary for the proper performance of the duties of said Board.

ARTICLE XIV: BANKS AND BANKING

Section 1. Banking Department

General laws shall be enacted by the legislature providing for the creation of a Banking Department, to be under the control of a Bank Commissioner, who shall be appointed by the Governor for a term of four years, by and with the consent of the Senate, with sufficient power and authority to regulate and control all State Banks, Loan, Trust and Guaranty Companies, under laws which shall provide for the protection of depositors and individual stockholders.

Section 2. Classification of Loans and Lenders - Licenses - Maximum Rates of Interest

The Legislature shall have authority to classify loans and lenders, license and regulate lenders, define interest and fix maximum rates of interest; provided, however, in the absence of legislation fixing maximum rates of interest, all contracts for a greater rate of interest than ten percent(10%) per annum shall be deemed usurious; provided, further, that in contracts where no rate of interest is agreed upon, the rate shall not exceed six percent (6%) per annum.

Section 3. Excessive Rate - Forfeiture of Interest - Recovery of Double Interest

The taking, receiving, reserving, or charging a rate of interest greater than is allowed by the preceding section, when knowingly done, shall be deemed a forfeiture of the entire interest which the note, bill, or other evidence of debt carries with it, or which has been agreed to be paid thereon. In case a greater rate of interest has been paid, the person by whom it has been paid, or his legal representatives, may recover from the person, firm, or corporation taking or receiving the same, in an action in the nature of an action of debt, twice the amount of the interest so paid: Provided, such action shall be brought within two years after the maturity of such usurious contract: Provided, However, That this section may be subject to such changes as the Legislature may prescribe.

ARTICLE XV: OATH OF OFFICE

Section 1. Officers Required to Take Oath or Affirmation - Form
All public officers, before entering upon the duties of their
offices, shall take and subscribe to the following oath or
affirmation:

"I, ..., do solemnly swear (or affirm) that I will support, obey,
and defend the Constitution of the United States, and the
Constitution of the State of Oklahoma, and that I will not,
knowingly, receive, directly or indirectly, any money or other
valuable thing, for the performance or nonperformance of any
act or duty pertaining to my office, other than the compensation
allowed by law; I further swear (or affirm) that I will faithfully
discharge my duties as .... to the best of my ability."

The Legislature may prescribe further oaths or affirmations.

Section 2. Administration and Filing of Oath - Refusal to Take -
False Swearing

The foregoing oath shall be administered by some person
authorized to administer oaths, and in the case of State officers
and judges of the Supreme Court, shall be filed in the office of
the Secretary of State, and in case of other judicial and county
officers, in the office of the clerk of the county in which the same
is taken; any person refusing to take said oath, or affirmation,
shall forfeit his office, and any person who shall have been
convicted of having sworn or affirmed falsely, or having violated
said oath, or affirmation, shall be guilty of perjury, and shall be
disqualified from holding any office of trust or profit within the
State. The oath to members of the Senate and House of
Representatives shall be administered in the hall of the house to
which the members shall have been elected, by one of the
judges of the Supreme Court, or in case no such judge is
present, then by any person authorized to administer oaths.

ARTICLE XVI: PUBLIC ROADS, HIGHWAYS, AND INTERNAL IMPROVEMENTS

Section 1. Power of Legislature Respecting Highways

The Legislature is directed to establish a Department of Highways, and shall have the power to create improvement districts and provide for building and maintaining public roads, and may provide for the utilization of convict and punitive labor thereon.

Section 2. Acceptance of Lands Granted or Reserved for Highway

The State of Oklahoma hereby accepts all reservations and lands for public highways made under any grant, agreement, treaty, or act of Congress: Provided, This section shall not be construed to prejudice the vested rights of any tribe, allottee, or other person to any such land.

Section 3. System of Levees, Drains, and Ditches and Irrigation

The Legislature shall have power and shall provide for a system of levees, drains, and ditches and of irrigation in this State when deemed expedient, and provide for a system of taxation on the lands affected or benefited by such levees, drains, and ditches and irrigation, or on crops produced on such land, to discharge such bonded indebtedness or expenses necessarily incurred in the establishment of such improvements; and to provide for compulsory issuance of bonds by the owners or lessees of the lands benefited or affected by such levees, drains, and ditches or irrigation.

ARTICLE XVII: COUNTIES

Section 1. Counties to Be Bodies Politic and Corporate
Each county in this State, now or hereafter organized, shall be a body politic and corporate.

Section 2. County and Township Offices

There are hereby created, subject to change by the Legislature, in and for each organized county of this State, the offices of Judge of the County Court, County Attorney, Clerk of the District Court, County Clerk, Sheriff, County Treasurer, Register of Deeds, County Surveyor, Superintendent of Public Instruction, three County Commissioners, and such municipal township officers as are now provided for under the laws of the Territory of Oklahoma, except as in this Constitution otherwise provided.

Section 3. Provision for Persons in Need

The several counties of the State shall provide, as may be prescribed by law, for those inhabitants who, by reason of age, infirmity, or misfortune, may have claims upon the sympathy and aid of the county.

Section 4. Legislature to Provide for Creation or Alteration - Submission to Vote - Area, Population and Taxable Wealth
The Legislature shall provide by general laws for the creation of new counties or altering or changing lines and the equitable division of assets and of liabilities, and the original location of county seats in such new counties: Provided, That every such question shall be submitted to the vote of the qualified electors residing in the territory to be formed into such new county or transferred to another county, and shall be approved by sixty per centum of the votes cast in said election: Provided, That no new county shall be formed of less than four hundred square miles taxable area, nor with a population less than fifteen thousand people, nor with taxable wealth less than two and one-half million dollars, as shown by the current tax rolls. Nor shall any

territory be taken from an existing county for any purpose bringing the newly created line of such existing county nearer than ten miles to the county seat thereof. Nor shall the taxable area, population, or taxable wealth of said existing county be reduced below that required for a new county. Nor shall any territory, in any case, be transferred from one county to an existing county, if, by such transfer of territory, the county from which the territory be taken will then be smaller in area than the county to which the addition is made: Provided, That when territory is to be transferred from an existing county to either a new or an existing county, there must be sixty per centum of the vote cast in such particular territory in favor of the transfer, and, in case the transfer be to an existing county, the acceptance of such territory must first be approved by a majority vote of the electors of said county, at an election to be called and held therefore, as may be provided by law. The limitation as to area, valuation and population shall not be increased by the Legislature.

Section 5. Disorganization of County

When, at any time hereafter, the aggregate value of all taxable property in any one county be a sum total less than two and one-half million dollars, upon petition of one-fourth or more of the qualified electors of such county, as shown by the last general election, signed, verified, and filed with the county commissioners thereof, not less than sixty days before the date of any general election, such county commissioners shall submit, upon the ballot at such next ensuing general election, to the qualified electors of the county, the question: "Shall the county be an unorganized county?" "Yes" or "No." If a majority of the votes cast on this question at such election shall be in the affirmative, such county shall thereafter be unorganized and be attached to and be a part of the adjoining county having the lowest valuation of taxable property, and shall so remain as a district in such county until such time as the qualified electors of such unorganized county shall, by similar petition and vote, declare in favor of separate organized county existence:

Provided, however, That at all times during such unorganized existence, such county shall have four terms of county court at the county seat therein each year, and the judge of the county court shall appoint a clerk of the county court of said district, from among the qualified electors thereof, who shall keep and maintain his office at such county seat: Provided, further, That while so unorganized, such county shall, in all respects, be part and parcel of the county with which it is united.

Section 6. Procedure for Removal of County Seat

The towns herein named as county seats shall be and remain the county seats of their respective counties until changed by vote of the qualified electors of such county, in the following manner:

(a) Upon a petition or petitions in writing, signed by twenty-five per centum of the qualified electors of the county, such per centum to be determined by the total vote cast in such county for the head of the State ticket in the next preceding general election, said petition or petitions being verified by an affidavit showing that the petitioners are qualified electors of said county, and such petition or petitions having been filed with the Governor at any time after four months after the admission of the State into the Union, the Governor shall within thirty days issue his proclamation calling an election to be held in such county not less than sixty nor more than seventy days from the date of his proclamation. Such election shall be held under the provisions of the election laws of the State, and upon such public notice of such election as the Governor in his proclamation may direct; and the Governor shall cause to be placed upon the tickets to be voted at such election, only the names of such towns as may, more than twenty days prior to such election, file with the Governor verified petitions therefore, as above mentioned, signed by not less than three hundred qualified electors of said county. (The word "town," as herein used, shall be construed to mean town, city, or place.)

(b) Upon the holding of any such election the board of canvassers shall certify and return said vote to the Governor, who shall thereupon at once declare the result and cause the will of the electors to be carried into effect: Provided, That in all elections for the removal of any of the county seats named in this Constitution the following rules shall govern, until the county seat is once located by vote of the people, but not later than the first day of April, nineteen hundred and nine: Provided further, in case the necessary and proper petition for the holding of an election for the removal of a county seat shall be filed with the Governor, for over six months prior to the first day of April, nineteen hundred and nine (1909), in accordance with the foregoing provisions, and if such election or elections are delayed or postponed on account of any injunction or legal proceedings then the time limit provided in the subdivision of this section, shall be extended the length of time that such election or elections are delayed or postponed by such injunction or legal proceedings. If a majority of all the votes cast in the county at such county seat election shall be in favor of any town, such town shall thereafter be the county seat: Provided, however, that where the county seat named in this Constitution is within six miles of the geographical center of the county (said geographical center to be determined by certificate from the Secretary of State, and said distance to be determined by measurement from said geographical center to the nearest corporate limits of such county seat as they existed on the twenty-first day of January, Nineteen Hundred and Seven), it shall require sixty per centum of the total vote cast at such election by the competing town to effect the removal of such county seat, unless such competing town be more than one mile nearer the geographical center of said county, in which event a majority vote shall suffice; but, if more than two towns are voted for and no town receive the requisite proportion of all the votes cast, then all names of towns voted for on said ballot, except the two receiving the greatest number of votes, shall be dropped; and the Governor shall, in like time and manner, cause to be called and held a second election, at which only the two towns which received the greatest number of votes cast at the first election shall be voted for; and the town receiving the requisite proportion of the votes cast at the second election shall be the county seat: Provided, that, after the first day of April, Nineteen Hundred and Nine, all county seats shall be subject to removal under the above named provisions; but, the town to which removal is sought must receive two-thirds of all votes cast in such county at the election held therefore, and such elections shall not occur at intervals of less than ten years: Provided further, that until after the first day of April, Nineteen Hundred and Nine, no public money shall be expended for court house or jail construction unless a vote of the people of such county shall have been taken on the relocation of the county seat.

Section 7. Bribery

Any person or corporation offering money or other thing of value, either directly or indirectly, for the purpose of influencing any voter for or against any competing town in such election, shall be deemed guilty of bribery.

Section 8. Description of Counties - Designation of County Seats

The State of Oklahoma is hereby divided into Counties named and described as follows (all descriptions are referred to the Indian Meridian and base line established by the United States Geological Survey, 1895-1899; unless otherwise specifically mentioned):

Adair County: Beginning on the township line between townships nineteen and twenty North, at its intersection with the range line between ranges twenty-three and twenty-four East; thence east along said township line to its intersection with the Arkansas State line; thence southward along said Arkansas State line to its intersection with the township line between townships thirteen and fourteen North; thence west along said township line to its intersection with the range line between ranges twenty-three and twenty-four East; thence north along said range line to the point of beginning. Westville is hereby designated the County Seat of Adair County.

Alfalfa County: Beginning on the Kansas and Oklahoma State line at its intersection with the range line between ranges twelve and thirteen West; thence eastward along said State line to its intersection with the range line between ranges eight and nine West; thence south along said range line to its intersection with the east and west center section line of township twenty-three North; thence west along said center section line to its intersection with the range line between ranges twelve and thirteen West; thence north along said range line to the point of beginning. Cherokee is hereby designated the County Seat of Alfalfa County.

Atoka County: Beginning at the northwest corner of township two North, range twelve East; thence east along the township line between townships two and three North, to its intersection with the range line between ranges thirteen and fourteen East; thence south along said range line to its intersection with the township line between townships one and two North; thence east along said township line to its intersection with the range line between ranges fifteen and sixteen East; thence south along said range line to its intersection with the base line; thence west along said base line to its intersection with the range line between ranges fourteen and fifteen East; thence south along said range line to its intersection with the township line between townships four and five South; thence west along said township line to its intersection with the range line between ranges eight and nine East; thence north along said range line to its intersection with the township line between townships one and two South; thence east along said township line to its intersection with the north and south center section line across range eleven East; thence north along said center section line to its intersection with the base line; thence east along said base line to its intersection with the range line between ranges eleven and twelve East; thence north to the point of beginning. Atoka is hereby designated the County Seat of Atoka County.

Beaver County: Beginning at the point where the one hundredth meridian intersects the south line of the State of Kansas; thence westward along the south line of the State of Kansas to its intersection with the range line between ranges nineteen and twenty East of Cimarron meridian; thence south along said range line to its intersection with the north boundary line of the State of Texas; thence eastward along the boundary line between Texas and Oklahoma to its intersection with the one hundredth meridian; thence north along said one hundredth meridian to the point of beginning. Beaver is hereby designated the County Seat of Beaver County.

Beckham County: Beginning on the State line between Texas and Oklahoma at its intersection with the east and west center section line across township eleven North; thence east along said section line to its intersection with the range line between ranges twenty-two and twenty-three West; thence north along the said range line to its intersection with the east and west center section line across township twelve North; thence east along said center section line to its intersection with the range line between ranges twenty and twenty-one West; thence south along said range line to its intersection with the township line between townships seven and eight North; thence west along said township line to its intersection with the center line of the North Fork of Red River; thence up along the center line of said river to its most westerly intersection with the township line between townships seven and eight North; thence west along said township line to its intersection with the range line between ranges twenty-three and twenty-four West; thence south along said range line to its intersection with the township line between townships six and seven North; thence west along said township line to its intersection with the State line between Texas and Oklahoma; thence north along said State line to the point of beginning. Sayre is hereby designated the County Seat of Beckham County.

Blaine County: Said County shall be and remain as it now exists under the Territory of Oklahoma, until hereafter changed under the provisions of this Constitution. Watonga is hereby designated the County Seat of Blaine County.

Bryan County: Beginning on the township line between townships four and five South, at its intersection with the boundary line between the Chickasaw and the Choctaw nations; thence east along said township line to its intersection with the center line of Clear Boggy Creek; thence down along the center line of said Clear Boggy Creek to its intersection with the north and south center section line across range thirteen East; thence south along said center section line to its intersection with the center-line of Whitegrass Creek; thence down along the center line of said Whitegrass Creek to its intersection with the State line between Texas and Oklahoma; thence westward along said State line to the center line of the mouth of the Washita River; thence up along the center line of the said Washita River to its intersection with the east and west center section line of township five South; thence east along said center section line to its intersection with the boundary line between the Chickasaw and the Choctaw nations; thence north along said boundary line to the point of beginning. Durant is hereby designated the County Seat of Bryan County.

Caddo County: Beginning on the range line between ranges thirteen and fourteen West, at its intersection with the township line between townships twelve and thirteen North; thence east along said township line to its intersection with the range line between ranges ten and eleven West; thence south along said range line to its intersection with the township line between townships ten and eleven North; thence east along said township line to its intersection with the center line of the Canadian River; thence down along the center line of said Canadian River to its intersection with the ninety-eighth meridian; thence south along said ninety-eighth meridian to its intersection with the east and west center section line across township eight North; thence west along said center section line to its intersection with the range line between ranges eight and nine West; thence south along said range line to its intersection with the township line between townships four and five North; thence west along said township line to its intersection with the range line between ranges thirteen and fourteen West; thence north along said range line to the point of beginning. Anadarko is hereby designated the County Seat of Caddo County.

Canadian County: Said County shall be and remain as it now exists under the Territory of Oklahoma until hereafter changed under the provisions of this Constitution. El Reno is hereby designated the County Seat of Canadian County.

Carter County: Beginning on the base line at its intersection with the range line between ranges three and four West; thence east along said base line to its intersection with the range line between ranges one and two West; thence south along said range line to its intersection with the east and west center section line of township two South; thence east along said center section line to its intersection with the center line of the Washita River; thence southwardly along the center line of said Washita River to its intersection with the township line between townships two and three South; thence east along the said township line to its intersection with the range line between ranges three and four East; thence south along said range line to the northeast corner of section thirty-six, township four South, range three East; thence west to the northwest corner of section thirty-five in said township and range; thence south along the section line to its intersection with the township line between townships five and six South; thence west along said township line to its intersection with the range line between ranges three and four West; thence north along said range line to the point of beginning. Ardmore is hereby designated the County Seat of Carter County.

Cherokee County: Beginning at the northwest corner of township nineteen North, range twenty-one East; thence east along the township line to its intersection with the range line between ranges twenty-three and twenty-four East; thence south along said range line to its intersection with the township line between townships thirteen and fourteen North; thence west along said township line to its intersection with the range line between ranges twenty and twenty-one East; thence north along said range line to its intersection with the township line between townships fifteen and sixteen North; thence west along said township line to its intersection with the center line of the Grand River; thence up along the center line of said Grand River to its intersection with the township line between townships eighteen and nineteen North; thence east along said township line to its intersection with the range line between ranges twenty and twenty-one East; thence north along the said range line to the point of beginning. Tahlequah is hereby designated the County Seat of Cherokee County.

Choctaw County: Beginning on the center line of Clear Boggy Creek at its intersection with the township line between townships four and five South; thence east along said township line to its intersection with the range line between ranges twenty and twenty-one East; thence south along said range line to its intersection with the State line between Texas and Oklahoma; thence westwardly along said state line to the center line of the mouth of Whitegrass Creek; thence up along the center line of said Whitegrass Creek, to its intersection with the north and south center section line across range thirteen East; thence north along said center section line to its intersection with the center line of Clear Boggy Creek; thence up along the center line of said Clear Boggy Creek to the point of beginning. Hugo is hereby designated the County Seat of Choctaw County.

Cimarron County: Beginning on the State line between Kansas and Oklahoma at its intersection with the range line between ranges nine and ten East of the Cimarron Meridian; thence westward along the State line of Kansas and of Colorado to its intersection with the Cimarron Meridian; thence south along the Cimarron Meridian to its intersection with the north boundary line of the State of Texas; thence eastward along the Texas State line to its intersection with the range line between ranges nine and ten East of the Cimarron Meridian; thence north along said range line to the point of beginning. Kenton is hereby designated the County Seat of Cimarron County.

Cleveland County: Said County shall be and remain as it now exists under the Territory of Oklahoma, until hereafter changed under the provisions of this Constitution. Norman is hereby designated the County Seat of Cleveland County.

Coal County: Beginning at the northwest corner of township three North, range nine East; thence east along the township line between townships three and four North, to its intersection with the range line between ranges eleven and twelve East; thence south along said range line to its intersection with the base line; thence west along said base line to its intersection with the north and south center section line across range eleven East; thence south along said center section line to its intersection with the township line between townships one and two South; thence west along said township line to its intersection with the range line between ranges seven and eight East; thence north along said range line to its intersection with the township line between townships two and three North; thence east along said township line to its intersection with the range line between ranges eight and nine East; thence north along said range line to the point of beginning. Lehigh is hereby designated the County Seat of Coal County.

Comanche County: Beginning on the township line between townships four and five North, at its intersection with the range line between ranges fifteen and sixteen West; thence east along said township line to its intersection with the range line between ranges eight and nine West; thence south along said range line to its intersection with the township line between townships two and three North; thence west along said township line to its intersection with the north and south center section line across range nine West; thence south along said center section line to its intersection with the State line between Texas and Oklahoma; thence west along said State line to its intersection with the range line between ranges thirteen and fourteen West; thence north along said range line to its intersection with the north line of township three South; thence west along said township line to the north and south center section line across range fourteen West; thence north along said center section line to the base line; thence west along the base line to the range line between ranges fifteen and sixteen West; thence north along said range line to the point of beginning. Lawton is hereby designated the County Seat of Comanche County.

Craig County: Beginning on the State line between Kansas and Oklahoma at its intersection with the range line between ranges seventeen and eighteen East; thence eastward along said State line to its intersection with the center line of the Neosho River; thence down along the center line of said Neosho River to its intersection with the range line between ranges twenty-one and twenty-two East; thence south along said range line to its intersection with the township line between townships twenty-three and twenty-four North; thence west along said township line to its intersection with the range line between ranges eighteen and nineteen East; thence north along said range line to its intersection with the township line between townships twenty-four and twenty-five North; thence west along said township line to its intersection with the range line between ranges seventeen and eighteen East; thence north along said range line to the point of beginning. Vinita is hereby designated the County Seat of Craig County.

Creek County: Beginning at the northwest corner of the Creek nation, extending thence east along the boundary line between the Creek nation and Pawnee county to its intersection with the range line between ranges nine and ten East; thence south along said range line to the township line between townships eighteen and nineteen North; thence east along the said township line to its intersection with the north and south center section line across range twelve East; thence south along said center section line to the southeast corner of section sixteen, in township sixteen North, range twelve East; thence west along the section line to its intersection with the range line between ranges ten and eleven East; thence south along said range line to its intersection with the township line between townships thirteen and fourteen North; thence west along said township line to its intersection with the west boundary line of the Creek nation; thence northward along the said boundary line to the point of beginning. Sapulpa is hereby designated the County Seat of Creek County.

Custer County: Said County shall be and remain as it now exists under the Territory of Oklahoma, until hereafter changed under the provisions of this Constitution. Arapaho is hereby designated the County Seat of Custer County.

Delaware County: Beginning at the southwest corner of section six, township twenty-five North, range twenty-two East; thence east along the section line to the Missouri State line; thence southward along the State line of Missouri and of Arkansas to the township line between townships nineteen and twenty North; thence west along said township line to its intersection with the range line between ranges twenty-one and twenty-two East; thence north along said range line to the point of beginning. Grove is hereby designated the County Seat of Delaware County.

Dewey County: Said County shall be and remain as it now exists under the Territory of Oklahoma, until hereafter changed under the provisions of this Constitution. Taloga is hereby designated the County Seat of Dewey County.

Ellis County: Beginning on the one hundredth meridian at its intersection with the township line between townships twenty-four and twenty-five North; thence east along said township line to the range line between ranges twenty-two and twenty-three West; thence south along said range line to its intersection with the township line between townships nineteen and twenty North; thence east along said township line to its intersection with the range line between ranges twenty and twenty-one West; thence south along said range line to its intersection with the center line of the Canadian River (sometimes called South Canadian); thence up along the center line of said river to its intersection with the State line between Texas and Oklahoma; thence north along said State line and the one hundredth meridian to the point of beginning. Grand is hereby designated the County Seat of Ellis County.

Garfield County: Said County shall be and remain as it now exists under the Territory of Oklahoma, until hereafter changed under the provisions of this Constitution. Enid is hereby designated the County Seat of Garfield County.

Garvin County: Beginning on the range line between ranges four and five West, at its intersection with the township line between townships four and five North; thence east along said township line to its intersection with the range line between ranges three and four East; thence south along said range line to its intersection with east and west center section line across township two North; thence west along said center section line to its intersection with the range line between ranges one and two East; thence south along said range line to its intersection with the section line, two miles north of and parallel to the township line between townships one and two North; thence west along said section line to its intersection with the center line of the Washita River; thence southward along the center line of the said Washita River to its intersection with the base line; thence west along said base line to its intersection with the range line between ranges three and four West; thence north along said range line to its intersection with the township line between townships two and three North; thence west along said township line to its intersection with the range line between ranges four and five West; thence north along said range line to the point of beginning. Pauls Valley is hereby designated the County Seat of Garvin County.

Grady County: Beginning on the center line of the Canadian River (sometimes called South Canadian), at its intersection with the ninety-eighth meridian; thence southeastwardly along the center line of said Canadian River to its intersection with the range line between ranges four and five West; thence south along said range line to its intersection with the township line between townships two and three north; thence west along said township line to its intersection with the range line between ranges eight and nine West; thence north along said range line to the east and west center section line across township eight North; thence east along said center section line to its intersection with the ninety-eighth meridian; thence north along said ninety-eighth meridian to the point of beginning. Chickasha is hereby designated the County Seat of Grady County.

Grant County: Said County shall be and remain as it now exists under the Territory of Oklahoma, until hereafter changed under the provisions of this Constitution. Pond Creek is hereby designated the County Seat of Grant County.

Greer County: Beginning on the State line between Texas and Oklahoma at its intersection with the township line between townships six and seven North; thence east along said township line to its intersection with the range line between ranges twenty-three and twenty-four West; thence north along said range line to its intersection with the township line between townships seven and eight North; thence east along said township line to its intersection with the center line of the North Fork of Red River; thence down along the center line of said North Fork of Red River to its intersection with the range line between ranges nineteen and twenty West; thence south along said range line to its intersection with the east and west center section line of township four North; thence west along said center section line to the north and south center section line across range twenty-one West; thence south along said center section line to its intersection with the township line between townships three and fourth North; thence west along said township line to its intersection with the center line of the Salt Fork of Red River; thence down along the center line of said river to its intersection with the east and west center section line of township three North; thence west along said center section line to its intersection with the range line between ranges twenty-three and twenty-four West; thence south along said range line to its intersection with the base line; thence west along said base line to its intersection with the State line between Texas and Oklahoma; thence westward and northward along said State line to the point of beginning. Mangum is hereby designated the County Seat of Greer County.

Harper County: Beginning on the one-hundredth meridian at its intersection with the Kansas and Oklahoma State line; thence east along said State line to its second intersection with the center line of the Cimarron River, in range twenty-one West; thence southeastwardly along the center line of said Cimarron River to its intersection with the range line between ranges nineteen and twenty West; thence south along said range line to its intersection with the township line between townships twenty-four and twenty-five North; thence west along said township line to its intersection with the one hundredth meridian; thence north along said meridian to the point of beginning. Buffalo is hereby designated the County Seat of Harper County.

Haskell County: Beginning on the center line of the Canadian River at its intersection with the range line between ranges seventeen and eighteen East; thence down along the center line of said Canadian River to its intersection with the center line of the Arkansas River; thence down along the center line of said Arkansas River to its intersection with the range line between ranges twenty-three and twenty-four East; thence south along the said range line to its intersection with the township line between townships eight and nine North; thence west along said township line to its intersection with the range line between ranges twenty-two and twenty-three East; thence south along said range line to the northeast corner of section twenty-five, township seven North, range twenty-two East; thence west along the section line to its intersection with the range line between ranges eighteen and nineteen East; thence north along said range line to its intersection with the east and west center section line across township eight North; thence west along said center section line to its intersection with the range line between ranges seventeen and eighteen East; thence north along said range line to the point of beginning. Stigler is hereby designated the County Seat of Haskell County.

Hughes County: Beginning on the township line between townships nine and ten North, at the southwest corner of section thirty-five, township ten North, range eight East; thence east along said township line to its intersection with range line between ranges thirteen and fourteen East; thence south along said range line to its intersection with the center line of the Canadian River (sometimes called South Canadian); thence up along the center line of said Canadian River to its intersection with the range line between ranges eleven and twelve East; thence south along said range line to its intersection with the township line between townships three and four North; thence west along said township line to its intersection with the range line between ranges eight and nine East; thence north along said range line to its intersection with the center line of the Canadian River; thence up along the center line of said Canadian River to its intersection with the east line of the Seminole nation; thence north along the said east line of the Seminole nation to its intersection with the township line between townships seven and eight North; thence east along said township line to the southwest corner of section thirty-five, township eight North, range eight East; thence north to the point of beginning. Holdenville is hereby designated the County Seat of Hughes County.

Jackson County: Beginning on the range line between ranges nineteen and twenty West, at its intersection with the center line of the North Fork of Red River; thence down along the center line of said river to the State line between Texas and Oklahoma; thence westwardly along said State line to its intersection with the base line; thence east along said base line to its intersection with the range line between ranges twenty-three and twenty-four West; thence north along said range line to its intersection with the east and west center section line of township three North; thence east along said center section line to its intersection with the center line of Salt Fork of Red River; thence up along the center line of said river to its intersection with the township line between townships three and four North; thence east along said township line to the southeast corner of section thirty-three, township four North, range twenty-one West; thence north to the southwest corner of section fifteen of said township and range; thence east along the section line to its intersection with the range line between ranges nineteen and twenty West; thence north along said range line to the point of beginning. Altus is hereby designated the County Seat of Jackson County.

Jefferson County: Beginning at the southwest corner of section fifteen, township three South, range nine West; thence east along the section line to its intersection with the range line between ranges three and four West; thence south along said range line to its intersection with the center line of Mud Creek; thence southeastwardly along the center line of said Mud Creek to the State line between Texas and Oklahoma; thence westwardly along said state line to its intersection with the north and south center section line of range nine West; thence north along said center section line to the point of beginning. Ryan is hereby designated the County Seat of Jefferson County.

Johnston County: Beginning on the base line at the southeast corner of section thirty-three, township one North, range four East; thence east along said base line to its intersection with the range line between ranges seven and eight East; thence south along said range line to its intersection with the township line between townships one and two South; thence east along said township line to its intersection with the range line between ranges eight and nine East; thence south along said range line to its intersection with the township line between townships four and five South; thence west along said township line to its intersection with the boundary line between the Choctaw and Chickasaw nations; thence south along said boundary line to its intersection with the east and west center section line across township five South; thence west along said center section line to its intersection with the center line of the Washita River; thence up along the center line of said Washita River to its intersection with the section line one mile north of and parallel to the township line between townships four and five South; thence west along said section line to its intersection with the range line between ranges three and four East; thence north along said range line to its intersection with the township line between townships two and three South; thence east along said township line to its intersection with the north and south center section line across range four East; thence north along said center section line to the point of beginning. Tishomingo is hereby designated the County Seat of Johnston County.

Kay County: Said County shall be and remain as it now exists under the Territory of Oklahoma, until hereafter changed under the provisions of this Constitution. Newkirk is hereby designated the County Seat of Kay County.

Kingfisher County: Said County shall be and remain as it now exists under the Territory of Oklahoma, until hereafter changed under the provisions of this Constitution. Kingfisher is hereby designated the County Seat of Kingfisher County.

Kiowa County: Said County shall be and remain as it now exists under the Territory of Oklahoma, until hereafter changed under the provisions of this Constitution. Hobart is hereby designated the County Seat of Kiowa County.

Latimer County: Beginning at the northwest corner of section thirty, township seven North, range nineteen East; thence east along the section line to its intersection with the range line between ranges twenty-two and twenty-three East; thence south along said range line to its intersection with the township line between townships five and six North; thence west along said township line to its intersection with the section line two miles east of the range line between ranges twenty-one and twenty-two East; thence south along said section line to its intersection with the township line between townships four and five North; thence west along said township line to its intersection with the section line one mile west of the range line between ranges twenty-one and twenty-two East; thence south along said section line to its intersection with the township line between townships two and three North; thence west along said township line to its intersection with the south and north center section line across range seventeen East; thence north along said center section line to its intersection with the township line between townships six and seven North; thence east along said township line to its intersection with the range line between ranges eighteen and nineteen East; thence north along said range line to the point of beginning. Wilburton is hereby designated the County Seat of Latimer County.

Le Flore County: Beginning on the center line of the Arkansas River at its intersection with the range line between ranges twenty-three and twenty-four East; thence down along the center line of said Arkansas River to its intersection with the

State line between Arkansas and Oklahoma; thence southward along said State line to its intersection with the base line; thence west along said base line to its intersection with the range line between ranges twenty-two and twenty-three East; thence north along said range line to its intersection with the township line between townships two and three North; thence west along said township line to its intersection with the section line one mile west of the range line between ranges twenty-one and twenty-two East; thence north along said section line to its intersection with the township line between townships four and five North; thence east along said township line to the section line two miles east of the range line between ranges twenty-one and twenty-two East; thence north along said section line to its intersection with the township line between townships five and six North; thence east along said township line to its intersection with the range line between ranges twenty-two and twenty-three East; thence north along said range line to its intersection with the township line between townships eight and nine North; thence east along said township line to its intersection with the range line between ranges twenty-three and twenty-four East; thence north along said range line to the point of beginning. Poteau is hereby designated the County Seat of Le Flore County.

Lincoln County: Said County shall be and remain as it now exists under the Territory of Oklahoma, until hereafter changed under the provisions of this Constitution. Chandler is hereby designated the County Seat of Lincoln County.

Logan County: Said County shall be and remain as it now exists under the Territory of Oklahoma until hereafter changed under the provisions of this Constitution. Guthrie is hereby designated the County Seat of Logan County.

Love County: Beginning on the township line between townships five and six South, at its intersection with the range line between ranges three and four West; thence east along said township line to its intersection with the section line between sections two and three, township six South, range three East;

thence south along said section line to the northwest corner of section twenty-six in said township; thence east along the section line to the range line between ranges three and four East; thence south along said range line to its intersection with the State line between Texas and Oklahoma; thence westward along said State line to the center line of the mouth of Mud Creek; thence up along the center line of said Mud Creek to its intersection with the range line between ranges three and four West; thence north along said range line to the point of beginning. Marietta is hereby designated the County Seat of Love County.

Major County: Beginning on the township line between townships twenty-three and twenty-four North, at its intersection with the range line between ranges sixteen and seventeen West; thence east along said township line to its intersection with the center line of the Cimarron River; thence down along the center line of said Cimarron River to its intersection with the range line between ranges twelve and thirteen West; thence north along said range line to its intersection with the east and west center section line of township twenty-three North; thence east along said center section line to its intersection with the range line between ranges eight and nine West; thence south along said range line to the north line of Kingfisher County; thence westward along the north line of Kingfisher, Blaine, and Dewey Counties to the intersection with the range line between ranges sixteen and seventeen West; thence north along said range line to the point of beginning. Fairview is hereby designated the County Seat of Major County.

Marshall County: Beginning at the northwest corner of section thirty-five, in township four South, range three East; thence east along the section line to its intersection with the center line of the Washita River; thence down along the center line of said Washita River to its intersection with the State line between Texas and Oklahoma; thence westward along said state line to its intersection with the range line between ranges three and four East; thence north along said range line to the northeast corner of section twenty-five, township six South, range three East; thence west along the section line to the northwest corner of section twenty-six, in said township and range; thence north to the point of beginning. Madill is hereby designated the County Seat of Marshall County.

Mayes County: Beginning on the township line between townships twenty-three and twenty-four North, at its intersection with the range line between ranges seventeen and eighteen East; thence east along said township line to its intersection with the range line between ranges twenty-one and twenty-two East; thence south along said range line to its intersection with the township line between townships nineteen and twenty North; thence west along said township line to its intersection with the range line between ranges twenty and twenty-one East; thence south along said range line to its intersection with the township line between townships eighteen and nineteen North; thence west along said township line to its intersection with the range line between ranges seventeen and eighteen East; thence north along said range line to the point of beginning. Pryor Creek is hereby designated the County Seat of Mayes County.

Murray County: Beginning on the base line at its intersection with the range line between ranges one and two West; thence east along said base line to its intersection with the center line of the Washita River; thence up along the center line of said Washita River to its intersection with the section line two miles north of and parallel to the township line between townships one and two North; thence east along said section line to its intersection with the range line between ranges one and two East; thence north along said range line to its intersection with the east and west center section line across township two North; thence east along said center section line to its intersection with the range line between ranges three and four East; thence south along said range line to its intersection with the township line between townships one and two North; thence east along said township line to its intersection with the range line between ranges four and five East; thence south along said range line to its intersection with the base line; thence west along said base line to its intersection with the north and south center section line across range four East; thence south along said center section line to its intersection with the township line between townships two and three South; thence west along said township line to its intersection with the center line of the Washita River; thence up along the center line of said Washita River to its intersection with the east and west center section line across township two South; thence west along said center section line to its intersection with the range line between ranges one and two West; thence north along said range line to the point of beginning. Sulphur is hereby designated the County Seat of Murray County.

Muskogee County: Beginning on the range line between ranges fourteen and fifteen East, at its intersection with the east and west center section line of township sixteen North, range fifteen East; thence east along said center section line to its intersection with the Arkansas River; thence down along the center line of said Arkansas River to its second intersection with the township line between townships fifteen and sixteen North, in range eighteen East; thence east along said township line to its intersection with the range line between ranges twenty and twenty-one East; thence south along said range line to its intersection with the center line of the Arkansas River; thence down along the center line of said Arkansas River to its intersection with the center line of the Canadian River; thence up along the center line of said Canadian River to its intersection with the range line between ranges eighteen and nineteen East; thence north along said range line to its intersection with the township line between townships twelve and thirteen North; thence west along said township line to the north and south center section line of township thirteen North, range fifteen East; thence north along said center section line to its intersection with the township line between townships fourteen and fifteen North; thence west along said township line to its intersection with the range line between ranges fourteen and fifteen East; thence north along said range line to the point of beginning. Muskogee is hereby designated the County Seat of Muskogee County.

McClain County: Beginning on the center line of the Canadian River (sometimes called South Canadian), at its intersection with the range line between ranges four and five West; thence down along the center line of said Canadian River to its intersection with the range line between ranges three and four East; thence south along said range line to its intersection with the township line between townships four and five North; thence west along said township line to its intersection with the range line between ranges four and five West; thence north along said range line to the point of beginning. Purcell is hereby designated the County Seat of McClain County.

McCurtain County: Beginning on the base line at its intersection with the range line between ranges twenty-one and twenty-two East; thence east along said base line to its intersection with the State line between Arkansas and Oklahoma; thence southward along said State line to its intersection with the State line between Texas and Oklahoma; thence northwestward along said state line to its intersection with the range line between ranges twenty and twenty-one East; thence north along said range line to its intersection with the township line between townships three and four South; thence east along said township line to its intersection with the range line between ranges twenty-one and twenty-two East; thence north along said range line to the point of beginning. Idabel is hereby designated the County Seat of McCurtain County.

McIntosh County: Beginning on the township line between townships twelve and thirteen North, at its intersection with the range line between ranges thirteen and fourteen East; thence east along said township line to its intersection with the range line between ranges eighteen and nineteen East; thence south along said range line to its intersection with the center line of the Canadian River; thence up along the center line of said Canadian River to its intersection with the range line between ranges thirteen and fourteen East; thence north along said range line to its intersection with the township line between townships nine and ten North; thence west along said township line to its intersection with the range line between ranges twelve and thirteen East; thence north along said range line to its intersection with the township line between townships ten and eleven North; thence east along said township line to its intersection with the range line between ranges thirteen and fourteen East; thence north along said range line to the point of beginning. Eufaula is hereby designated the County Seat of McIntosh County.

Noble County: Said County shall be as it now exists under the Territory of Oklahoma, with township twenty North, range one East, and township twenty North, range one West, added thereto. Perry is hereby designated the County Seat of Noble County.

Nowata County: Beginning on the State line between Kansas and Oklahoma at its intersection with the north and south center section line of range fourteen East; thence eastward along said State line to its intersection with the range line between ranges seventeen and eighteen East; thence south along said range line to its intersection with the township line between townships twenty-four and twenty-five North; thence west along said township line to its intersection with the north and south center section line across range fourteen East; thence north along said center section line to the point of beginning. Nowata is hereby designated the County Seat of Nowata County.

Okfuskee County: Beginning on the west boundary line of the Creek nation at its intersection with the township line between townships thirteen and fourteen North; thence east along said township line to its intersection with the range line between ranges ten and eleven East; thence south along said range line to its intersection with the township line between townships twelve and thirteen North; thence east along said township line to its intersection with the range line between ranges eleven and twelve East; thence south along said range line to its intersection with the township line between townships ten and eleven North; thence east along said township line to its intersection with the range line between ranges twelve and thirteen East; thence south along said range line to its intersection with the township line between townships nine and ten North; thence west along said township line to its intersection with section line two miles west of and parallel to the range line between ranges eight and nine East; thence north along said section line to its intersection with the center line of the North Fork of the Canadian River; thence up along the center line of said river to the southwest corner of the Creek nation in township eleven North; thence along the west boundary line of said Creek nation to the point of beginning. Okemah is hereby designated the County Seat of Okfuskee County.

Oklahoma County: Said County shall be and remain, as it now exists under the Territory of Oklahoma, until hereafter changed under the provisions of this Constitution. Oklahoma City is hereby designated the County Seat of Oklahoma County.

Okmulgee County: Beginning on the range line between ranges ten and eleven East, at its intersection with the east and west center section line across township sixteen North; thence east along said center section line to its intersection with the range line between ranges fourteen and fifteen East; thence south along said range line to its intersection with the township line between townships fourteen and fifteen North; thence east along said township line to its intersection with the north and south center section line across range fifteen East; thence south along said center section line to its intersection with the township line between townships twelve and thirteen North; thence west along said township line to its intersection with the range line between ranges thirteen and fourteen East; thence south along said range line to its intersection with the township line between townships ten and eleven North; thence west along said township line to its intersection with the range line between ranges eleven and twelve East; thence north along said range line to its intersection with the township line between townships twelve and thirteen North; thence west along said township line to its intersection with the range line between ranges ten and eleven East; thence north along said range line to the point of beginning. Okmulgee is hereby designated the County Seat of Okmulgee County.

Osage County: The Osage Indian Reservation with its present boundaries is hereby constituted one county to be known as Osage County; the present boundaries to remain unchanged until all the lands of the Osage Tribe of Indians shall have been allotted, and until the same shall be changed as provided by the Legislature for changing county lines. Pawhuska is hereby designated the County Seat of Osage County.

Ottawa County: Beginning on the State line between Kansas and Oklahoma at its intersection with the center line of the Neosho River; thence east along said State line to its intersection with the Missouri State line; thence southward along the Missouri State line to its intersection with the section line one mile south of and parallel to the south line of township twenty-six North; thence west along said section line to its intersection with the range line between ranges twenty-one and twenty-two East; thence north along said range line to its intersection with the center line of the Neosho River; thence up along the center line of said Neosho River to the point of beginning. Miami is hereby designated the County Seat of Ottawa County.

Pawnee County: Said County shall be and remain as it now exists under the Territory of Oklahoma, until hereafter changed under the provisions of this Constitution. Pawnee is hereby designated the County Seat of Pawnee County.

Payne County: Said County shall be as it now exists under the Territory of Oklahoma, with township twenty North, range one East, and township twenty North, range one West, taken therefrom. Stillwater is hereby designated the County Seat of Payne County.

Pittsburg County: Beginning on the center line of the Canadian River (sometimes called South Canadian), at its intersection with the range line between ranges eleven and twelve East; thence down along the center line of said Canadian River to its intersection with the range line between ranges seventeen and eighteen East; thence south along said range line to its intersection with the east and west center section line of township eight North; thence east along said center section line to its intersection with the range line between ranges eighteen and nineteen East; thence south along said range line to its intersection with the township line between townships six and seven North; thence west along said township line to its intersection with the north and south center section line across range seventeen East; thence south along said center section line to its intersection with the township line between townships one and two North; thence west along said township line to its intersection with the range line between ranges thirteen and fourteen East; thence north along said range line to its intersection with the township line between townships two and three North; thence west along said township line to its intersection with the range line between ranges eleven and twelve East; thence north along said range line to the point of beginning. McAlester is hereby designated the County Seat of Pittsburg County.

Pontotoc County: Beginning on the center line of the Canadian River (sometimes called South Canadian), at its intersection with the range line between ranges three and four East; thence down along the center line of said Canadian River to its intersection with the range line between ranges eight and nine East; thence south along said range line to its intersection with the township line between townships two and three North; thence west along said township line to its intersection with the range line between ranges seven and eight East; thence south down along said range line to its intersection with the base line; thence west along said base line to its intersection with the range line between ranges four and five East; thence north along said range line to its intersection with the township line between townships one and two North; thence west along said township line to its intersection with the range line between ranges three and four East; thence north along said range line to the point of beginning. Ada is hereby designated the County Seat of Pontotoc County.

Pottawatomie County: Said County shall be and remain as it now exists under the Territory of Oklahoma, until hereafter changed under the provisions of this Constitution. Tecumseh is hereby designated the County Seat of Pottawatomie County.

Pushmataha County: Beginning on the township line between townships two and three North, at its intersection with the north and south center section line across range seventeen East; thence east along said township line to its intersection with the range line between ranges twenty-two and twenty-three East; thence south along said range line to its intersection with the base line; thence west along said base line to its intersection with the range line between ranges twenty-one and twenty-two East; thence south along said range line to its intersection with the township line between townships three and four South; thence west along said township line to its intersection with the range line between ranges twenty and twenty-one East; thence south along said range line to its intersection with the township line between townships four and five South; thence west along said township line to its intersection with the range line between ranges fourteen and fifteen East; thence north along said range line to its intersection with the base line; thence east along said base line to its intersection with the range line between ranges fifteen and sixteen East; thence north along said range line to its intersection with the township line between townships one and two North; thence east along said township line to its intersection with the north and south center section line across range seventeen East; thence north along said center section line to the point of beginning. Antlers is hereby designated the County Seat of Pushmataha County.

Roger Mills County: Beginning on the State line between Texas and Oklahoma at its intersection with the center line of the Canadian River (sometimes called South Canadian); thence down along the center line of said river to its intersection with the range line between ranges twenty and twenty-one West; thence south along said range line to its intersection with the east and west center section line across township twelve North; thence west along said section line to its intersection with the range line between ranges twenty-two and twenty-three West; thence south along said range line to its intersection with the east and west center section line across township eleven North; thence west along said section line to its intersection with the State line between Texas and Oklahoma; thence northward along said State line to the point of beginning. Cheyenne is hereby designated the County Seat of Roger Mills County.

Rogers County: Beginning on the township line between townships twenty-four and twenty-five North at its intersection with the north and south center section line across range fourteen East; thence east along said township line to the range line between ranges eighteen and nineteen East; thence south along said range line to the township line between townships twenty-three and twenty-four North; thence west along said township line to the range line between ranges seventeen and eighteen East; thence south along said range line to its intersection with the township line between townships eighteen and nineteen North; thence west along said township line to its intersection with the center line of the Verdigris River; thence up along the center line of said Verdigris River to its intersection with the township line between townships nineteen and twenty North; thence west along said township line to its intersection with the north and south center section line across range fourteen East; thence north along said center section line to the township line between townships twenty-one and twenty-two North; thence west along said township line to the range line between ranges thirteen and fourteen East; thence north along said range line to the township line between townships twenty-two and twenty-three North; thence east along said township line to the north and south center section line across range fourteen East; thence north along said center section line to the point of beginning. Claremore is hereby designated the County Seat of Rogers County.

Seminole County: Beginning at a point where the east boundary line of the Seminole nation intersects the center line of the South Canadian River; thence north along the east boundary line of said Seminole nation to its intersection with the township line between townships seven and eight North; thence east along said township line to the southwest corner of section thirty-five, township eight North, range eight East; thence north along the section line between sections thirty-four and thirty-five, in said township and range, projected to its intersection with the center line of the North Canadian River; thence westward along the center line of said river to its intersection with the east boundary line of Pottawatomie County; thence southward along said east boundary line to its intersection with the center line of the South Canadian River; thence down along the center line of said river to the point of beginning. Wewoka is hereby designated the County Seat of Seminole County.

Sequoyah County: Beginning on the township line between townships thirteen and fourteen North, at its intersection with the range line between ranges twenty and twenty-one East; thence east along said township line to its intersection with the state line between Arkansas and Oklahoma; thence southward along said state line to its intersection with the center line of the Arkansas River; thence up along the center line of said Arkansas River to its intersection with the range line between ranges twenty and twenty-one East; thence north along said range line to the point of beginning. Sallisaw is hereby designated the County Seat of Sequoyah County.

Stephens County: Beginning on the township line between townships two and three North, at its intersection with the north and south center section line across range nine West; thence east along said township line to its intersection with the range line between ranges three and four West; thence south along said range line to its intersection with the east and west center section line across township three South; thence west along said center section line to its intersection with the north and south center section line across range nine West; thence north along said center section line to the point of beginning. Duncan is hereby designated the County Seat of Stephens County.

Texas County: All that part of the former county of Beaver, Territory of Oklahoma, extending from the range line between ranges nineteen and twenty East of the Cimarron Meridian, to the range line between ranges nine and ten East of the Cimarron Meridian. Guymon is hereby designated the County Seat of Texas County.

Tillman County: Beginning on the base line at its intersection with the center line of the North Fork of Red River; thence east along said base line to its intersection with the north and south center section line across range fourteen West; thence south along said center section line to its intersection with the township line between townships two and three South; thence east along said township line to its intersection with the range line between ranges thirteen and fourteen West; thence south along said range line to its intersection with the State line between Texas and Oklahoma; thence westwardly and northwardly along said State line to its intersection with the center line of the mouth of the North Fork of Red River; thence up along the center line of said North Fork of Red River to the point of beginning. Frederick is hereby designated the County Seat of Tillman County.

Tulsa County: Beginning at the northeast corner of township nineteen North, range fourteen East; thence south along the range line between ranges fourteen and fifteen East, to its intersection with the township line between townships seventeen and eighteen North; thence west along said township line to its intersection with the range line between ranges thirteen and fourteen East; thence south along said range line to its intersection with the east and west center section line across township sixteen North; thence west along said center section line to its intersection with the north and south center section line across range twelve East; thence north along said center section line to its intersection with the township line between townships eighteen and nineteen North; thence west along said township line to its intersection with the range line between ranges nine and ten East; thence north along said range line to its intersection with the north boundary line of the Creek nation; thence eastward along said boundary line to the southeast corner of the Osage nation; thence north along the east boundary line of the Osage nation to its intersection with the township line between townships twenty-two and twenty-three North; thence east along said township line to the range line between ranges thirteen and fourteen East; thence south along said range line to its intersection with the township line between townships twenty-one and twenty-two North; thence east along said township line to its intersection with the north and south center section line across range fourteen East; thence south along said center section line to its intersection with the township line between townships nineteen and twenty North; thence east along said township line to the point of beginning. Tulsa is hereby designated the County Seat of Tulsa County.

Wagoner County: Beginning on the township line between townships nineteen and twenty North, at its intersection with the range line between ranges fourteen and fifteen East; thence east along said township line to its intersection with the center line of the Verdigris River; thence down along the center line of said river to its intersection with the township line between townships eighteen and nineteen North; thence east along said township line to its intersection with the center line of Grand River; thence down along the center line of said Grand River to its intersection with the township line between townships fifteen and sixteen North; thence west along said township line to its intersection with the center line of the Arkansas River, in range eighteen East, to correspond with the description of Muskogee County; thence up along the center line of said Arkansas River to its intersection with the east and west center section line across township sixteen North, range fifteen East; thence west along said center section line to its intersection with the range line between ranges thirteen and fourteen East; thence north along said range line to its intersection with the township line between townships seventeen and eighteen North; thence east along said township line to its intersection with the range line between ranges fourteen and fifteen East; thence north along said range line to the point of beginning. Wagoner is hereby designated the County Seat of Wagoner County.

Washington County: Beginning on the State line between Kansas and Oklahoma at its intersection with the east boundary line of the Osage nation; thence eastward along said State line to its intersection with the north and south center section line across range fourteen East; thence south along said center section line to its intersection with the township line between townships twenty-two and twenty-three North; thence west along said township line to its intersection with the east boundary line of the Osage nation; thence northward along said boundary line to the point of beginning. Bartlesville is hereby designated the County Seat of Washington County.

Washita County: Said County shall be and remain, as it now exists under the Territory of Oklahoma, until hereafter changed under the provisions of this Constitution. Cordell is hereby designated the County Seat of Washita County.

Woods County: Beginning on the State line between Kansas and Oklahoma at its intersection with the center line of the Cimarron River in range twenty-one West; thence eastward along said State line to its intersection with the range line between ranges twelve and thirteen West; thence south along said range line to its intersection with the center line of the Cimarron River; thence up along the center line of said Cimarron River to its intersection with the township line between townships twenty-three and twenty-four North; thence west along said township line to its intersection with the range line between ranges sixteen and seventeen West; thence north along said range line to its intersection with the center line of the Cimarron River; thence up along the center line of said Cimarron River to the point of beginning. Alva is hereby designated the County Seat of Woods County.

Woodward County: Beginning on the center line of the Cimarron River at its intersection with the range line between ranges nineteen and twenty West; thence southeastwardly along the center line of said Cimarron River to its intersection with the range line between ranges sixteen and seventeen West; thence south along said range line to its intersection with the south boundary line of said County, as it now exists under the Territory of Oklahoma; thence westward along said line to its intersection with the range line between ranges twenty-two and twenty-three West; thence north along said range line to its intersection with the township line between townships twenty-four and twenty-five North; thence east along said township line to its intersection with the range line between ranges nineteen and twenty West; thence north along said range line to the point of beginning. Woodward is hereby designated the County Seat of Woodward County.

ARTICLE XVIII: MUNICIPAL CORPORATIONS

Section 1. Creation - General or Special Laws – Classification

Municipal corporations shall not be created by special laws, but the Legislature, by general laws shall provide for the incorporation and organization of cities and towns and the classification of same in proportion to population, subject to the provisions of this article.

Section 2. Existing Municipal Corporations Continued - Rights and Powers
Every municipal corporation now existing within this State shall continue with all of its present rights and powers until otherwise provided by law, and shall always have the additional rights and powers conferred by the Constitution.

Section 3(a). Framing and Adoption of Charter - Approval by Governor - Effect - Record – Amendment

Any city containing a population of more than two thousand inhabitants may frame a charter for its own government, consistent with and subject to the Constitution and laws of this State, by causing a board of freeholders, composed of two from each ward, who shall be qualified electors of said city, to be elected by the qualified electors of said city, at any general or special election, whose duty it shall be, within ninety days after such election, to prepare and propose a charter for such city, which shall be signed in duplicate by the members of such board or a majority of them, and returned, one copy of said charter to the chief executive officer of such city, and the other to the Register of Deeds of the county in which said city shall be situated. Such proposed charter shall then be published in one or more newspapers published and of general circulation within said city, for at least twenty-one days, if in a daily paper, or in three consecutive issues, if in a weekly paper, and the first publication shall be made within twenty days after the completion of the charter; and within thirty days, and not earlier than twenty days after such publication, it shall be submitted to the qualified electors of said city at a general or special election, and if a majority of such qualified electors voting thereon shall ratify the same, it shall thereafter be submitted to the Governor for his approval, and the Governor shall approve the same if it shall not be in conflict with the Constitution and laws of this State. Upon such approval it shall become the organic law of such city and supersede any existing charter and all amendments thereof and all ordinances inconsistent with it. A copy of such charter, certified by the chief executive officer, and authenticated by the seal of such city, setting forth the submission of such charter to the electors and its ratification by them shall, after the approval of such charter by the Governor, be made in duplicate and deposited, one in the office of the Secretary of State, and the other, after being recorded in the office of said Register of Deeds, shall be deposited in the archives of the city; and thereafter all courts shall take judicial notice of said charter. The charter so ratified may be amended by proposals therefore, submitted by the legislative authority of the city to the qualified electors thereof (or by petition as hereinafter provided) at a general or special election, and ratified by a majority of the qualified electors voting thereon, and approved by the Governor as herein provided for the approval of the charter.

Section 3(b). Election of Board of Freeholders

An election of such board of freeholders may be called at any time by the legislative authority of any such city, and such election shall be called by the chief executive officer of any such city within ten days after there shall have been filed with him a petition demanding the same, signed by a number of qualified electors residing within such city, equal to twenty-five per centum of the total number of votes cast at the next preceding general municipal election; and such election shall be held not later than thirty days after the call therefore. At such election a vote shall be taken upon the question of whether or not further proceedings toward adopting a charter shall be had in pursuance to the call, and unless a majority of the qualified electors voting thereon shall vote to proceed further, no further proceeding shall be had, and all proceedings up to that time shall be of no effect.

Section 4(a). Reservation of Powers

The powers of the initiative and referendum, reserved by this Constitution to the people of the State and the respective counties and districts therein, are hereby reserved to the people of every municipal corporation now existing or which shall hereafter be created within this State, with reference to all legislative authority which it may exercise, and amendments to charters for its own government in accordance with the provisions of this Constitution.

Section 4(b). Petition - Signature – Filing

Every petition for either the initiative or referendum in the government of a municipal corporation shall be signed by a number of qualified electors residing within the territorial limits of such municipal corporation, equal to twenty-five per centum of the total number of votes cast at the next preceding election, and every such petition shall be filed with the chief executive officer of such municipal corporation.

Section 4(c). Presentation of Petition to Legislative Body - Submission to Voters

When such petition demands the enactment of an ordinance or other legal act other than the grant, extension, or renewal of a franchise, the chief executive officer shall present the same to the legislative body of such corporation at its next meeting, and unless the said petition shall be granted more than thirty days before the next election at which any city officers are to be elected, the chief executive officer shall submit the said ordinance or act so petitioned for, to the qualified electors at said election; and if a majority of said electors voting thereon shall vote for the same, it shall thereupon become in full force and effect.

Section 4(d). Submission to Referendum Vote

When such petition demands a referendum vote upon any ordinance or any other legal act other than the grant, extension, or renewal of a franchise, the chief executive officer shall submit said ordinance or act to the qualified electors of said corporation at the next succeeding general municipal election, and if, at said election, a majority of the electors voting thereon shall not vote for the same, it shall thereupon stand repealed.

Section 4(e). Submission of Amendment to Charter

When such petition demands an amendment to a charter, the chief executive officer shall submit such amendment to the qualified electors of said municipal corporation at the next election of any officers of said corporation and if, at said election, a majority of said electors voting thereon shall vote for such amendment, the same shall thereupon become an amendment to and a part of said charter, when approved by the Governor and filed in the same manner and form as an original charter is required by the provisions of this article to be approved and filed.

Section 5(a). Grant, Extension or Renewal - Approval by Voters – Term

No municipal corporation shall ever grant, extend, or renew a franchise, without the approval of a majority of the qualified electors residing within its corporate limits, who shall vote thereon at a general or special election; and the legislative body of any such corporation may submit any such matter for approval or disapproval to such electors at any general municipal election, or call a special election for such purpose at any time upon thirty days' notice; and no franchise shall be granted, extended, or renewed for a longer term than twenty-five years.

Section 5(b). Petition - Calling Election - Result of Election

Whenever a petition signed by a number of qualified electors of any municipal corporation equal to twenty-five per centum of the total number of votes cast at the next preceding general municipal election, demanding that a franchise be granted, extended, or renewed, shall be filed with the chief executive officer of said corporation, the chief executive officer shall, within ten days thereafter, call a special election, at which he shall submit the question of whether or not such franchise shall be granted, extended, or renewed, and if, at said election, a majority of the said electors voting thereon shall vote for the grant, extension, or renewal of such franchise, the same shall be granted by the proper authorities at the next succeeding regular meeting of the legislative body of the city.

Section 6. Business or Enterprise - Right to Engage In

Every municipal corporation within this State shall have the right to engage in any business or enterprise which may be engaged in by a person, firm, or corporation by virtue of a franchise from said corporation.

Section 7. Control and Regulation Not Divested - Surrender of Powers - Exclusive Franchises

No grant, extension, or renewal of any franchise or other use of the streets, alleys, or other public grounds or ways of any municipality, shall divest the State, or any of its subordinate subdivisions, of their control and regulation of such use and enjoyment. Nor shall the power to regulate the charges for public services be surrendered; and no exclusive franchise shall ever be granted.

ARTICLE XIX: INSURANCE

Section 1. Foreign Insurance Companies - Conditions of Doing Business

No foreign insurance company shall be granted a license or permitted to do business in this State until it shall have complied with the laws of the State, including the deposit of such collateral or indemnity for the protection of its patrons within this State as may be prescribed by law, and shall agree to pay all such taxes and fees as may at any time be imposed by law or act of the Legislature, on foreign insurance companies, and a refusal to pay such taxes or fees shall work a forfeiture of such license.

Section 2. Entrance Fees - Annual Tax

Until otherwise provided by law, all foreign insurance companies, including surety and bond companies, doing business in the State, except fraternal insurance companies, shall pay to the Insurance Commissioner for the use of the State, an entrance fee as follows:

Each foreign Life Insurance Company, per annum, two hundred dollars; each Foreign Fire Insurance Company, per annum, one hundred dollars; each Foreign Accident and Health Insurance Company, jointly, per annum, one hundred dollars; each Surety and Bond Company, per annum, one hundred and fifty dollars; each Plate Glass Insurance Company, (not accident), per annum, twenty-five dollars; each foreign live stock insurance company, per annum, twenty-five dollars. Until otherwise provided by law, domestic companies excepted, each insurance company, including surety and bond companies, doing business in this State, shall pay an annual tax of two per centum on all premiums collected in the State, after all cancellations are deducted, and a tax of three dollars on each local agent.

Section 3. Non-Profit Insurance Organizations

The revenue and tax provisions of this Constitution shall not include, but the State shall provide for, the following classes of insurance organizations not conducted for profit, and insuring only their own members:

First, farm companies insuring farm property and products thereon; second, Trades Insurance Companies insuring the property and interest of one line of business; third, Fraternal Life, Health, and Accident Insurance in Fraternal and Civic Orders, and in all of which the interests of the members of each respectively shall be uniform and mutual.

Section 4. Fees Paid to State Treasurer

All fees collected by the Insurance Commissioner shall be paid to the State Treasurer monthly.

ARTICLE XX: MANUFACTURE AND COMMERCE

Section 1. Denaturized Alcohol - Manufacture and Sale
Nothing herein shall prevent the manufacture or sale of
denaturized alcohol under such regulations as may be prescribed
by law.

Section 2. Kerosene Oil - Flash Test - Specific Gravity Test
Until changed by the Legislature, the flash test provided for
under the laws of Oklahoma Territory for all kerosene oil for
illuminating purposes shall be 115 degrees Fahrenheit; and the
specific gravity test for all such oil shall be 40 degrees Baume.

ARTICLE XXI: PUBLIC INSTITUTIONS

Section 1. Establishment and Support

Educational, reformatory, and penal institutions and those for the benefit of the insane, blind, deaf, and mute, and such other institutions as the public good may require, shall be established and supported by the State in such manner as may be prescribed by law.

ARTICLE XXII: ALIEN AND CORPORATE OWNERSHIP OF LANDS

Section 1. Aliens - Ownership of Land Prohibited - Disposal of Lands Acquired

No alien or person who is not a citizen of the United States, shall acquire title to or own land in this state, and the Legislature shall enact laws whereby all persons not citizens of the United States, and their heirs, who may hereafter acquire real estate in this state by devise, descent, or otherwise, shall dispose of the same within five years upon condition of escheat or forfeiture to the State: Provided, This shall not apply to Indians born within the United States, nor to aliens or persons not citizens of the United States who may become bona fide residents of this State: And Provided Further, That this section shall not apply to lands now owned by aliens in this State.

Section 2. Corporations - Buying, Acquiring or Dealing in Real Estate

No corporation shall be created or licensed in this State for the purpose of buying, acquiring, trading, or dealing in real estate other than real estate located in incorporated cities and towns and as additions thereto; nor shall any corporation doing business in this State buy, acquire, trade, or deal in real estate for any purpose except such as may be located in such towns and cities and as additions to such towns and cities, and further except such as shall be necessary and proper for carrying on the business for which it was chartered or licensed; and provided further that under limitations prescribed by the legislature, any corporation may acquire real estate for lease or sale to any other corporation, if such latter corporation could have legally acquired the same in the first instance; nor shall any corporation be created or licensed to do business in this State for the purpose of acting as agent in buying and selling or leasing land for agricultural purposes; provided, however, that corporations shall not be precluded from taking mortgages on real estate to secure loans or debts, or from acquiring title thereto upon foreclosure of such mortgages or in the collection of debts, conditioned that such corporation or corporations shall not hold such real estate for a longer period than seven (7) years after acquiring such title; and provided, further, that this Section shall not apply to trust companies taking only the naked title to real estate in this State as a trustee, to be held solely as security for indebtedness pursuant to such trust; and provided, further, that no public service corporation shall hold any land, or the title thereof, in any way whatever in this State, except as the same shall be necessary for the transaction and operation of its business as such public service corporation.

ARTICLE XXIII: MISCELLANEOUS

Section 1. Hours of Labor on Public Work

Eight hours shall constitute a day's work in all cases of employment by and on behalf of the State or any county or municipality.

Section 2. Contracting Prohibited

The contracting of convict labor is hereby prohibited.

Section 3. Children under Fifteen

The employment of children, under the age of fifteen years, in any occupation, injurious to health or morals or especially hazardous to life or limb, is hereby prohibited.

Section 4. Employment Underground - Hours of Labor Underground

Boys and girls under the age of eighteen years shall not be employed, underground, in the operation of mines; and, except in cases of emergency, eight hours shall constitute a day's work underground in all mines in the State.

Section 5. Health and Safety of Employees

The Legislature shall pass laws to protect the health and safety of employees in factories, in mines, and on railroads.

Section 6. Contributory Negligence - Assumption of Risk - Questions for Jury

The defense of contributory negligence or of assumption of risk shall, in all cases whatsoever, be a question of fact, and shall, at all times, be left to the jury.

Section 7. Right of Action - Amount of Recovery - Exclusiveness of Remedy under Workers' Compensation Law

The right of action to recover damages for injuries resulting in death shall never be abrogated, and the amount recoverable shall not be subject to any statutory limitation, provided however, that the Legislature may provide an amount of compensation under the Workers' Compensation Law for death resulting from injuries suffered in employment covered by such law, in which case the compensation so provided shall be exclusive, and the Legislature may enact statutory limits on the amount recoverable in civil actions or claims against the state or any of its political subdivisions.

Section 8. Contracts Waiving Benefits of Constitution Invalid
Any provision of a contract, express or implied, made by any person, by which any of the benefits of this Constitution is sought to be waived, shall be null and void.

Section 9. Notice or Demand, Stipulation for

Any provision of any contract or agreement, express or implied, stipulating for notice or demand other than such as may be provided by law, as a condition precedent to establish any claim, demand, or liability, shall be null and void.

Section 10. Change of Salary During Term - Extension of Term - Continuance until Qualification of Successor

Except wherein otherwise provided in this Constitution, in no case shall the salary or emoluments of any public official be changed after his election or appointment, or during his term of office, unless by operation of law enacted prior to such election or appointment; nor shall the term of any public official be extended beyond the period for which he was elected or appointed: Provided, That all officers within this State shall continue to perform the duties of their offices until their successors shall be duly qualified.

Section 12. On Use of Monies

All the proceeds, assets and income of any public retirement system administered by an agency of the State of Oklahoma shall be held, invested, or disbursed as provided for by law as in trust for the exclusive purpose of providing for benefits, refunds, investment management, and administrative expenses of the individual public retirement system, and shall not be encumbered for or diverted to any other purposes.

ARTICLE XXIV: CONSTITUTIONAL AMENDMENTS

Section 1. Amendments Proposed by Legislature - Submission to Vote

Any amendment or amendments to this Constitution may be proposed in either branch of the Legislature, and if the same shall be agreed to by a majority of all the members elected to each of the two (2) houses, such proposed amendment or amendments shall, with the yeas and nays thereon, be entered in their journals and referred by the Secretary of State to the people for their approval or rejection, at the next regular general election, except when the Legislature, by a two-thirds (2/3) vote of each house, shall order a special election for that purpose. If a majority of all the electors voting on any proposed amendment at such election shall vote in favor thereof, it shall thereby become a part of this Constitution. No proposal for the amendment or alteration of this Constitution which is submitted to the voters shall embrace more than one general subject and the voters shall vote separately for or against each proposal submitted; provided, however, that in the submission of proposals for the amendment of this Constitution by articles, which embrace one general subject, each proposed article shall be deemed a single proposal or proposition.

Section 2. Constitutional Convention to Propose Amendments or New Constitution

No convention shall be called by the Legislature to propose alterations, revisions, or amendments to this Constitution, or to propose a new Constitution, unless the law providing for such convention shall first be approved by the people on a referendum vote at a regular or special election, and any amendments, alterations, revisions, or new Constitution, proposed by such convention, shall be submitted to the electors of the State at a general or special election and be approved by a majority of the electors voting thereon, before the same shall become effective: Provided, That the question of such proposed convention shall be submitted to the people at least once in every twenty years.

Section 3. Right of Amendment by Initiative Petition Not Impaired

This article shall not impair the right of the people to amend this Constitution by a vote upon an initiative petition therefore.

ARTICLE XXV: SOCIAL SECURITY

Section 1. Relief and Care of Needy Aged and Disabled Persons - Co-operation with Federal Plan

In order to promote the general welfare of the people of the State of Oklahoma and for their protection, security, and benefit, the Legislature and the people by initiative petition are hereby authorized to provide by appropriate legislation for the relief and care of needy aged persons who are unable to provide for themselves, and other needy persons who, on account of immature age, physical infirmity, disability, or other cause, are unable to provide or care for themselves; Provided, the Legislature or the people by initiative petition, are further authorized, in co-operation with and under any plan authorized by the Federal Government for State participation, to provide by appropriate legislation for the relief and care of aged or needy persons. The levy of taxes, other than ad valorem taxes, necessary to carry into effect legislation enacted pursuant thereto, is hereby authorized.

Section 2. Repealed

Section 3. Repealed

Section 4. Repealed

Section 5. Effect of Legislation Contemporaneously Adopted

Any legislation under the authority herein granted, adopted contemporaneously with the adoption of this amendment, shall have the same force and effect as if same had been initiated and adopted subsequent to the adoption of this amendment.

ARTICLE XXVI: DEPARTMENT OF WILDLIFE CONSERVATION

Section 1. Creation of Department - Wildlife Conservation Commission - Membership - Appointment - Tenure - Vacancies - Oath and Bonds

There is hereby created a Department of Wildlife Conservation of the State of Oklahoma and an Oklahoma Wildlife Conservation Commission. The Department of Wildlife Conservation shall be governed by the Wildlife Conservation Director, hereinafter created, under such rules, regulations and policies as may be prescribed from time to time by the Oklahoma Wildlife Conservation Commission. Such rules and regulations and amendments thereof shall be filed and recorded in the office of the Secretary of State, and shall become effective on the tenth (10th) day following such filing.

Said Commission shall be composed of eight (8) members to be appointed by the Governor by and with the consent of the Senate and shall be removable only for cause, as provided by law for the removal of officers not subject to impeachment; one (1) member from each of eight (8) districts as the same are presently defined by Title 29 O.S.1951, Section 104. The term of office of each such member shall be eight (8) years, except that the first appointed members shall hold office for terms as follows: the member appointed from the first district shall hold office until July 1st following his appointment, and the members appointed from the second, third, fourth, fifth, sixth, seventh and eighth districts shall hold office until July 1st of the second, third, fourth, fifth, sixth, seventh and eighth succeeding calendar years, respectively. In the event the Governor fails to fill a vacancy within thirty (30) days following such vacancy, the remaining members of the Commission may appoint a qualified person to fill such vacancy for the unexpired portion of the term. The members of the Commission shall receive no salary or other compensation for their services, other than per diem and expenses as may be authorized by the Legislature.

Each member of the Commission shall take the oaths required of other State officers, and each shall execute a good and sufficient corporate surety bond in the sum of Ten Thousand Dollars ($10,000.00) payable to the State of Oklahoma, and conditioned upon the faithful performance of duty, and the premium thereon shall be payable by the State.

Section 2. Game and Fish Laws Not Repealed - Acquisition of Property

Nothing in this Act shall repeal any existing laws now on the Statute, pertaining to game and fish. The Commission may acquire by purchase, gift, grants-in-aid from the Federal Government, or otherwise, all property necessary, useful or convenient for its use in carrying out the objects and purposes of this Article.

Section 3. Director of Wildlife Conservation

A Director of Wildlife Conservation shall be appointed by a majority vote of the entire Commission, who shall be removed only for cause and after public hearing by the Commission. His duties and compensation for his services shall be fixed by a majority vote of the entire Commission. The Director shall, with the approval of the Commission, appoint such assistants and employees as the Commission may deem necessary. The Commission shall determine the qualifications of the Director, all assistants and employees. No Commissioner shall be eligible for employment as Director or otherwise.

Section 4. Disposition of Funds

The fees, monies, or funds arising from the operation and transactions of said Commission and from the application and the administration of the laws and regulations pertaining to the bird, fish, game and wildlife resources of the State and from the sale of property used for said purposes shall be expended and used by said Commission for the control, management, restoration, conservation and regulation of the bird, fish, game and wildlife resources of the State, including the purchase or other acquisition of property for said purposes, and for the administration of the laws pertaining thereto and for no other purpose.

ARTICLE XXVIII: ALCOHOLIC BEVERAGE LAWS AND ENFORCEMENT (Repealed)

Section 1. Creation of Commission - Appointment - Membership - Powers – Tenure / Repealed

Section 1.A. Transition from The Alcoholic Beverage Control Board To The Alcoholic Beverage Laws Enforcement Commission / Repealed

Section 2. Exclusion of Beer or Cereal Malt Beverages Containing not More than 3.2% Of Alcohol by Weight / Repealed

Section 3. Enactment of Laws by Legislature - Indiscriminate Sales to Licensed Wholesale Distribution / Repealed

Section 4. Retail Sales by Package Stores and by the Individual Drink / Repealed

Section 5. Prohibition of Sales to Certain Persons - Limitation on Advertising - Penalties / Repealed

Section 6. Prohibition of Sales on Certain Days - Penalties / Repealed

Section 7. Taxation and Licensing - Distribution of Funds / Repealed

Section 8. State and Political Subdivisions Prohibited from Engaging in Business / Repealed

Section 9. Occupation Tax / Repealed

Section 10. Restrictions on Issuance of Licenses / Repealed

Section 11. Repealed

ARTICLE XXIX: ETHICS COMMISSION

Section 1. Ethics Commission - Appointments - Qualifications - Terms - Vacancies – Quorum

A. There is hereby created the Ethics Commission which shall consist of five members. The Governor, Attorney General, President Pro Tempore of the Senate, Speaker of the House of Representatives, and Chief Justice of the Supreme Court shall each appoint a person who is a registered voter of this State to the Commission. The initial terms of the Governor's and Attorney General's appointees shall be one year; the initial terms of the President Pro Tempore's and Speaker's appointees shall be three years, and the initial term of the Chief Justice's appointee shall be five years.

B. No congressional district shall be represented by more than one Commissioner, and no more than three persons of the same political registration shall serve on the Ethics Commission at the same time.

C. After the initial terms, members of the Ethics Commission shall serve terms of five years. No person shall be appointed to the Commission more than two times in succession, except the initial members who serve less than five-year terms may be appointed three times in succession. A vacancy on the Commission shall be filled for the remainder of the unexpired term by the appointing authority.

D. The members of the Commission shall choose a chair from among themselves.

E. The term of office for a Commissioner shall commence at noon on the second Monday in July.

F. No member of the Ethics Commission shall be eligible for elected office for two years after completing his or her term.

G. A majority of the members serving shall constitute a quorum.

Section 2. Appropriation - Compensation – Staff

A. The Ethics Commission shall receive an annual appropriation by the Legislature sufficient to enable it to perform its duties as set forth in this Constitutional Amendment. Any funds appropriated to the Ethics Commission, which remain unspent at the end of the fiscal year shall be returned to the general revenue fund. The Commission shall present its proposed budget to the Governor and the Legislature on the second day of each legislature session.

B. The Commissioners shall receive reimbursement for travel, lodging, and meals while on official business as provided for other officers of the State, but they shall not be otherwise compensated.

C. The Commission may employ an executive director and other staff, including attorneys, necessary to fulfill its duties.

Section 3. Ethics Rules

A. After public hearing, the Ethics Commission shall promulgate rules of ethical conduct for campaigns for elective state office and for campaigns for initiatives and referenda, including civil penalties for violation of these rules.

B. After public hearing, the Ethics Commission shall promulgate rules of ethical conduct for state officers and employees, including civil penalties for violation of these rules.

C. Newly promulgated rules shall be presented to each House of the Legislature and to the Governor on the second day of each session of the Legislature. If these rules are not disapproved by joint resolution, subject to veto by the Governor, during the same legislative session, they shall be effective. In the event the Governor vetoes a joint resolution disapproving any Ethics

Commission's rules, the procedure shall be the same as for the veto of any other bill or joint resolution. Effective Ethics Commission rules shall be published in the official statutes of the State.

D. Effective Ethics Commission rules may be repealed or modified by the Commission, and the repeal or modification shall be submitted to the Legislature and the Governor in the same manner as newly promulgated rules. Effective Ethics Commission rules may also be repealed or modified by law passed by a majority vote of each House of the Legislature. If the Governor vetoes such a law, the procedure shall be the same as for the veto of any other bill or joint resolution.

Section 4. Investigation - Decision - Subpoena Power

A. The Ethics Commission shall investigate and, when it deems appropriate, prosecute in the District Court of the County where the violation occurred violations of its rules governing ethical conduct of campaigns, state officers, and state employees. Where uncertainty exists, as to the County in which the violation occurred, the Commission may prosecute in any County in which the evidence indicates the violation might have been committed. The Court may assess penalties for violation of ethical standards established by the Commission as provided in the Commission's rules. The Commission may settle investigations and accept payment of fines without Court order. Fines paid shall be deposited in the general revenue fund of the State.

B. The Commission shall also enforce other ethics laws as prescribed by law.

C. For purposes of its investigations, the Ethics Commission shall have subpoena power.

Section 5. Ethics Interpretations

The Ethics Commission may respond, pursuant to its rules, to questions of specific individuals seeking an interpretation of the Commission's rules governing ethical conduct for campaigns, state officers, or state employees. Any such official interpretation of ethics rules shall be binding on the Commission.

Section 6. Criminal Penalties

This Article shall not prevent enactment of laws prohibiting certain conduct by political candidates, government officers, government employees, or other persons and providing criminal penalties for such conduct. It also shall not prevent enactment of laws governing ethical conduct of local political subdivision officers and employees, nor shall it prevent enactment of law governing conditions of state government employment.

Section 7. Removal

A Commissioner shall only be removed from office pursuant to the provisions of Article VIII of this Constitution.

SCHEDULE:

Preamble:

In order that no inconveniences may arise by reason of a change from the forms of government now existing in Indian Territory and in the Territory of Oklahoma, it is hereby declared as follows:

Section 1. Existing Rights, Actions, Proceedings, Contracts, Claims, and Processes

No existing rights, actions, suits, proceedings, contracts, or claims shall be affected by the change in the forms of government, but all shall continue as if no change in the forms of government had taken place. And all processes which may have been issued previous to the admission of the State into the Union under the authority of the Territory of Oklahoma or under the authority of the laws in force in the Indian Territory shall be as valid as if issued in the name of the State.

Section 2. Laws of the Territory of Oklahoma – Extended and to Remain in Force

All laws in force in the Territory of Oklahoma at the time of the admission of the State into the Union, which are not repugnant to this Constitution, and which are not locally inapplicable, shall be extended to and remain in force in the State of Oklahoma until they expire by their own limitation or are altered or repealed by law.

Section 3. Debts, Fines, Penalties and Forfeitures Accruing to the Territory of Oklahoma

All debts, fines, penalties, and forfeitures which have accrued or may hereafter accrue to the Territory of Oklahoma shall inure to the State of Oklahoma, and may be sued for and recovered by the State.

Section 4. Constitution Takes Effect and Force – When

This Constitution shall take effect and be in full force immediately upon the admission of the State into the Union.

Section 5. Notaries Public - Continuation of Duties of Office

Until otherwise provided by law, notaries public appointed under the laws of the Territory of Oklahoma, or under the authority of the laws heretofore in force in the Indian Territory, may continue to exercise and perform the duties of the office of notary public until the expiration of their commissions: Provided, That any notary public appointed in the Indian Territory for any district, or in the Territory of Oklahoma for any county, shall, after this Constitution takes effect, exercise the powers, privileges, and rights of a notary public only of the county formed in whole or in part out of the district or county for which such person is a notary public, and in which such person resides at the time the State is admitted into the Union; but before any such notary public, except notaries public for those counties in the Territory of Oklahoma, the boundaries of which have not been changed by the Constitution, shall exercise the powers, privileges, and rights of a notary public of such county, he shall have filed in the office of the county clerk of the county in which he resides his commission as notary public and an affidavit stating that he is a resident of such county, whereupon he shall become a notary public for such county.

Section 6. Female Persons as Notaries - Females Eligible to Office of County Superintendent of Public Instruction

The appointments of female persons as notaries public, heretofore made by the Governor of Oklahoma, and by the United States courts for the Indian Territory, and by the judges of said courts, are hereby confirmed and made valid, and all official acts of such notaries public heretofore performed are hereby validated, in so far as the acts of such notaries public may be affected by any ineligibility of such persons to appointment as notaries public. Female persons possessing the other qualifications prescribed by law shall be eligible to the office of notary public and of County Superintendent of Public Instruction.

Section 7. Property, Credits, Claims, and Choses in Action Belonging to Territory of Oklahoma

All property, real and personal, credits, claims, and choses in action, belonging to the Territory of Oklahoma at the time the State is admitted into the Union, shall be vested in and become the property of the State of Oklahoma.

Section 8. Judgments and Property Records in Indian Territory and Osage Reservation Effectual to Impart Notice

All judgments and records of deeds, mortgages, liens, and other instruments, filed or recorded, affecting the title to real and personal property in the Indian Territory and Osage Indian Reservation, are hereby made as effectual to impart notice and for all other purposes under the laws of the Territory of Oklahoma extended in force in the State, as they were under the laws heretofore in force in the Indian Territory and Osage Indian Reservation.

Section 9. Judgments and Property Records of Oklahoma Territory Effectual to Impart Notice

All judgments and records of deeds, mortgages, liens, and other instruments, filed or recorded, affecting title to real and personal property in new counties that have been created out of the territory of any county or counties of the Territory of Oklahoma or out of the territory of any county or counties of the Territory of Oklahoma and of any recording district or districts of the Indian Territory, are hereby made as effectual to impart notice and for all other purposes under the laws of the Territory of Oklahoma, extended in force in the State, as the same would have been if no changes had been made by the provisions of this Constitution in the boundaries of the counties as they existed in the Territory of Oklahoma, or of the boundaries of the recording districts as they existed in the Indian Territory.

Section 10. Continued Corporate Existence of Cities and Towns - Officers – Ordinances

Until otherwise provided by law, incorporated cities and towns, heretofore incorporated under the laws in force in the Territory of Oklahoma or in the Indian Territory, shall continue their corporate existence under the laws extended in force in the State, and all officers of such municipal corporations at the time of the admission of the State into the Union shall perform the duties of their respective offices under the laws extended in force in the State, until their successors are elected and qualified in the manner that is or may be provided by law: Provided, That all valid ordinances now in force in such incorporated cities and towns shall continue in force until altered, amended, or repealed.

Section 11. Taxes Assessed or Due in Incorporated Cities and Towns

All taxes assessed or due to incorporated cities and towns in the Indian Territory, and all taxes levied by such incorporated cities and towns for the year nineteen hundred and seven shall, until otherwise provided by law, be levied and collected in the same manner as now provided by law in force in the Indian Territory, and under the laws and ordinances now in force in such municipal corporations.

Section 12. Local Improvements and Public Buildings Being Made or Constructed in Indian Territory

In all incorporated cities and towns in the Indian Territory, all local improvements or public buildings in process of being made or constructed under the laws in force in the Indian Territory, or for which proceedings having been commenced under such laws at the time of the admission of the State into the Union, shall be completed under said laws, and said laws are hereby extended in force as to such improvements or public buildings until such local improvements or public buildings are completed and paid for, as by such laws provided.

Section 13. Congressional Acts Concerning Mining - Chief Mine Inspector to Perform Duties of Oil Inspector

The Act of Congress entitled "An Act for the protection of the Lives of Miners in the Territories," approved March 3, 1891, and the Act of Congress entitled "An Act to Amend an Act Entitled 'An Act for the Protection of the Lives of Miners in the Territories,' " approved July 1, 1902, are hereby extended to and over the State of Oklahoma until otherwise provided by law: Provided, That the words, Governor of the State are hereby substituted for the words, "Governor of such organized territory," and for the words "Secretary of Interior," wherever the same appear in said Acts, and the words, Chief Mine Inspector, for the words, "Mine Inspector," wherever the same appear in said Acts. The Chief Mine Inspector shall also perform the duties required by laws of the Territory of Oklahoma of the Territorial Oil Inspector until otherwise provided by law.

Section 14. Licensure of Dental Surgeons

Until otherwise provided by law, all dental surgeons licensed to practice in the Territory of Oklahoma and all dental surgeons who were residents of the Indian Territory on the sixteenth day of June, nineteen hundred and six, and also all graduates of some reputable school or college of dental surgery, shall be eligible and be licensed to practice in the State without examination.

Section 15. Compensation of Certain State Officers

Until otherwise provided by law, the officers of the State shall receive annually as compensation for their services, the following sums:

The Governor, four thousand, five hundred dollars;

Lieutenant Governor, one thousand dollars;

Secretary of State, two thousand, five hundred dollars;

Attorney General, four thousand dollars;

State Treasurer, three thousand dollars;

State Auditor, two thousand, five hundred dollars;

State Examiner and Inspector, three thousand dollars;

Chief Mine Inspector, three thousand dollars;

Labor Commissioner, two thousand dollars;

Commissioner of Charities and Corrections, one thousand, five hundred dollars;

Corporation Commissioners, four thousand dollars each;

Superintendent of Public Instruction, two thousand, five hundred dollars;

Insurance Commissioner, two thousand, five hundred dollars.

Section 16. Salaries of Supreme Court Justices and Judges of District Court

The salary of the Justices of the Supreme Court of the State shall be four thousand dollars per annum, each, and that of the judges of the District Court, three thousand dollars per annum, each, until changed by the Legislature.

Section 17. Compensation of Other State Officers

The members of the Board of Agriculture, Bank Commissioner, Clerk of the Supreme Court, and all other State officers, except as herein provided, or such as may be created, and all clerks and assistants, shall receive such compensation for their services as may be provided by law.

Section 18. Terms, Duties, Powers, Qualifications, and Compensation of County and Township Officers

Until otherwise provided by law, the terms, duties, powers, qualifications, and salary and compensation of all county and township officers, not otherwise provided by this Constitution, shall be as now provided by the laws of the Territory of Oklahoma for like named officers, and the duties and compensation of the probate judge under such laws shall devolve upon and belong to the judge of the county court: Provided, That the term of office of those elected at the time of the adoption of this Constitution, or first appointed under the provisions of the laws extended in force in the State, shall expire on the second Monday of January in the year nineteen hundred and eleven: And Provided Further, That county attorneys and judges of the county court of the several counties of the State, having a population of more than twenty thousand shall be paid a salary of two thousand dollars per annum; and of counties having a population of more than thirty thousand, a salary of twenty-five hundred dollars per annum; and of counties having a population of more than forty thousand, a salary of three thousand dollars per annum; such salaries to be paid in the same manner as is provided by law in force in the Territory of Oklahoma for the payment of salaries to county attorneys.

Section 19. Boards of Regents of Certain Colleges, Schools, and Universities

Until otherwise provided by law, the boards of regents of the University of Oklahoma, of the Agricultural and Mechanical

College, of the Normal schools now established, of the University Preparatory School, and of the Colored Agricultural and Normal University, shall continue to hold their offices and exercise the functions thereof until their successors are elected or appointed and qualified.

Section 20. Division of Property, Assets and Liabilities Among Existing and New Counties

The Legislature shall provide by general, special, or local law for the equitable division of the property, assets, and liabilities of any county existing in the Territory of Oklahoma between such county and any new county or counties created in whole or in part out of the territory of such county.

Section 21. Property, Credits, Claims, Choses in Action, and Liabilities of Day County

All property, real and personal, and credits, claims, and choses in action, belonging to the county of Day at the time of the admission of the State into the Union, shall be vested in and become the property of the County of Ellis: Provided, The Legislature shall provide, by general, special, or local law, for the equitable division of the assets of Day County, thus transferred to Ellis County, and of the liabilities of Day County, between the Counties of Roger Mills and Ellis.

Section 22. Procurement, Sufficiency, and Necessity of Official Seals

The Clerk of the Supreme Court shall procure a seal and cause such inscription to be placed thereon as may be prescribed by the Supreme Court. Each clerk of the District Court shall procure a seal, and, under the direction of the Judge of the District Court, cause to be inscribed thereon the style of his office and the name of his County. Each County Clerk, County Treasurer, Register of Deeds, County Surveyor, and County Superintendent of Public Instruction, shall procure a seal, and, under the direction of the County Judge, cause to be inscribed thereon the style of his office and the name of his county. Said seals shall be sufficient and used for all lawful purposes until otherwise provided by law: Provided, That, until any of such officers shall have procured a seal, the signature of any such officer shall be sufficient for all purposes without a seal.

Section 23. Transfer of Books, Records, Papers of County Probate Courts

When this Constitution shall go into effect, the books, records, papers, and proceedings of the probate court in each county, and all causes and matters of administration and guardianship, and other matters pending therein, shall be transferred to the county court of such county, except of Day County, which shall be transferred to the county court of Ellis County, and the county courts of the respective counties shall proceed to final decree or judgment, order, or other termination in the said several matters and causes as the said probate court might have done if this Constitution had not been adopted. The District Court of any county, the successor of the United States Court for the Indian Territory, in each of the counties formed in whole or in part in the Indian Territory, shall transfer to the county court of such county all matters, proceedings, records, books, papers, and documents appertaining to all causes or proceedings relating to estates: Provided, That the Legislature may provide for the transfer of any of said matters and causes to another county than herein prescribed.

Section 24. Seal of Probate Courts and County Courts
Until otherwise provided by law, the seal of the probate courts in the counties of the Territory of Oklahoma shall be the seal of the county courts, and in that part of the State heretofore comprising the Indian Territory and Osage Indian Reservation, and in the new counties created in the Territory of Oklahoma, until the county court shall have procured a proper seal, the signature of the county judge shall be sufficient for all purposes without a seal.

Section 25. Indebtedness of County, City, or Other Municipality
Any county, city, incorporated town, township, board of
education, school district, or other municipality, either in the
Territory of Oklahoma or the Indian Territory, that shall owe, at
the time of the admission of the State into the Union, any
indebtedness, evidenced by warrants, script, or other evidence of
indebtedness, is authorized, through the proper officers thereof,
to make provision for the payment of, and to pay, such
indebtedness, either by tax levy or by issuing bonds in lieu
thereof, in accordance with and under the provision of the laws
extended in force in the State: Provided, That the limitation upon
the amount of indebtedness that may be created by any county,
city, incorporated town, township, board of education, school
district, or other municipality, and upon the amount of taxes that
may be levied by any county, city, incorporated town, township,
board of education, school district, or other municipality, under
the provisions of this Constitution, or of law, shall not apply to
the indebtedness, the levying of taxes, and the issuing of bonds
provided for herein.

Section 26. Transfer of Papers, Records, Proceedings, and Seal
to Supreme Court of State

All cases, civil and criminal, pending, upon the admission of the
State into the Union, in the Supreme Court of the Territory of
Oklahoma, on appeal or writ of error from the district or probate
courts of any county or subdivision within the limits of the State,
and the papers, records, proceedings, and seal of said court shall
be transferred to the Supreme Court of the State, except as is
otherwise provided in the Enabling Act of Congress. And all
cases, civil and criminal, pending, on the admission of the State
into the Union, in the United States Court of Appeals, for the
Indian Territory, and the papers, records, and proceedings of said
court, shall be transferred to the Supreme Court of the State,
except as is otherwise provided by the Enabling Act of Congress
and the amendments thereto.

Section 27. Transfer of Cases from District Court of the Territory to District Courts of the State

All cases, civil and criminal, pending, at the time of the admission of the State into the Union, in the District Courts of the Territory of Oklahoma, in any county within the district, and the records, papers, and proceedings of said District Court, and the seal and other property appertaining thereto, shall be transferred into the District Court of the State for such county, except as is provided in the Enabling Act of Congress, and all cases, civil and criminal, pending, at the time of the admission of the State into the Union, in the United States Court for the Indian Territory, within the limits of any county created in whole or in part within the limits of what was heretofore the Indian Territory, and all records, papers, and proceedings of said United States Courts for the Indian Territory, and the seal and other property appertaining thereto, shall be transferred to the District Court of the State for such county, except as is provided in the Enabling Act of Congress and the amendments thereto: Provided, That the Legislature may provide for the transfer of any such cases from one county to another county.

Section 28. Amendment of Enabling Act Accepted

The terms and provisions of an Act of Congress, entitled "An Act to Amend Section Sixteen, Seventeen and Twenty, of an Act Entitled 'An Act to Enable the People of Oklahoma and Indian Territory to form a Constitution and State government and be admitted into the Union on an equal footing with the original states; and to enable the people of New Mexico and Arizona to form a Constitution and State government and be admitted into the Union on an equal footing with the original states,' " are hereby accepted, and the jurisdiction of the cases enumerated therein is hereby assumed by the Courts of the State.

Section 29. Eligibility to Be Elected Judge of District Court

Any person who shall be a qualified elector of any county of a judicial district at the time of the election held to ratify this Constitution, and who shall, in all other respects, be eligible under the provisions of the Constitution, to be elected judge of the District Court of such district, shall be eligible to be elected judge of the District Court of such district at the first election held for the election of State officers.

Section 30. Eligibility to Be Elected to State Office

Any person who shall have been a resident of the territory within the limits of the State for a period of one year next preceding the date on which the election for the ratification of the Constitution is held, and who shall otherwise be eligible, under the provisions of this Constitution, to be elected to any State office, shall be eligible to be elected to any such State office at the first election held for the election of State officers.

Section 31. Osage County – Taxation – Assessments, Tax Books, Records, Collections

The assessment of property in the Osage Indian Reservation for the year nineteen hundred and seven, by the authorities of Pawnee County, shall be the assessment of Osage County for the year nineteen hundred and seven, and the proper authorities of Pawnee County shall levy a tax on the property of the Osage Indian Reservation for the year nineteen hundred and seven, as now provided by law, and immediately upon the admission of the State into the Union, the county treasurer of Pawnee County shall turn over to the county treasurer of Osage County the tax books and records of taxes in the Osage Indian Reservation, so made for the year nineteen hundred and seven, and the treasurer of Osage County shall proceed and have the authority to receive all such taxes in the Osage Indian Reservation for the year nineteen hundred and seven, and such taxes shall be collected and enforced in the manner provided by law. And there shall also be collected, in addition to the tax so levied by the authorities of Pawnee County, a county school tax of ten mills on the dollar of the assessed valuation, and the same shall be and become the property of said Osage County: Provided, That out of the funds so collected, the county treasurer of Osage County shall pay to the county treasurer of Pawnee County the cost and expenses of making such assessment and the levying of such taxes.

Section 32. New and Existing School Districts - Equitable Division of Property, Assets and Liabilities

The Legislature shall provide by general, special, or local law for the equitable division of the property, assets, and liabilities of any school district existing in the Territory of Oklahoma between such school district and any new school district created in whole or in part of the territory of any such school district, as may be affected by a change in the county boundaries under this Constitution.

Section 33. Licensed Attorneys - Eligibility to Practice without Examination

All attorneys-at-law licensed to practice in any court of record of the Territory of Oklahoma, or in any of the United States Courts for the Indian Territory, or any court of record of any of the Five Civilized Tribes, shall be eligible to practice in any court of the State without examination.

Section 34. Newspapers Entitled to Publish Legal Notices, Advertisements, Etc.

Until otherwise provided by law, any newspaper, published at the time of the admission of the State into the Union, in any new county, created in whole or in part out of the territory of any county of Oklahoma Territory, or in any county, created in whole or in part, out of territory within the limits of the Indian Territory or Osage Indian Reservation, shall, under the laws extended in force in the State, be considered, in law, to have been published continuously for fifty-two weeks in said county and shall be a newspaper entitled to publish all legal notices, advertisements, or publications of any kind required or provided by any law of the State.

Section 35. Debts of Constitutional Convention - Expenses of Holding Ratification Election

All debts and indebtedness, authorized to be incurred by the Constitutional Convention of the proposed State of Oklahoma, and all expenses of holding the election for the ratification or rejection of this Constitution and for the election of officers of a full state government, which shall remain unpaid after the appropriation made by the Congress of the United States has been exhausted, are hereby assumed by the State; and it is hereby made the duty of the Legislature, at its first session, to provide for the payment of same: Provided, That the debts and indebtedness, the payment of which is hereby assumed by the State, shall not include any debt or expense as a salary or compensation of the delegates of the Constitutional Convention.

Section 36. Ordinance of Constitutional Convention – Ratification and Validity

The Ordinance adopted by the Constitutional Convention, entitled, "An Ordinance, providing for an election, at which the proposed Constitution for the proposed State of Oklahoma, shall be submitted to the people thereof for ratification or rejection, and submitting separately to the people of the proposed State of Oklahoma the proposed prohibition article, making substantially the terms of the Enabling Act uniformly applicable to the entire State, for ratification or rejection, and for the election of certain State, district, county and township officers provided for by said proposed Constitution, and for the election of members of the Legislature of said proposed State of Oklahoma and for five Representatives to Congress," is hereby ratified and shall be valid for all the purposes thereof.

Section 37. Illegal or Invalid Indebtedness Not Legalized or Made Valid

Nothing in this Constitution contained shall legalize or make valid any illegal or invalid indebtedness of any county, city, incorporated town, township, board of education, school district, or other municipality, either in the Territory of Oklahoma or the Indian Territory, or impair any defense against the payment of the same.

Section 38. Jurisdiction to Make Equitable Division of County Property, Assets, and Liabilities

Should the first session of the Legislature, provided by this Constitution, fail to provide for the division of the property, assets and liabilities of any county existing in the Territory of Oklahoma between such county and any county or counties created in whole or in part out of such county, original jurisdiction is hereby conferred upon the Supreme Court to make equitable division of such property, assets and liabilities, and for the purpose of hearing and receiving evidence and reporting findings of law and fact may appoint a special Master in Chancery in any such case.

Section 39. Superintendents of Public Instruction in Indian Territory and Osage Reservation

The qualifications prescribed by the laws of Oklahoma shall not apply to Superintendents of Public Instruction, elected at the time of the ratification of this Constitution, in the Indian Territory, and Osage Indian Reservation.

Section 40. Terms of Officers of State Government
The terms of all officers of the State government elected at the time of the adoption of this Constitution shall begin upon the admission of the State into the Union.

Section 41. Qualification of Constitutional Officers – Oath and Bond

All persons elected at the time of the adoption of this Constitution to any of the offices provided under the Constitution shall be deemed to have duly qualified upon their taking the oath of office before any officer authorized by law to administer oaths, and executing such bond as may be required by law.

Section 42. Officers Elected at Time of Adoption of Constitution - Official Bonds

All officers elected at the time of the adoption of the Constitution shall execute such official bond as may then be required by law or thereafter required by act of the Legislature; and such bonds shall inure to the benefit of the State or other beneficiary, for whose protection or security the same shall be required.

Section 43. Filing and Preservation of Constitution - Secretary of State

When this Constitution shall have been ratified by the people of the State of Oklahoma and the State admitted into the Federal Union, under the same, as engrossed on parchment and signed by the officers and members of this Constitutional Convention, it shall be filed in the office of the Secretary of State and sacredly preserved by him, as the fundamental law of the State of Oklahoma.